WARFARE IN HISTORY

In the Steps of the Black Prince

The Road to Poitiers, 1355–1356

WARFARE IN HISTORY

ISSN 1358–779X

Series editor
Matthew Bennett, Royal Military Academy, Sandhurst
Anne Curry, University of Southampton
Stephen Morillo, Wabash College, Crawfordsville, USA

This series aims to provide a wide-ranging and scholarly approach to military history, offering both individual studies of topics or wars, and volumes giving a selection of contemporary and later accounts of particular battles; its scope ranges from the early medieval to the early modern period.

New proposals for the series are welcomed; they should be sent to the publisher at the address below.

Boydell and Brewer Limited, PO Box 9, Woodbridge, Suffolk, IP12 3DF

Previously published volumes in this series are listed at the back of this volume

In the Steps of the Black Prince

The Road to Poitiers, 1355–1356

Peter Hoskins

THE BOYDELL PRESS

First published 2011
The Boydell Press, Woodbridge
Reprinted 2012
Paperback edition 2013

ISBN 978 1 84383 611 7 hardback
ISBN 978 1 84383 874 6 paperback

The Boydell Press is an imprint of Boydell & Brewer Ltd
PO Box 9, Woodbridge, Suffolk IP12 3DF, UK
and of Boydell & Brewer Inc.
668 Mt Hope Avenue, Rochester, NY 14620–2731, USA
website: www.boydellandbrewer.com

A CIP catalogue record for this book is available
from the British Library

The publisher has no responsibility for the continued existence or accuracy of
URLs for external or third-party internet websites referred to in this book,
and does not guarantee that any content on such websites is,
or will remain, accurate or appropriate.

Papers used by Boydell & Brewer Ltd are natural, recyclable products
made from wood grown in sustainable forests

Printed and bound in Great Britain by
CPI Group (UK) Ltd, Croydon, CR0 4YY

To Josephine, a Black Prince widow as I tramped the French countryside, with grateful thanks for her tolerance, love, and encouragement.

Contents

Part V Epilogue

Illustrations

Acknowledgements

I owe thanks to many people. First, those employed in the *mairies* and tourist offices on my route for much local historical information and helping me to make contact with those with an interest in their local history and heritage. These contacts gave me invaluable help and deserve a mention. Françoise Delahaie at Castelnau, Gérard Temple at Nogaro, Alain Lagors in Plaisance, Anne-Marie Seguy of Castanet-Tolosan, Jean Odol in Bazièege, Jean-Louis Bonnet at Carcassonne, Roger Maguer in Castelnaudary, Julien Aussenac in Ouveillan, Françoise Paraire in Fanjeaux, Corinne Marcou in Mazères, Christine Peyre and Auguste Armengaud in Belpech, Annie Prat and Roger Ycart in Cintegabelle, Louis Latour in Auterive, Francis Bop and Jean-Yves Canal in Miremont, Madame Douleau in Noé and Claude Ferre in Carbonne were all very helpful with information on their towns and regions during the 1355 *chevauchée*. For the 1356 campaign, my thanks go to Guy Penaud in Périgueux, Gérard Durand de Ramefort for his help and guided visit to his château of Ramefort, Guy Goss for his advice on Bourges and events in the Berry, to François Reix for his help with information on Quinsac, Sylvine Verpaalen-Bessaguet in Lesterps, Nicole Raynaud in Bussière-Boffy, the Marquis de Fraisse for a tour of his château thanks to Nicole's introduction, Stéphane Hilaire in Lussac-les-Eglises, Anne Barbier for a tour of St-Benoît-du-Sault, Jocelyn Chauvat in Argenton-sur-Creuse, Sébastien Delaveau of the Amis du Viel Issoudun, Harry and Jacqueline Atterton, the seigneurs of the Château of Montbazon, Noel de Linares at St-Maure-de-Touraine. My thanks are also due to Elisabeth Stuart, the Archivist at the Duchy of Cornwall, for letting me have a transcription of the journal of John Henxteworth and granting permission for its use in this book, and to Jo Bartholomew, Librarian at Winchester Cathedral, for help with copies of campaign letters in the Chartulary of the Cathedral. The archivists in the bishopric of Carcassonne and of the departments of the Aude, Charente, Dordogne and Hérault, and the staff of the Bibliothèque Nationale de France were also all most helpful. I am grateful to Oxford University Press for permission to use the translation by A. H. Burne of Baker's description of the battlefield in 'The Battle of Poitiers', *English Historical Review*, vol. 53, no. 209, 1938, pp. 27–8. Similarly, I am grateful to Pennsyvania State University Press for permission to quote from Christine de Pizan, *The Book of Deeds of Arms and of Chivalry*, translated by Sumner Willard, edited by Charity Cannon Willard. I also owe thanks to two experts in the field for their patience in response to inquiries and requests for opinions. I am particularly grateful to Andrew Ayton, senior lecturer in history at the University of Hull, for his support and encouragement as this project progressed, and to Professor Clifford Rogers at the US

Military Academy, West Point, for answering many questions with great patience and allowing me to quote from some of his unpublished replies. I find reading books with a myriad of place-names and no maps extremely frustrating, and I am grateful to Phillip Judge for turning my sketches into the maps in this book. Finally, a word of thanks to those who accompanied me on my walks: Martin and Lindsey Hoskins, Rodger Barker, and my very good friend Richard Kinnear who walked around 800 miles with me, carrying stoically for many of them a knee injury sustained on the march near Issoudun.

Preface to the Paperback Edition

Since the publication of the hardback edition in 2011 I have come across some further material which sheds additional light on the events of the Black Prince's *chevauchées* of 1355 and 1356.

Recent work indicates that the Black Prince arrived in Bordeaux on 16 September 1355,[1] and not four days later as has generally been accepted (Chapter 2). Also in respect of Chapter 2, it has been brought to my attention that ruins remain of the castle of Ornave,[2] where the Black Prince is said to have stayed the first night after leaving Bordeaux. They are to be found in Gradignan, about two miles to the west of Villenave-d'Ornon.

There is a small town, Couffoulens, between Carcassonne and Limoux, which appears to have suffered fire damage in the fourteenth century.[3] This village can perhaps be added to the list of the numerous places destroyed during the passage of the Black Prince, either while the army was moving towards the east (Chapter 5) or during the return to Gascony (Chapter 6). The village of Milhan, close to Trèbes and said to have been destroyed by fire in 1355, may be the village now called Barbaira,[4] about five miles south-east of Trèbes (Chapter 5).

Jean Capbon, an inhabitant of Montlaur, a village to the south of the Montagne d'Alaric, declared in a report addressed to the French king 'that he was taken prisoner with his family by the English who had burned his houses and all his papers'.[5] This evidence adds weight to the argument that the Black Prince's army crossed the Montagne d'Alaric, passing to the south of Carcassonne, on its return to Gascony (Chapter 6).

More detail can also be added to events at Narbonne (Chapter 6). At the time of the *chevauchée* of 1355 the defences had recently been repaired, with permission given in 1349 by the French king's lieutenant in the Languedoc, renewed in 1352 by King Jean, for the consuls to raise taxes for restoration, reinforcement and construction of defences of the *cité*, the *bourg*, and the suburbs. These suburbs were extensive and on all sides. They had not been walled, but arrangements had been made to install chains across streets to impede cavalry. There was ready access to these suburbs across a ford just to the north of the *bourg*. When the army departed it is said to have set the *bourg* alight with flaming arrows. There was also extensive destruction throughout the suburbs as they left, although it appears that the religious buildings, including two leper houses, were spared. After the departure of the Black Prince the consuls turned their thoughts to reconstruction. Meeting ten days after the departure of the prince, they had to take into account 'damages and attacks which had just been inflicted on their town', which had entailed 'dangers and ravages which are almost irreparable'. Six days later a programme of work was started with a range of indirect taxes imposed for five years to pay for the reconstruction.[6]

I refer in Chapter 11 to two un-named castles between Le Dorat and Lussac-les-Eglises taken by assault on 18 August 1356, in one of which the prince is said to have lodged. It has been suggested that these two castles may have been those in the village of Tersannes: the *château du bourg* and the manor of La Mothe.[7]

Notes

1. Guilhem Pépin, 'La collégiale Saint-Seurin de Bordeaux aux XIIIe–XIVe siècles et son élaboration d'une historiographie et d'une idéologie du duché d'Aquitaine anglo-gascon', *Le Moyen Age, Revue d'histoire et de philologie*, CXVII (2011), pp. 43–66.

2. My thanks to Dr Guilhem Pépin for this information.

3. Excavations at the castle of Couffoulens have revealed extensive evidence of fire damage in the space between an external wall, constructed in the fourteenth century, and an inner wall built in the eleventh century. A coin, issued by Louis I, count of Flanders, and lord of Crécy, dated 1340, was found among the debris of the fire. Its provenance and date were interpreted as indicating that the fire damage could date from the passage of the Black Prince in 1355.

4. J. Sarrand, 'La chevauchée du Prince Noir dans la région de Carcassonne – Novembre 1355', paper delivered to La Société des Arts et Sciences de Carcassonne, 1963.

5. Alphonse Mahul, *Cartulaire et Archives des Communes de l'Ancien Diocèse et de l'Arrondissement Administratif de Carcassonne*, (Paris, 1857–1882), vol. 5, p. 565, cited in J. Sarrand, 'La chevauchée du Prince Noir'.

6. Jacqueline Caille, 'Nouveaux Regards sur l'Attaque du Prince Noir contre Narbonne en Novembre 1355', *Bulletin de la Société d'Études Scientifiques de l'Aude*, vol. 109, 2009, pp. 89–103.

7. Nicole Raynaud, 'Du Périgord au Berry: l'itinéraire du Prince Noir en Limousin durant l'été 1356', *Travaux d'Archéologie Limousine*, vol. 30, 2010, pp. 71–8.

Abbreviations

Anonimalle   *Anonimalle Chronicle 1333–1381*, ed. V. H. Galbraith, Manchester 1927.

Avesbury   Robertus de Avesbury, *De gestis mirabilibus Regis Edwardi Tertii*, ed. E. M. Thompson, London 1889.

Baker   Galfridi Le Baker de Swynebroke, *Chronicon*, ed. E. M. Thompson, Oxford 1889.

BPE   H. J. Hewitt, *The Black Prince's Expedition of 1355–1357*, Barnsley, 2004.

BPR   *The Black Prince's Register*, 4 vols., London, 1933.

Cassini   *Carte de Cassini: La France du XVIIIe siècle, d'après les originaux d'IGN*, CD-ROM, 2 vols, *France Sud* and *France Nord*.

Chandos   *The Life and Feats of Arms of Edward the Black Prince by Chandos Herald*, trans. Francisque-Michel, London and Paris, 1883.

Chroniques   Jean Froissart, *Chroniques*, vol. 5, ed. Siméon Luce, Paris, 1874.

Delachenal   R. Delachenal, *Histoire de Charles V*, Paris, 1909.

Denifle   Henri Denifle, *La desolation des monastères, églises, et hôpitaux en France pendant la Guerre de Cent Ans*, Paris 1899.

Eulogium   *Eulogium Historiarum*, vol. 3, ed. F. S. Haydon, London 1863.

Henxteworth   Journal of John Henxteworth, trans. Edmund Rollo Laird Clowes. Manuscript in the Duchy of Cornwall Archive and Library.

Le Bel   Jean Le Bel, *Chronique*, ed. J. Viard and E. Déprez, Paris, 1904–5.

Life and Campaigns   Richard Barber, *Life and Campaigns of the Black Prince*, Woodbridge, 1979.

Oeuvres   Jean Froissart, *Oeuvres de Froissart, Chroniques*, ed. Kervyn de Lettenhove, Brussels, 1867–77.

WCS   Clifford J. Rogers, *War Cruel and Sharp: English Strategy Under Edward III, 1327–1360*, Woodbridge, 2000.

Full details of works cited in the footnotes will be found in the bibliography.

Introduction

Edward of Woodstock, eldest son of Edward III, Prince of Wales, duke of Cornwall, earl of Chester, and in due course prince of Aquitaine, or the Black Prince as he was to become known many years after his death, was a remarkable man. He fought with distinction at Crécy at only sixteen years of age, was present at the siege of Calais, and at a little over twenty-six years old was the victor at Poitiers.

To some he was a skilled general, an effective lieutenant for his father in Aquitaine, and a fine example of chivalry. To others he was little more than a figurehead, reliant on the experience of those who served him and the tactical skills of his men, a brigand, and a spendthrift during his time as Prince of Aquitaine. In those parts of France through which he passed he is often known simply as *le terrible Prince Noir*. Whatever the truth, which probably lies somewhere in the middle, he was completely loyal to his father at a time when disloyalty within royal families was commonplace. Henry II, with his rebellious and troublesome brood of Henry the Young King, Geoffrey Duke of Brittany and the future kings of England Richard the Lionheart and the much maligned John, would surely have looked with envy at the good fortune of Edward III. Most unusually for a royal prince next in line to succeed to the throne, the prince did not marry until he was thirty-one and, equally unusually, he did not do so for dynastic reasons but married Joan, 'The Fair Maid of Kent', apparently for love, after the death of her husband Thomas Holland, a companion in arms of the prince at Crécy.

The prince's expedition to France in 1355 and 1356, culminating in his victory on the battlefield near Poitiers, was the pinnacle of his career. There is a good deal of information available about his itineraries in these years, but, inevitably, there is some uncertainty about some places on the routes. Atlases, road maps and even large-scale 1:25,000 maps give an idea of the nature of the terrain but no real feel for either the lie of the land or the problems that the terrain might present tactically and for movement. Also maps do not answer such questions as: Why did they go that way? Why did they travel so far on that day? I was interested to know what the routes would be like on the ground, and what the countryside that I saw could tell me about events during the expedition. One way to expand my understanding was to travel the route. This would also be a means of exploring local traditions relating to the *chevauchées* and seeing what local history might add to the story. Since I do not ride a horse, what better way than to go on foot, as so many of the prince's army would have done? The result was a walk of more than 1,300 miles through France.

Tracing the route at a large scale is straightforward enough, but it becomes more problematic when the scale is enlarged and the maps are examined in more detail. Some towns have either shrunk or disappeared altogether over time, and there are frequently no surviving traces of castles mentioned in the sources. The spelling of some places in the source documents requires judgement, and sometimes guesswork, to determine their modern names, and some names give rise to ambiguities. Even today there are frequently differences between the maps and the signposts in spellings of small habitations. In the First World War British troops gave French and Belgian towns informal, more pronounceable names, such as Ocean Villas for Auchenvillers and Wipers for Ypres. Few Britons pronounce Rheims in a way that would be recognisable to the French, so it is not surprising that the clerks who wrote the chronicles made errors as a town name, perhaps originally in Occitan, was passed to them by an English knight, whose first language was probably Anglo-Norman French, for transcription into Latin. Finally, the army split into three divisions for much of the campaign. The divisions often marched in parallel, and sometimes it is not clear whether or not places were visited by the prince's division or by one of the other divisions. Another problem is that, although regional maps of Britain survive from the thirteenth century, there were no large-scale maps of France in the period to help us locate place-names.

In choosing my routes I have, as far as possible, tried to follow roads and tracks which seem the most appropriate topographically. I have used both the modern 1:25,000 scale maps produced by the Institut Géographique National and reproductions of the Cassini maps made in the eighteenth century. In some areas Roman roads are still evident and they provide an obvious route, in part because they were in existence in the fourteenth century and some were in a reasonable state of repair, at least in comparison with many other tracks and roads. Sites of minor medieval settlements and churches are also an indication of routes likely to have been in existence in the Middle Ages. I also considered the likely approaches to towns, bearing in mind river crossing points and the position of the towns. A further consideration is that, once in hostile territory, the army often burnt and pillaged a band five leagues (fifteen miles or more) in width.[1] Professor Clifford Rogers has described how the army 'would progress as a sort of cloud dispersed to both sides of a major road, in order to facilitate foraging and devastation'. It is reasonable to assume that the roads would have been used for wagons and foot-soldiers, and they can be considered as the main axes of advance.[2] In addition, the summer of 1355 has been reported as being unusually dry with river levels at their lowest for twenty years, and therefore I have assumed that rivers were not in flood and that flood-plains would have been useable for the 1355 chevauchée.[3] It was a different matter in 1356 when a wet summer made rivers much more challenging and the Loire impassable. Finally, I had to take account of the facts of modern life. I have had to find accommodation, I have had to respect property rights and boundaries, and I had no wish to share my route with thundering juggernauts. In sum, I can claim to have followed reasonably accurately the general axis of the routes taken, and in some places I will have incontrovertibly walked in the steps of the Black Prince. For the rest, my track will have been a good approximation.

My principal primary sources for the routes are widely acknowledged as the most authoritative sources for the campaign diaries of the two *chevauchées*: the *Chronicon*, by Geoffrey le Baker, or Galfridi Le Baker de Swynebroke (hereafter Baker) for 1355 and *Eulogium Historiarum* for 1356 (*Eulogium*).[4] Baker was most probably a clerk writing for his patron Sir Thomas de la More, an Oxfordshire knight. He is believed to have died between 1358 and 1360, and he was therefore writing very soon after the events he describes. Baker was also most probably writing with reference to an itinerary written by a member of the prince's division.[5] The *Eulogium*, or at least the part that concerns us, is believed to have been written by a monk called Thomas at Malmesbury Abbey. It is thought that Thomas had access to and transcribed the itinerary for 1356 written by someone present on the *chevauchée*. He is believed to have stopped his work in 1366, so again he was writing reasonably contemporaneously. Like Baker, he deals mainly with the prince's division.[6] Another valuable contemporary primary source is the journal of John Henxteworth, a member of the Black Prince's household in France in 1355/1356, which as well as detailing income and expenditure records a number of locations on the 1355 *chevauchée*. Other important contemporaneous primary documents are several letters written by the prince and his companions. Collectively these sources carry the greatest weight. However, there are also a number of other near-contemporary sources which, although carrying less weight, are nonetheless useful. One of these sources in particular, the work of Jean Froissart, requires comment. Froissart (*c.* 1337–*c.* 1404), a Hainaulter, was in the household of Edward III's Queen Philippa of Hainault in the 1360s and had access to many involved in both the French and the Anglo-Gascon armies. He also travelled extensively in Europe gathering material for his chronicles. On the face of it, his work should be of great value, and in many instances it is. However, he was writing some years after the events described, and it is probable that some of the eyewitness accounts he drew on had become embellished or hazy over the years and he had to balance differing accounts. In addition, there are variations between different redactions of his chronicles. Overall, his chronicles are valuable but need to be treated with caution. There are also later chronicles and local accounts, some preserved in oral tradition, which can fill gaps and help to resolve difficulties but which clearly deserve less weight than the principal primary sources.

The most useful secondary sources which deal with the itineraries in depth are H. J. Hewitt's *The Black Prince's Expedition of 1355–1357*, Clifford J. Rogers' *War Cruel and Sharp: English Strategy Under Edward III, 1327–1360*, and Richard Barber's *Edward, Prince of Wales and Aquitaine: A Biography of the Black Prince*. In considering Baker, the translation by Richard Barber of the text relating to the 1355 *chevauchée* in his *Life and Campaigns of the Black Prince* has been a most valuable adjunct to the editorial work and annotation by E. M. Thompson of the original Latin text, and I am very grateful to him for his permission to use his translation.

A few words on currency: in medieval England the main currency was based on sterling silver and the pound, divided, as it would remain until 1971, into twenty shillings (s) each of which was in turn divided into twelve pennies (d). A mark was worth 13s 4d (two-thirds of a pound) and the gold noble 6s 8d. In France the basic division into *livre*, *sou* and *denier* was the same as that for English pounds, shillings and pence. However, the French *livre* was of a different value to the pound sterling, and within France *livres* of different values were minted in Paris, Bordeaux and Tours. The French used a variety of coins but for the most part values in the context of this book are quoted in *écus* and *florins*.[7] I have made approximate conversions to the pound sterling, using an exchange rate of 2s and 10d to the *écu* or *florin* to give some means of comparison. It is difficult to make comparisons to modern wages and values, but a man-at-arms was paid 1s a day, a foot archer 3d a day, and a mounted archer in the English armies can be considered reasonably well paid with a wage of 6d a day which compared favourably with the wages of a skilled artisan. In terms of purchase value, 1d would buy a gallon of ale.[8]

As for measures, I have in general used imperial measures, but I have used metric measures when quoting from modern documents or measurements where a conversion back into imperial would serve no useful purpose. On occasion leagues are mentioned, a league generally being taken to be three miles.

PART I

PROLOGUE

1

Origins

> Since therefore the kingdom of France has by divine disposition devolved upon us by the clearest right owing to the death of Charles of noted memory, the last king of France, brother to our lady mother, and since the lord Philippe de Valois, son of the King's uncle and thus further removed in blood from the said king, has intruded himself by force into the kingdom while we were yet of tender years ... we have recognised our right to the kingdom and have undertaken the burden of the rule of that kingdom, as we ought to do, resolving with unshakeable purpose ... to cast out the usurper when opportunity shall seem most propitious.
>
> Edward III assumes the title and arms of the king of France, 1340[1]

On 11 April 1357, William Pierres, master of the *Sainte-Marie*, took on board his ship at Bordeaux King Jean II of France. Jean had been taken prisoner the previous September at the Battle of Poitiers, and he, along with numerous other prisoners captured at the battle, was on his way to London. The *Sainte-Marie* reached Plymouth on 5 May. For his troubles William received £20 from the prince, and his crew of 100 mariners shared a further £66 13s 4d.[2] On 24 May King Jean, riding a white courser, entered London as the prisoner of Edward the Black Prince. The prince rode behind the king on a modest black hackney, probably to emphasise the eminent rank of his captive.[3] The occasion was accompanied by much pomp and theatre from the moment Edward and Jean were met by the mayor and leading citizens on their approach to London. As they passed through the city they were escorted by 1,000 mounted men and crowds of Londoners thronged the streets to watch the triumphant return of the prince. Members of the guilds and companies, dressed in their rich livery, were drawn up in his honour, and the prince was met by the bishop of London at St Paul's Churchyard. He and King Jean then moved off towards the Savoy Palace, which was to be Jean's residence. The throng was so dense that this last part of his journey took three hours.[4]

To Londoners it must have seemed that King Edward III was making something of a hobby of collecting kings, since David II of Scotland was already a guest in the Tower of London. But this was altogether more significant. This triumphant entry was the culmination of an extraordinary period since the prince had left Plymouth for Bordeaux in September 1355. He had done so in response to an appeal by the Gascon lords to King Edward III for assistance in keeping the French at bay. He could not then have expected to have returned in such triumph.

Ten years after the Black Prince had fought alongside his father at Crécy he had, on 19 September 1356, won a great battle in his own right. His Anglo-Gascon army of some 6,000 men had defeated a much larger French army a few miles from Poitiers. Crécy had been a great victory for Edward III, but on that occasion King Philippe VI had escaped from the battlefield. In the ten years that followed, despite the nature and scale of that great victory, it had not been possible to secure the treaty that Edward III wanted to bring the war to a favourable conclusion for the English. This time, however, the French king was in English hands. Furthermore, morale in France was shattered. After the Battle of Poitiers the country sank into chaos amid recriminations over the defeat. Not only had the king been captured but also around 2,000 other members of the French nobility and men-at-arms had been taken prisoner and almost 2,500 nobles and men-at-arms killed. As Jean II settled into the Savoy Palace in London and negotiations began, which culminated in the Treaty of Brétigny in 1360, it must have seemed to the Black Prince and his father that this was the decisive victory that was needed. The future must have looked rosy indeed for Edward III and the Black Prince.

This book looks at the events during 1355 and 1356 leading to the Battle of Poitiers and resulting in the very favourable position in which the English Crown found itself in the early summer of 1357. It does so by following the routes taken by the Black Prince during his raids in France in 1355 and 1356. However, an account of those events only makes sense within the context of the under-lying causes of the war and its progress until the prince's departure for France in September 1355.

The root cause of the outbreak of war in 1337 was the homage due from Edward III to the king of France for his lands in France, since this affected the degree of sovereignty that he exercised over these lands. This dispute was long-running and deep-seated. It has been argued that the origins of the conflict go back to the Norman Conquest, with the creation of the paradox whereby William was an independent sovereign king of England but also a vassal of the king of France for the dukedom of Normandy.[5] The marriage of Henry Plantagenet to Eleanor of Aquitaine in 1152 exacerbated this anomalous situation. By that marriage Henry (King Henry II of England from 1154), acquired extensive lands in the south-west of France which covered much of the modern regions of Aquitaine and Poitou-Charentes, and some of the Midi-Pyrénées. These lands, when added to those that he already held as duke of Normandy and Anjou as a vassal of the king of France, gave him control of a very large part of modern France. He did not pay homage for Aquitaine, but that was to come for his successors when Henry III conceded homage for the duchy under the Treaty of Paris in 1259. By that treaty the Angevin Empire all but disappeared since Henry III also renounced all his rights to Normandy, Anjou, Touraine, Maine and Poitou.

Map 1 Angevin possessions in France under Henry II.

On the eve of the Hundred Years War the French possessions of Edward III were much smaller than those of Henry II and comprised just Aquitaine and Ponthieu, in northern France, for which the English kings owed homage to the king of France.[6] This homage was not an abstract concept. It brought with it the real obligation for English kings to acknowledge the French king's sovereignty for matters relating to all the lands they held in France as vassals. They were also required to support the king of France in his wars. There were great practical difficulties when both parties were kings in their own right, and the issue of homage for Aquitaine was a running sore in the relations between the French and English kings.

In 1328 the death of the French king Charles IV brought in its train a disputed succession to add to the problems of homage. The crux of the matter was the question of whether the crown could be passed through the female line. This was of critical importance since the closest male successor to Charles was Edward III of England through his mother Isabella, sister to Charles IV and daughter of Philippe IV. Some in England were of the opinion that the crown should pass to Edward. However, the French nobility took the view that a woman could not inherit the crown and that by inference she could not pass this right to her son. Their support went to the next closest male successor, Philippe de Valois, who could trace his lineage back to Philippe III through an unbroken male line. On 1 April 1328 he assumed the title of King Philippe VI.[7] There was a somewhat desultory attempt to lay claim to the throne on behalf of the fifteen-year-old Edward III with an embassy by the bishops of Coventry and Worcester. This received short shrift in France. In May 1328 Philippe called upon Edward III to pay homage for Aquitaine. The response by Queen Isabella, Philippe's first cousin and the young King Edward's mother and co-regent, was an uncompromising rejection. There then followed the despatch of commissioners acting for Philippe to sequestrate Edward's revenues from Aquitaine until he agreed to pay homage. Further measures were threatened, and rather than risk the forfeiture of the duchy of Aquitaine, Edward III went to Amiens to render homage to Philippe on 6 June 1329. However, this was not quite what Philippe was looking for. He wanted full 'liege' homage whereby Edward would recognise him as his sovereign. Edward was not prepared to go that far and, declining to join hands with Philippe, gave only 'simple' homage to recognise Philippe as his landlord. This was not the end of the matter. Shortly thereafter Philippe demanded once again that Edward give full liege homage or forfeit Aquitaine. The English stalled for as long as they could, and during July 1330 Edward failed to meet a deadline for paying homage. Edward was declared to be in default, and Philippe decided on military action to seize Aquitaine.

However, in October 1330, Edward took power for himself from his mother, Queen Isabella, and Roger Mortimer, who had been acting as regents, and a change of English policy followed. He stated to Philippe that he now wished his homage given at Amiens to be considered as liege homage. Philippe was happy to accept this on the basis of an exchange of letters without requiring Edward to submit to a further ceremony. So far so good, but then Edward turned his attention to Scotland and success in his wars north of the border between 1331 and 1335 brought a renewed deterioration in relations between England and France.

One of the unfortunate implications for Edward of the system of homage was the right of appeal of a vassal to higher authority against a judgment made by his own lord. This opened the way for vassals of Edward to appeal to Philippe. By late 1336 there were a number of such cases before Parlement in Paris, and in due course one case brought matters to a head with a large award of damages being made against Edward. He refused to pay, and Philippe gave orders to seize assets from Aquitaine in settlement of the award. In later years the Black Prince was faced with the inconvenience of the practical implications of homage. In 1369, when the terms of the Treaty of Brétigny, which should have resolved this problem, had not been fulfilled by either side, some of the Black Prince's

Edward III's claim to the throne of France

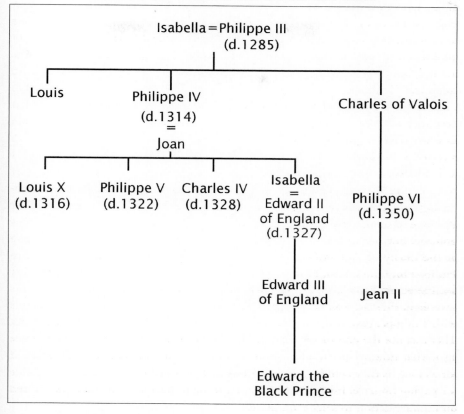

vassals lodged an appeal with King Charles V of France. The Black Prince was summoned to appear before Parlement in Paris in May 1369. The prince's response was 'that willingly and certainly would he come at his bidding, if God granted him health and life, himself with all his company, helmed to the head'.[8]

While the issue of homage continued to simmer throughout 1336, Philippe decided to make a *cause célèbre* of the case of Robert of Artois. Robert was a former advisor to Philippe who had devoted a great deal of energy and scheming to take possession of the county of Artois which, due to the vagaries of the inheritance laws, had passed first to his aunt and then, on her death, to the duchess of Burgundy. It was no help to Robert that there was an inconsistency whereby what he saw as his rightful inheritance passed to a female claimant, while Philippe was king of France because Edward's claim through the female line had been rejected. Nor was Robert's case helped by the duke of Burgundy being Philippe's brother-in-law. Robert fell into extreme disfavour with Philippe and was exiled in 1332. In 1334 he sought asylum at Edward's court, and in December 1336 Philippe issued a letter demanding Robert's surrender. Edward did not comply. This was taken as the final *casus belli* by Philippe, and in May

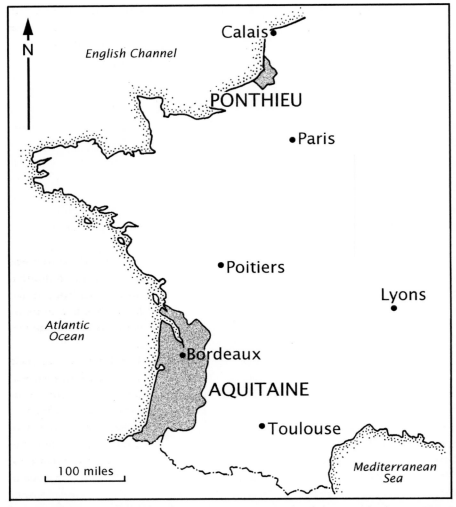

Map 2 English possessions in France at the outbreak of the Hundred Years War.

1337 it was ruled by Philippe and his Great Council that, by giving asylum and support to Robert, Edward was in breach of his duties as a vassal of Philippe. The council agreed that the duchy of Aquitaine should be forfeit and taken into the French king's hands. By late April Philippe had already rejected final attempts by the English to negotiate, and had instigated measures to raise a royal army through proclamation of the *arrière-ban* to oblige those subject to his sovereignty to muster troops for his service.[9]

By October 1337 it was clear that war was coming. Edward revoked both his homage to Philippe and his allegiance for lands held in France. Edward intended to apply pressure on France from Aquitaine in the south and from Flanders in the north. His endeavours in the north centred on attempts to buy the services of mercenaries and to build alliances with those princes in the Low Countries and Germany who might support him in his quarrel with Philippe. In January 1340 Edward formally staked his claim to the French crown. It was a breach of homage to wage war on one's lord; Edward's decision actively to pursue his claim seems intended largely to give the Flemings a legal basis for joining his alliance against Philippe. The argument was that if Edward were king of France they could legitimately pursue their interests by waging war against the usurper Philippe.

It is one of those quirks of continuity of history that, much as many in the United Kingdom are now troubled by pooling of sovereignty within the European Union, many in England in the fourteenth century were wary of transfer of sovereignty abroad if Edward took the throne of France. Edward felt it necessary to state that England would not be subject to him as king of France but solely in his capacity as king of England.[10]

The main result of Edward's endeavours in the early years of the war was a great deal of expense to try to keep the interest of less than fully committed allies. There was little to show for the considerable treasure expended. He had gained a victory over the French at sea near Sluys in June 1340, but Philippe would not be drawn into a set-piece battle on land. This first phase of the war came to an end with the Truce of Espléchin in late 1340.

Hostilities resumed in April 1341, and then Edward had a stroke of luck. The duke of Brittany died that month, and Brittany descended into civil war between the two contenders for the duchy, Jean de Montfort and Charles de Blois. Jean, who was also earl of Richmond, called on Edward for help. He was only too willing to assist, and sent two English forces to Brittany during 1342, one of which defeated a French army under Charles de Blois near Morlaix in September 1342. At last, after almost five years of war, a French army had been brought to battle on land and defeated. Edward landed with a further force in October 1342 and seemed set to do battle with a French army under the duke of Normandy. However, an intervention by papal emissaries secured the Truce of Malestroit which it was agreed would last until September 1346. Despite the truce, however, fighting continued in Brittany and by the spring of 1345 the duchy was effectively under the control of the English.

Although the truce still had a year to run, in June 1345 Edward III renounced it and began to prepare for the renewal of hostilities. Plans for Flanders that year came to nought with the killing by a mob of Jacob Van Artevelde, Edward's principal ally in the Low Countries. However, the earl of Northampton set out for Brittany and en route completed the reoccupation of the Channel Islands, which had been lost to the French in 1338 and only partially recaptured in 1340. The earl of Derby, who had landed in Bordeaux in August 1345, started to drive the French back from their garrisons in the south-west. He defeated a French army at the Battle of Auberoche in October, and went on to make further gains during the remaining months of the year.

When campaigning started once again in the spring of 1346 the erstwhile earl of Derby, now Henry earl of Lancaster, made greater inroads into French possessions in the south-west, and fighting continued in Brittany. On 12 July Edward III disembarked with an army in Normandy, and nine days later Hugh Hastings landed in Flanders with a small force of men-at-arms and archers to rally Edward's Flemish allies to march into Artois and Picardy. The campaign that followed took Edward through Normandy and to within twenty miles of Paris, where he turned north towards the Channel coast. The French had secured or destroyed crossings of the river Somme, but Edward's army forced a passage at the ford at Blanchetaque as French troops arrived to defend the crossing. Once across the river Edward moved on to Crécy-en-Ponthieu. He now drew up his army for the battle with the French king that he had sought since the start of the war and which now seemed inevitable. Unfortunately, Hugh Hastings had been unable to hold his volatile allies together, and on the very day that the king crossed the Somme Hastings' army dispersed and turned for home. It is not clear whether or not Edward had planned for their support, but in any case he now stopped at Crécy and prepared to face the French. On 26 August 1346, Philippe's much larger army was comprehensively defeated by Edward III, with the Black Prince in the forefront of the fighting, sending shock waves across Europe.

The next objective was Calais. The town fell to Edward after a protracted siege in August 1347 and remained in English hands for more than 200 years until it fell to the duke of Guise in 1558 during the reign of Queen Mary. There had been further success in Brittany and Aquitaine, and Philippe's France was in disarray. The time had come for a truce which was duly signed in September 1347, to be renewed annually. How long it would have lasted in the normal course of events is impossible to tell; as it was, in the autumn of 1348 the Black Death spread to western Europe. It has been estimated that around 35 per cent of the population of western Europe died due to the plague or the effects of the consequent famine. The economic and social impact in both England and France was devastating. The ability to resume the war on any scale was severely limited, and the truce held for eight years, save for sporadic breaches short of full-scale campaigns and the continuing civil war in Brittany.

In 1350 King Philippe died, to be succeeded by Jean II, and two years later a new pope came to the throne in Avignon. Innocent VI decided that the time had come to try to bring peace to France and England and brokered a peace conference held at Guînes in 1353. The negotiations concluded in the spring of the following year. Edward had to cease all hostilities and renounce his claim to the crown of France, but his rewards were to be rich indeed, with the removal of the need to pay homage for Aquitaine and the cession to him of Poitou, Touraine, Anjou, Maine and Normandy. The treaty, which was to be ratified in the autumn in the presence of the pope, was much to the liking of the English; the French, however, had second thoughts and repudiated it in early 1355. War broke out again during the summer.[11]

Meanwhile, in January 1355, senior Gascon nobles, including Jean de Grailly, holder of the ancient feudal title peculiar to Gascony of the captal de Buch, Guillaume Sans, lord of Lesparre, and Auger de Montaut, lord of Mussidan, came to England to argue that, when the truce expired in the summer, Edward should take the offensive in the south. What fighting there had been during the truce had not gone particularly badly but neither had it gone well, and there was concern over raids being made on Aquitaine by Jean I, count of Armagnac, who was King Jean's lieutenant in the Languedoc. The Gascons were looking not only for military support but also for leadership from the king's son. Edward held a Great Council in April which, *inter alia*, agreed that the Black Prince should go to Gascony with an army and the earls of Warwick, Suffolk, Salisbury and Oxford.[12] An indenture with the king appointed the Black Prince:

> to go as his lieutenant to Gascony with 433 men-at-arms and seven hundred archers, four hundred mounted and three hundred on foot, as his own retinue, and with the men-at-arms and archers in the companies of the earls of Warwick, Suffolk, Oxford, and Salisbury, Sir John de Lisle and Sir Reynold [Reginald] de Cobham, who are to go with the prince to the said parts.[13]

This was an experienced team of advisors for the prince. Thomas Beauchamp, earl of Warwick, who was forty-one or forty-two in 1355, had fought on several of Edward III's campaigns since 1339 and had been in the prince's division at Crécy. Robert Ufford, earl of Suffolk, had also fought alongside the prince at Crécy, and at fifty-seven brought the wisdom of older age. John Vere, earl of Oxford, was of similar age to Warwick, with military experience in Scotland, Flanders and Brittany. He had also fought in the prince's division at Crécy. Salisbury, at twenty-eight, was only two years older than the prince. They had a sometimes uneasy relationship but they had been knighted together when they landed in France in 1346 and fought alongside each other at Crécy. Cobham, amongst the older heads at sixty years of age, and de Lisle, thirty-seven, had also been at Crécy. With the prince went three other veterans of Crécy who were to play a major part in the coming events: James Audley, forty, Bartholomew de Burghersh, around the prince's age, and John Chandos, forty to forty-five.[14] Thus, at the core of the force which the prince was to take to France was a group of experienced men, used to living and fighting together and alongside the prince. Their comradeship would be progressively reinforced over the months ahead, and would stand the army in good stead. The force that would leave with them is believed to have numbered around 2,600 comprising approximately 1,000 men-at-arms, 1,000 mounted archers, 300 to 400 foot archers, and 170 'Welshmen' who were most probably foot-soldiers or pike-men, a specialist arm provided by the Welsh.[15]

The indenture between the king and the prince was dated 10 July and was signed in London. However, preparations had been put in hand to gather the expeditionary force at Plymouth some while earlier, with the first request for ships being issued on 10 March 1355.[16] In Cheshire orders had been issued on 26 June for 300 archers to be sent to arrive in Plymouth by 'three weeks from

Midsummer'.[17] The prince arrived in Plymouth by 30 July, and by then it was
clear that, for want of sufficient shipping and due to contrary winds, an immediate departure would not be possible. This unforeseen event placed additional
demands on the prince and on 30 July he instructed his chamberlain for North
Wales, Robert de Parys, to 'do all that he can to borrow one hundred pounds
for the prince over and above the sum mentioned above [two hundred pounds],
and to send the same to the prince at Plymouth within fifteen days from Sunday
next'.[18] While the ships and suitable weather were awaited, the prince and his
household were engaged in a range of activities. These included routine administration of his affairs, such as an order for the delivery to 'Henry de Berkhamp-
sted, yeoman of the prince's buttery, as a gift from the prince three beeches for
fuel in the foreign wood of Berkhamsted'. There were also final preparations for
the expedition with an order: 'to purvey for the prince's use four hundred bows
and one thousand sheaves of arrows, or as many as possible up to that number'.
There was also a settling of a wide variety of accounts, including payment to
Lambekyn, a German saddler, for saddles for the expedition and 26s 8d for the
prince's minstrel and 'his two fellows'. The volume of activity was extensive, with
179 entries recorded for 7 September alone.[19] No doubt this late flurry owed
something to imminent departure, for at long last the Black Prince's fleet sailed
for Aquitaine on 9 September with 179 ships drawn from thirty-five ports in
England and arrived in Bordeaux eleven days later on 20 September.[20] The
prince lodged in the archbishop's palace, which he seems to have retained as his
residence until his return to England in 1357.[21] He had embarked on a campaign
which was to be the apogee of his career.

Opinion is divided as to the overall plan for the coming campaigns. Some
believe that three operations were planned, with an army under Edward moving
out from Calais, a second in Normandy under the duke of Lancaster, and the
third with the Black Prince in Gascony.[22] An alternative interpretation is that
there were to be just two theatres of operation, one in the north and a second
in the south.[23] Whatever the plans, the result was a *chevauchée* by the king in
Picardy in late October and early November 1355. Both King Edward and King
Jean were apparently willing to do battle but vied for advantage in terms of place
and time. In the event Edward returned to England and Jean discharged his army
without battle. If there were plans for operations by the duke of Lancaster that
year they were postponed, and he was not to land in Normandy until June 1356.
Meanwhile the Black Prince had launched his first *chevauchée* in early October
1355 and was wreaking havoc in the Languedoc.

PART II

THE *CHEVAUCHÉE* IN THE LANGUEDOC,

OCTOBER TO DECEMBER 1355

2

Advance to Contact

Bordeaux to Arouille
Monday 5 to Sunday 11 October 1355

The Gascons are loud-mouthed, talkative, given to mockery, libidinous, drunken, greedy eaters, clad in rags, and poverty stricken; but they are skilled fighters.
The Pilgrim's Guide[1]

On 21 September 1355, the day after the prince's arrival in Bordeaux, King Edward's letters patent were read in the cathedral of St-André to an assembly of the lords, senior clergy and prominent citizens of Gascony and Bordeaux. The prince pledged to be a good and loyal lord and to respect the rights of the citizens. In return he received the homage of the lords and citizenry. This large assembly was followed by a council of war of the most prominent lords. The prince expressed his outrage at the activities of Jean, count of Armagnac, who had been making a series of successful and disconcerting raids into Aquitaine. It was decided that the war should be carried into the territory of Armagnac, and that the *chevauchée* should start in two weeks' time. This decision for a prompt departure appears to have taken some by surprise, but it was already getting late in the season for campaigning and the expedition would need to start soon to reduce the risk of being caught by winter weather. In addition, there would be an advantage if the Anglo-Gascon army could set off before the French had the chance to organise their defences. The objective first and foremost was to spread devastation throughout Languedoc, with the territory of the count of Armagnac as the first target. However, if the French forces in Languedoc could be brought to battle, so much the better. As the military historian Lieutenant-Colonel Burne put it, this could be achieved in two ways: 'by advancing straight toward him or, if he did not react to that, by devastating his country, until he was forced to take action in its defence.'[2]

The two weeks left before departure were busy for all concerned. Tasks for the English component included the unloading of stores and horses, the purchase of further horses, advances of money to be made to leaders, and no doubt some time for rest and recovery after the ten days or so at sea. For the prince there were purchases to be made of meat, fish, firewood, and salt. Money had to be provided for the prince's personal use, including gaming, and material acquired for clothing. In addition, to mark the importance of the prince's mission, new coins were struck and issued on 29 September with the production of gold and silver Leopards.[3]

Some idea of the variety and scale of the activity can be gleaned from the journal of John Henxteworth, controller of the prince's household. Much of his work was involved with settling debts owed to members of the army. A determined effort was clearly being made to get the accounts in order before departure. In addition to this, and the purchase of provisions, there are entries for a payment to archers for repairs made to the prince's ship on the voyage and for losses of their horses at sea. Evidently the crossing had not been plain sailing. Nineteen shillings, the daily wage of seventy-six foot archers, were also spent on sixteen pewter bottles for the prince's medicines. Disbursements were made to move victuals for the prince and bows and arrows to St-Macaire. The prince's tailor received 9s as an advance for the purchase and painting of two lances. Entertainers also had to be paid, with 4 marks paid as wages to jugglers and musicians. Two loans were also procured from Master John Strettle for a total of almost £1,000 to be repaid on 14 January 1356. As Henxteworth drew a line under his records for the first four days of October he could reflect on four busy days with 180 entries and no respite on Sunday. He had disbursed £512 4s 5d, and he carefully records a remaining balance of £3,024 16s 4¼d.[4] The Gascons, who probably contributed the greater part of the combined Anglo-Gascon army, would have needed to move fast to muster their forces. Equipment also had to be gathered at the supply depot at St-Macaire upstream on the river Garonne near Langon for resupply as the army advanced.

In the fourteenth century, Bordeaux was a large and thriving city. According to the French historian J. M. Tourneur-Aumont, London seemed to some to be a dependence of Bordeaux. He recounts how a Christian monk on a mission for the sovereign of Persia in 1282 visited Bordeaux and, considering it to be the capital of England, decided to forgo a visit to England itself.[5] The mistake was perhaps understandable since, with around 30,000 inhabitants, Bordeaux was broadly as populous as London.[6] It was the chief city of the large and prosperous duchy of Aquitaine and was firmly in the English camp both through the Plantagenet inheritance and by choice, for sound commercial reasons. Furthermore, the lighter administrative touch from London than that from Paris helped keep this fiercely independent city within the English sphere of influence. The enclosed part of Bordeaux covered some 400 acres within fortifications constructed during the early part of the century and completed in 1327. As was common in the Middle Ages the city had by 1355 outgrown its walls, and many buildings had been built outside the ramparts as it started to sprawl outwards.

It was from this great city on 5 October 1355 that the Black Prince set out with his Anglo-Gascon army. To the 2,600 men of his English and Welsh contingents were added the Gascon contribution and a smattering of German and Spanish lords. Baker claims a strength of 60,000 men for the army, including 11,000 men-at-arms. This is a gross exaggeration and the overall strength has been estimated as being between 6,000 and 8,000.[7] As the French historian Micheline Dupuy points out, with troops from such a range of countries the common soldiers must have found communicating with each other a challenge, with Welsh, English, French and Gascon being spoken.[8] English was becoming more widely used in England in the fourteenth century, and in 1362 parliament stipulated that English and not French would be the language for legal matters; the chancellor addressed parliament in English for the first time the following year.[9] However, Anglo-Norman French was still the language of the English aristocracy, so the senior elements of the army, having French as a common language, would not have faced the difficulties of the lower ranks.

The fighting men were supported by a large complement of non-combatants. We know that the prince was accompanied by William Stratton his tailor, as well as John Henxteworth, and his household would also have included administrators, servants and clerks. Other lords, and some men-at-arms, would also have had servants. Indeed, based on evidence from the Agincourt campaign of 1415 it may be that all men-at-arms would have had servants.[10] Then there would have been carpenters, farriers, bowyers, fletchers, smiths, armourers, cooks, bakers, saddlers and carters, amongst others. It has been estimated that in some cases during the fourteenth century the non-combatant element of an army could be as great as the strength of the fighting men. Even for a highly mobile operation such as a chevauchée a complement of non-combatants of 50 per cent of the fighting strength would not be unusual.[11] Thus, the overall strength of the army with its accompanying non-combatants was probably in the region of 10,000. Then there were the animals.

It is not possible to establish definitively how many horses were taken on the chevauchée, but it is useful to have some idea of the number simply to illustrate the scale of the operation and the logistic challenges faced by the leaders of the army in feeding and watering the accompanying horses. As a rule of thumb, we can say that in this period knights, esquires and men-at-arms typically took four, three and two horses respectively on campaign, and mounted archers would take at least one horse.[12] Whether or not the knights, men-at-arms and esquires took as many horses on this particular chevauchée is not known, but one estimate places the number of horses transported to Gascony at 6,500 and there were also provisions in the prince's indenture allowing for the purchase of horses in Gascony.[13] The Gascon element of the army would probably have brought a similar number. Thus, a figure of 13,000 horses for the use of combatants and non-combatants may not be an unreasonable estimate. In addition there was the logistic train. We know that the French typically allowed one horse-drawn wagon for fifty men.[14] On this basis, for 10,000 men we arrive at a figure of 200 horse-drawn vehicles. However, in his analysis of the information available from fourteenth-century campaigns, Yuval Noah Harari concludes that a ratio of one cart for twenty men was not excessive, which would give us a figure of 500 vehicles. He goes on to argue that, for a *chevauchée* campaign during which the army was living largely off the land, it would be reasonable to expect the army to carry food supplies only to supplement forage and plunder and to provide a contingency.[15] He has calculated, therefore, that for an army of 15,000 men a train of 100 carts, 850 pack horses and 520 cattle would provide sufficient food for ten days. If we extrapolate from this assumed ten days' supplies, then the supply train for the Black Prince's *chevauchée* in 1355 would be around seventy carts, carrying between 1,200 and 3,000 pounds each, depending on size, and 550 pack horses each carrying around 400 pounds.[16] There is no evidence that the Black Prince took livestock on this *chevauchée*. However, if this expedition followed this common practice, once more extrapolating from Harari's calculations, there could have been around 350 head of cattle. Harari points out that carts could be pulled by up to eight horses, but that four was a good average figure. On this basis we need to add a total of around 800 horses for the baggage train. In addition, some of the lords would have had pack animals for their own use.

It is also possible that a number of portable bridges were taken with the army. One historian thinks that this was the case, and certainly during the Crécy campaign a team of forty carpenters accompanied the army repairing bridges at Carentan, Pont-Hébert, and Poissy, albeit apparently largely using materials gathered locally rather than transported with the army.[17] Thus, yet more horses would be required for the bridging equipment. Finally, a wide range of equipment would be needed, not least reserve supplies of arrows, bows and bow-strings for the archers. Extrapolating from the calculations made by Andrew Ayton for the Crécy campaign of 1346, and figures quoted for the Flanders campaign of the same year, we can add another ten to twelve carts for equipment for English and Welsh archers with a further fifty horses.[18] Thus, we reach a figure of around 900 horses for the baggage train, giving a round total of 14,000 horses for the army.

Finding sufficient forage and water for the horses would be a daily preoccupation over the weeks ahead and, as we shall see, this gave rise to problems during the latter stages of the 1355 *chevauchée*. It was also probably a determining factor on occasions for the length of the day's march and the duration of halts. It was also a problem that was going to become more demanding: as the army gathered plunder it needed more transport. It has been said that by the time that the army returned home, their booty filled a thousand carts, pulled of course, by many more horses.[19]

Modern Bordeaux is a large city covering an area more than 300 times the size of its medieval predecessor, but in the fourteenth century the expedition would quickly have passed out of the city, through the suburbs, and into open country which would have been humming with activity in the midst of the annual grape harvest on which the wealth of the city was based.

Villenave-d'Ornon was the first staging point for the Black Prince after leaving Bordeaux, and here the army bought hay for the horses and rested overnight. Villenave now merges with Bordeaux proper, but then it was four miles outside

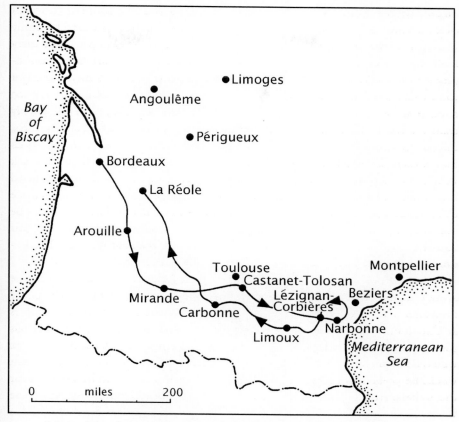

Map 3 The *chevauchée* in the Languedoc, October to December 1355.

the city, not the two miles that Baker states. There are no traces remaining of the castle of Ornon where the prince stayed for the night, and the only vestige of the medieval town is the church, parts of which date back to the twelfth and eleventh centuries. One explanation for a short first day's march of five miles could be that the army was not yet fully prepared. However, a more probable explanation is that Villenave-d'Ornon was the marshalling point for the army. Accommodating a large army with their wagons and horses in a city of the size of Bordeaux would not have been easy, and it is more likely that the troops were encamped and billeted in areas outside the city. Furthermore, as we shall see later, and as has been the case throughout the ages, troops with time on their hands can cause trouble, and it is entirely possible that many of the English and Welsh contingent were billeted outside the city to minimise this risk. In addition, there would have been little need for the gathering Gascon contingent to go to Bordeaux itself. It would be logical to select a marshalling point close to but outside the city, and it is possible that Villenave-d'Ornon filled this function. If this were the marshalling point, it is likely that only the prince, the great

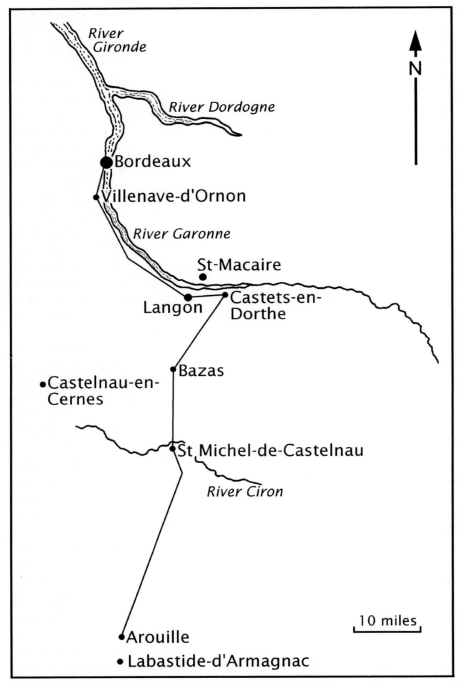

Map 4 Bordeaux to Arouille.

lords, and their immediate entourages, having been accommodated in Bordeaux, rode out on that first day to join the assembling army. Indeed, it is possible that elements of the Gascon troops coming from the east of the Garonne would join the army later, having crossed the river further to the south-east.

The next stop for the prince was to be at Castets-en-Dorthe, twenty-eight miles on from Villenave. The route keeps the river Garonne on the left, and Baker describes the march as being along a narrow track through woodland and then through the walled town of Langon.[20] The landscape now bears little relationship to Baker's description, with some farmland, woods and a predominance of vineyards. As will be seen later there was a significant economic dimension to the prince's *chevauchée* into the Languedoc in terms of its impact on the tax-raising capability of the French king for the following year. The other side of the coin was that, by carrying the war to the French, the English could protect the wealth of the Bordelais; the vineyards along the route are a reminder that the economic base for this wealth was founded on wine in the medieval period. The wine trade with Bordeaux was of great importance to England, and its significance was certainly not lost on King Louis XI who said, a hundred years later: 'If the city of Bordeaux is one of the biggest and best populated cities of the realm it owes it to the island of England ... The English brought their gold and silver which they converted into the wines of Gascony.'[21]

To meet demand for Gascon wine around 100,000 hectares were devoted to viticulture in Gascony. This is roughly the same as today although, with modern techniques, this area now produces three times as much wine.[22] Nevertheless, the scale of production was impressive and exports during the first half of the fourteenth century would not be matched or exceeded until after World War II. Although by 1355 wine production had fallen below the pre-war average it nevertheless remained at the heart of Gascon prosperity, in no small measure due to special tax privileges accorded by the English crown. The downside was that by 1315 Gascony, which had previously been the grain store of the south-west, was no longer self-sufficient in cereals.[23] Thus, it became dependent on English exports of grain, often at a time when England itself was stretched to meet its own needs.

Langon, through which the Black Prince passed on 6 October 1355, has little to show for its medieval past, other than some ecclesiastical buildings dating from the twelfth and thirteenth centuries. However, the army did not stop at Langon, despite the proximity of the supply depot across the river at St-Macaire a mile further upstream, but continued to Castets-en-Dorthe. They had had a gruelling twenty-five mile march, and lost many horses as a consequence. In normal circumstances a horseman could travel well in excess of twenty-five miles per day, twenty miles per day would be good going for infantry, and the baggage train would be doing well to exceed ten to twelve miles per day.[24] It is difficult to understand why the army made such a demanding forced march while still in friendly territory and so early in the campaign. Also the prince and his advisors would have known from experience that horses are susceptible to fever after long sea crossings, even up to two weeks after disembarking. It seems extraordinary that they should move at such a pace and risk losing valuable animals.

There is another conundrum to which we do not have an answer. Why did the army move past the St-Macaire supply depot at such speed? It seems very unlikely that the main body paused for any sort of resupply in view of the distance that they had to cover on 6 October. However, on arrival in Castets-en-Dorthe the army rested for a day, and it is possible that the baggage train took two days to travel from Villenave-d'Ornon to Castets-en-Dorthe and paused to collect supplies at Langon. Alternatively, it may be that the baggage train was assembling at Langon, drawing on the supplies shipped up the river from Bordeaux and then transported across the river by boat from St-Macaire for cross-loading to the vehicles, since there were no bridges at either St-Macaire or Langon in 1355. It is also possible that, in view of the relative haste with which the expedition had departed from Bordeaux, Gascon contingents from areas to the east of the Garonne were converging in the vicinity of Castets-en-Dorthe to rendezvous with the main body.

Castets-en-Dorthe also stands on the Garonne. Its castle, much modified over the years and with no obvious traces of the medieval building, was built on the authority given by King Edward II on 15 November 1313 and stands in a dominant position high above the river. At some time the castle passed into French hands, but it was retaken by Derby in 1345 and in 1355 was in the possession of Jean de Grailly, the captal de Buch, a prominent Gascon member of the prince's entourage.[25]

Hay and oats were bought at Castets-en-Dorthe. Unfortunately, rather a lot of wine was also purchased and distributed to the Welsh troops, and the age-old problem of soldiers with time on their hands and too much to drink manifested itself. John Henxteworth's accounts show that on 6 and 7 October £10 9s 2d was spent on over 1,000 gallons of wine, with 670 gallons being specifically attributed to the Welshmen. In this period ale and wine were preferred as beverages since water was dangerous, and ale would have been less common than wine in the southern half of France. Thus, a record of the purchase of large quantities of wine is to be expected. Nevertheless, in this case things seem to have got out of hand and the result was a substantial bill for compensation, with £11 5s paid out by Henxteworth to 'divers men of the town of Castets-en-Dorthe in recompense for the damage done to the same by divers Welshmen and other retainers of the Lord'. The damage must have been considerable since we find that on 7 October John paid £4 10s to Guillaume Brigan as recompense for the burning of his house.[26] If this was what the army were doing in friendly territory, the omens for what would happen when they got their hands on looted wine in enemy territory were not good.

From Castets-en-Dorthe the army turned south on Thursday 8 October 1355, leaving the Garonne behind for the first time, across terrain which now starts to become more undulating. The next place of any consequence is the cathedral town of Bazas, eleven miles on from Castets-en-Dorthe, and the Black Prince's next stopping point for the nights of Thursday 8 and Friday 9 October.

Approached from the north, Bazas is striking, rising on a steep rocky promontory between two valleys, with the medieval cathedral towering above the town. A large part of the ramparts, believed to date at the latest from the start of the fourteenth century, and therefore extant when the Black Prince passed this way, remains in place atop steep escarpments. The Gisquet gate in the north wall also still exists and it was through this narrow gateway that the Black Prince would most likely have made his entry. Although parts of the Cathedral of St-Jean-Baptiste have been rebuilt after suffering damage at the hands of the Protestants in the sixteenth- and seventeenth-century Wars of Religion, the west front, the bell tower and the choir were undamaged and are much as they were in the fourteenth century. According to one local resident, this piece of good fortune owed more to the task of its demolition being beyond the Protestants than to any scruples on their part. There are also vestiges of the medieval episcopal palace adjacent to the cathedral, and it is likely that the Black Prince would have lodged here during his stay.

Bazas was a prominent town in Aquitaine and one whose history took it back and forth between English and French allegiance. It had most recently come across to the English cause in 1347, thanks to the efforts of Henry of Lancaster, largely in return for the grant of a customs exemption on wine produced within one league of the town. In 1352 it had had to be hurriedly reinforced from Bordeaux to prevent its surrender to the French, and in 1355 Bazas remained in allegiance to the English.[27] Since it was the last large town before entering enemy territory it was a place to resupply and rest, and on Friday the army halted here and provisioned with wine and corn.

The order was given in Bazas that all in the army were henceforth to bear the red cross of St George. Somewhat enigmatically, Baker also says that it was rumoured that the enemy were doing the same. Whether or not it was standard practice at the time for English armies to wear the cross we do not know, but by 1385 it had been enshrined in the Ordinances of War of Richard II, the prince's son, which instructed that

> everyone … of our party, shall bear a large sign of the arms of St George before, and another behind, upon peril that if he be hurt or slain in default thereof, he who shall hurt or slay him shall suffer no penalty for it.[28]

Clearly there was much concern to avoid casualties from what we now euphemistically call 'friendly fire'.

On Saturday 10 October the army set off once more. After leaving Bazas the route south quickly enters the area known as the Landes. This was, and is today, an area of low population density, and there were few villages of any consequence before entering enemy territory, thirty-eight miles south of Bazas. Nowadays, following a programme of extensive forestation in the middle of the nineteenth century, the area is largely given over to forest, with parcels of land for arable farming. However, before the Landes were reclaimed from the sand, this was an area considered almost as desert: Voltaire compared it to the Sinai and Toulouse and Montpellier to the Promised Land for the unfortunate dwellers of the Landes.[29] We get an idea of how unpleasant this area was at the time of the Black Prince's passage from the author of the *Pilgrim's Guide* writing in the twelfth century:

> Then, for travellers who are already tired, there is a three days' journey through the Landes of Bordeaux. This is a desolate country lacking in everything: there is neither bread nor wine nor fish nor water nor any springs. There are few villages on this sandy plain, though it has honey, millet, and pigs in plenty. If you are going through the Landes in summer be sure to protect your face from wasps and horse flies which are particularly abundant in this region. And if you do not watch your feet carefully you will sink up to your knees in the sea sand which is found everywhere here.[30]

Although there were some trees, with oaks as well as conifers thriving on the sandy soil, the landscape was desolate with tough marsh plants growing in tufts and gorse and heather the main vegetation. In the winter it was wet and marshy; in summer the water evaporated to leave a dry, sandy plain. From autumn to spring the stagnant water was notorious for malaria. It was, and remains, renowned for its quicksands.

The first port of call in the Landes was Castelnau, but there is some ambiguity about the precise location of this town. Part of the problem of identifying the correct location is that the word *castelnau* is a common noun for a small walled town built around a keep or donjon. Thus, a *castelnau* was similar in concept to a motte and bailey castle, but designed to give protection to the local inhabitants on a permanent basis rather than as a refuge in times of need. Because of this generic name there is a host of villages and towns in south-west France with the name Castelnau appended. One nineteenth-century French historian believed that the Castelnau in question was the château of Castelnau-en-Cernes, largely it seems because this belonged to one of the principal Gascon lords in the Black Prince's army, Bernard d'Albret. This is probably the ruined château of Castelnau-de-Cernès, which was certainly in the d'Albret family, in the village of St-Léger-de-Balson.[31] Since it is fifteen miles to the west of Bazas and the general line of advance this was very unlikely to have been the Castelnau visited by the prince.

There is a Castelnau in the right place, even if now it is no more than a hamlet of a few buildings, not far off a direct line south from Bazas to Arouille, the first stop in enemy territory. Even here there remains some ambiguity because a mile to the south-east is the slightly larger St-Michel-de-Castelnau. There is further ambiguity because Baker says that 'On Saturday, the army reached Castelnau, where three castles belonging to three different lords can be seen from a long way off'.[32] However, there are remains and records of only one castle in the vicinity at Castelnau. It is clear that this castle existed at the time of the 1355 *chevauchée*, since it is recorded as having belonged to one Bertrand des Mames in 1294 with the seigneur of the area being from the La Mote family who was either related or allied to the powerful d'Albrets. There is little to show now of the castle, since in the 1930s the owner, unable to afford the costs of maintenance, demolished the building and sold the stone. All that remains of a castle that at one time covered an area 40 by 60 metres are some subterranean cellars in the hamlet of Castelnau.

There are only a few very minor streams en route from Bazas to Castelnau, and a substantial water supply would have been essential at the end of the day's march. The river Ciron is the first watercourse of any consequence since leaving Bazas. This river was once sufficiently well maintained to support navigation for the transport of timber, and it should have been an adequate source of water for the army. Its immediate proximity to the remains of the castle is consistent with St-Michel-de-Castelnau playing host to the Black Prince on 10 October 1355.[33]

Castelnau was the last opportunity for the army to buy provisions until their eventual return to friendly territory, and meat and wine were purchased here. By the end of the next day the army would be in enemy territory and largely reliant on supplies that could be obtained through forage and requisition. The revelry at Castets-en-Dorthe continued to figure in the work of John Henxteworth, with a late payment made for a pipe of wine, 105 gallons, to Sir Stephen de Cusyngton. This time the beneficiaries were Gascons.[34]

The next day, Sunday 11 October, brought a long march of twenty-five miles, almost certainly due to the difficulty of finding water and forage, through the difficult country of the Landes to Arouille. The possibility that it was made for tactical reasons to maximise surprise as to the timing of the prince's entry into Armagnac can probably be discounted since, as we shall see, the arrival seems to have been neither a surprise nor indeed unwelcome to the local French commander. Whatever the reason the result of the hard day's march was the loss of more horses.

When the army was two miles from Arouille, which was just inside enemy territory in the county of Armagnac, banners were unfurled and the army was divided into three divisions. The vanguard was commanded by the earl of Warwick, in the office of constable, and Sir Reginald Cobham, the marshal. With them were Lord Beauchamp of Somerset, Lord Clifford and Sir Thomas Hampton, the standard-bearer. The main body was commanded by the prince, and in his company were the Earl of Oxford, Sir Bartholomew de Burghersh, Sir John de Lisle, Lord Wilby, Lord de la Ware, Sir Maurice Berkeley, Sir John Bourchier, Sir John de Roos, mayor of Bordeaux, the captal de Buch, the lord of Caumont and the lord of Montferrand who was the standard-bearer. The rearguard was under the command of the earls of Suffolk and Salisbury in whose company was the lord of Pommiers.[35]

The nature of the campaign would now change: provisions would be seized from the enemy and not purchased, pillaging and burning would begin, and there would be the ever-present risk of hostile action. From now on they would generally advance in three columns on a broad front, which made for easier foraging and provisioning as they started to live off the land. It also enabled destruction to be extended across a wide area, so maximising the destructive potential of the army. But the divisions were generally close enough to come together quickly if needed for defence or a set-piece battle.[36]

The army had covered eighty-one miles in the seven days since leaving Bordeaux. It was now on the threshold of action for the first time as it embarked on the offensive phase of the *chevauchée*.

3

Armagnac

Arouille to Mirande
Monday 12 to Thursday 22 October 1355

So we rode afterwards through the land of Armagnac, harrying and wasting the country, whereby the lieges of our said most honoured lord, whom the count had before oppressed, were much comforted.

Letter from the Black Prince to the bishop of Winchester,
25 December 1355[1]

The approach to Arouille brought the army out of the Landes and into the territory of the count of Armagnac. With this came a change of terrain as the flat, forested landscape gave way to more open and undulating countryside intersected by small rivers and streams. It seems that the village of Vielle-Soubiran received the first hostile visitation from the Anglo-Gascon army, but it was at Arouille, four miles further south, that the first hostilities were recorded by Baker.[2]

We know little of Arouille other than that it was a *bastide* town founded by King Edward I and the viscount of Juliac in 1295. Over its life it has diminished in size and importance, to the extent that in 1965 it ceased to be a *commune* in its own right and was absorbed into the nearby town of St-Justin. All that remains now is a small hamlet with a cluster of houses. However, as a *bastide* town Arouille would have had much in common with similar new towns which have survived in south-west France. There would have been both economic and political motives for its foundation. Arouille would almost certainly have been founded to bring more land into cultivation in order to increase the income of the founders, but it would also have been seen as a means to strengthen the defence of the area, much as the charter for nearby Labastide-d'Armagnac was granted to Bernard VI of Armagnac by Edward I in 1294 to protect the lands of the English kings from the count of Foix.

Bastides, unlike *castelnaux* (see Chapter 2), were not necessarily fortified at their inception, but this often followed with the Crown normally paying for fortified gates and the inhabitants being responsible for the remainder of the

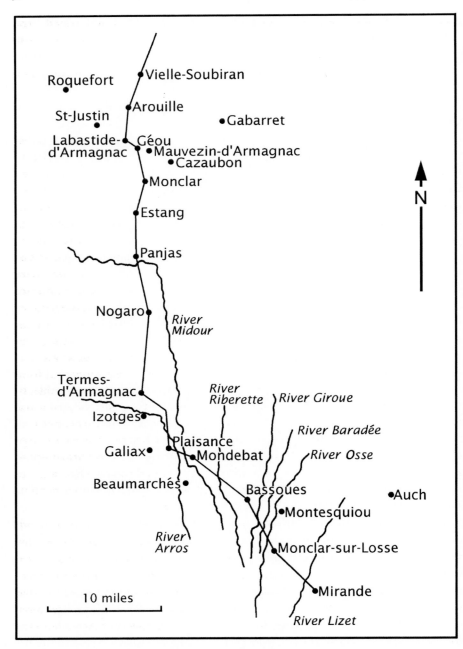

Map 5 Arouille to Mirande.

enclosure. By 1355 Arouille would almost certainly have been fortified. The Anglo-Gascon troops approaching Arouille would have seen a typical small, fortified *bastide* town, built on a grid pattern, surrounding a market hall at its centre, with a church set a little way apart and with a population probably of a few hundred.[3]

Arouille, together with three other local towns, was surrendered to the Anglo-Gascon army by the captain of the castle, Guillaume Raymond. Certainly the fortifications of a small town such as Arouille would have offered little protection from an assault by an army the size of the prince's, and surrender to such overwhelming force would have been prudent. However, it has also been suggested that Raymond had been engaged in secret negotiations with the English before the arrival of the army.[4] The identity of the other towns surrendered by Raymond is uncertain. In a letter to the bishop of Winchester written on Christmas Day, after his return to Bordeaux, the prince refers to passing through the land of Juliac, 'le pais de Juliak', but he does not name the towns which surrendered.[5] It has been suggested by Clifford Rogers that they were Juliac, Mauvezin-d'Armagnac, and Créon-d'Armagnac.[6] Today there is no trace of a town of Juliac, although there is a Château de Juliac marked on the modern large-scale map and the eighteenth-century Cassini map shows a small settlement with this name.[7] This was once the centre of the vicomté of Juliac, and since Arouille was held in fief from the viscount, it is likely that Juliac was one of the towns surrendered. Other fiefs of Juliac have long since disappeared from the map, save Labastide-d'Armagnac, two and a half miles south of Arouille. In an unusual family arrangement, this town was held by the count of Armagnac as a fief of the viscount, Roger d'Armagnac. As such it would have been an attractive prize for the prince, and the town is likely either to have been one of those which surrendered or to have been sacked.[8] In view of their proximity to Arouille, Mauvezin-d'Armagnac, five miles east, St-Justin, two and a half miles to the south-west, and Créon-d'Armagnac, five miles south-east, are other possible towns to have surrendered.

In the past these towns had been under English jurisdiction, and their hand-over was seen by the English as a return to their rightful allegiance. The army was billeted here for two nights, but nevertheless offensive operations started in earnest, with Baker recording that 'those who wished to do so went out and took provisions and forage, burning enemy territory, and doing everything that would bring the country to the king's peace'.[9] Indeed, it seems that these initial operations may have taken the army out ten miles to the west of Arouille to the town of Roquefort.[10]

On Tuesday 13 October the army moved on again eight miles south-east to Monclar. This is now a small village, but in 1355 it was a more substantial settlement with a castle and a town, founded by Alphonse de Poitiers in 1256. The castle surrendered, but during the night the town was set alight, with the fire being so intense that the Black Prince had to flee for his safety. We do not know whether the fire was started deliberately, either by a member of the prince's army or by a fleeing member of the garrison as a final act of defiance, or was simply an accident. Whatever the case, the prince drew a lesson from this experience, and for the rest of the campaign he would not sleep in captured towns, both to avoid the risk of similar incidents and to be better prepared in the event of the approach of the French. If a castle or a monastery were not available, he would sleep in his tent outside the walls.[11]

While the army was operating in the area around Monclar on Tuesday, three towns were entered and burnt. It is not clear whether one of these was Estang, a small town four miles south of Monclar, which has changed little in size over the centuries and has retained its twelfth-century church, the mound where the castle keep stood, and remnants of the town walls. However, this town, standing on a steep south-facing escarpment, and in 1355 surrounded by stone ramparts, with a castle and church in its centre, was certainly assaulted. It was here that one of the prince's company, Sir John de Lisle, was fatally wounded by a crossbow bolt. Baker describes this as happening on the Tuesday, with his death following the next day. However, Sir John Wingfield, in a post-campaign letter written from Bordeaux shortly before Christmas, in describing how Sir John de Lisle was killed 'most remarkably', gives slightly different dates to Baker and records the wounding as taking place on the third day after they had entered enemy territory, Wednesday 14 October, with the death following on Thursday 15 October. Sir John also tells us that this was the only loss of a knight or esquire in the prince's army on the entire *chevauchée*.[12] John Stretton, the prince's tailor, and others were knighted on the Tuesday, but we can be sure that the wounding and subsequent death of Sir John de Lisle would have cast a shadow over this event. Not only was he a prominent member of the prince's entourage, but he was also a veteran of the fighting both in Gascony in 1339–40 and at Crécy and one of the first members of King Edward's newly founded Order of the Garter.[13]

We cannot identify with certainty the towns said to be burnt on the Tuesday, although one historian lists places in Armagnac which he believes received the attentions of the prince's army. If churches and smaller hamlets are excluded from this list, then only a few places remain which might justify the description of a town in the vicinity of Monclar. The most likely to have been attacked on 13 October, in addition to Monclar and Estang, are: Géou, marked now simply by a chapel, three miles to the north-west of Monclar, Gabarret, ten miles to the north-east and Panjas, nine miles to the south.[14]

There is some circumstantial evidence that Panjas was indeed one of the three towns. It is recorded locally that the nave of its medieval church, which certainly existed in 1355 since it has some fine twelfth-century frescoes, was rebuilt in either the late fifteenth or early sixteenth century having been destroyed at an unspecified date during the Hundred Years War. Fortunately the extensive frescoes were in the chancel which evidently survived the destruction of the adjacent nave. They show, *inter alia*, scenes from St John's account of the Apocalypse. The portrayal of the Apocalypse, although predating the *chevauchée*, has a resonance with a late fourteenth-century portrayal in a French tapestry of the Black

Prince as one of the Riders of the Apocalypse. The village was fortified until the seventeenth century with a castle outside but adjoining the village with access through a gate. The castle has a dominant position above the valley of the Midour, and the approaching troops would have seen the town walls and gates and the adjoining castle surrounded by a curtain wall with six towers. However, as with so many of these minor castles, and despite its imposing position, it was a relatively modest affair. It is clear from the remaining buildings, which include the keep and some truncated corner towers, that it would have offered little resistance to a determined attack.[15]

The army remained encamped at Monclar for two days and on Friday 16 October moved on fourteen miles to Nogaro. The route passed through gently undulating countryside with the valley of the river Midour off to the right, before descending to cross the flood-plain of the Midour and climbing to traverse the southern side of the river valley to the town of Nogaro.

Accounts of the events after the destruction of Estang and the surrounding area differ. Baker states that the army halted for two days at Monclar and then advanced fourteen miles to Nogaro on Friday where it camped outside the town overnight before moving on again on Saturday. Others claim that the army spent three days fruitlessly attacking Nogaro before moving on.[16] Nogaro today is a bustling if rather uninspiring town and with little to show of its medieval past, but in 1355 it was, according to Baker, a 'strong place'. It is possible that the differing accounts of events at Nogaro are explained in part by its strength, and from Wednesday onwards it may have been subject to probing attacks by elements of the army while the main body of the army remained at Monclar until moving to the town on Friday. During the *chevauchée* as a whole the prince did not spend precious time and risk valuable resources on sieges. As Clifford Rogers, has pointed out, his strategy was focused on people rather than places.[17] Success did not hinge on reducing every town on the line of march. A demonstration that the king of France and his lieutenant in the Languedoc, the count of Armagnac, were powerless to stop the Anglo-Gascon army would convey a sufficiently powerful message. It is also likely that the prince had learnt from his experience in the Crécy campaign when Edward III refused his request to attack Beauvais. On that occasion the king was clear that the priority was to drive north to find a crossing of the Somme to avoid being trapped by the French. A battle with the main French army could be imminent and he did not wish to waste either time or resources on attacking Beauvais. The prince is described as going into a sulk and having done little or nothing to restrain his men from entering and burning the outskirts of Beauvais.[18] Nine years later he was more experienced, older and wiser, and it is possible that, probing attacks having failed over previous days to reveal weaknesses, he decided not to risk resources on a major assault and the army moved on again on Saturday 17 October.

The next halt for the army was to be Plaisance, thirteen miles south-east from Nogaro on the west bank of the river Arros. The likely axis of advance of the army would have been along the route of the modern roads from Nogaro to

Plaisance. The route climbs gently from Nogaro, and two miles from the town crests a ridge. On a clear day the mountains of the Pyrenees come into view for the first time, running like a majestic snow-clad rampart across the horizon more than sixty miles away. For men in the army who had never before seen anything higher than the mountains of Wales this must have been an impressive sight.

Five miles along the ridge is a tall castle keep. It is the last vestige of the castle at Termes-d'Armagnac. The keep rises 120 feet above the surrounding country-side, and, standing on an escarpment a further 150 feet above the valley of the Adour and Arros rivers, it dominates the countryside to the south and south-east. The castle was built either towards the end of the thirteenth or at the beginning of the fourteenth century, and later in the Hundred Years War one of its owners, Thibault d'Armagnac Termes, fought alongside Joan of Arc and was present at her trial. However, in 1355 the castle merited neither comment in the chronicles nor, apparently, attention from the prince.[19] Looking back from Plaisance, six miles away by line of sight, it stands clear on the horizon, and it seems strange that a castle in such a dominant position should not have been reduced. Perhaps it was too hard a nut to crack, or possibly, with the focus on people rather than places, it was better to leave it alone to demonstrate to the population of Plaisance the impotence of a local lord shut up in his castle to discharge his responsibility to protect his people.

Beyond Termes-d'Armagnac the route descends into the valley of the Arros for the approach to Plaisance. Once in the valley the army had two choices: to stay to the east of the river and cross on arrival at Plaisance, or to find a crossing of the river to the north-west near Izotges and approach the town from the land-side. The main considerations would be the practicability of river crossings, the state of the defences and the onward route. At Plaisance there was a ford across the river, and there is today a stone bridge, built in 1846, leading directly into the town. There were earlier wooden bridges in the same position which were frequently washed away by floods, and it is not clear if there was a bridge here in the fourteenth century. The local historian Alain Lagors believes that there may have been a wooden bridge across the Arros, but to the south of the town adjacent to the ford. The Arros is not very wide or deep to the north-west of Plaisance, but it has steep banks which would present problems for horse-drawn vehicles. No doubt the carpenters could have constructed a temporary bridge, but since the advance on subsequent days would be to the east of the Arros there would be no need to bring the baggage train across. It would be much more practical to remain to the east, with only the fighting troops needing to cross at the ford or the bridge for the assault on the town. There is circumstantial evidence to support the supposition that the approach was made from the east since the castle of Galiax, only two miles to the west of Plaisance, was attacked on the day following the arrival of the prince at Plaisance. If the approach had been made from the west of the river then the attack on Galiax would have been more probable during the approach march.

The civilian population had fled from Plaisance, despite the town being fortified with ditches, stone walls and towers. The count of Montluzon and other lords who remained were left with the garrison to defend the castle, which was of wooden construction on a grass mound and did not prove to be much of a challenge to the attackers. The defenders were captured by the captal de Buch, the lord of Montferrand, and Sir Adam de Louches.[20] De Louches was a bachelor of the prince, and he was knighted on the day that the castle at Plaisance was taken. He remained with the prince throughout the 1355−56 campaigns and served again with him in 1369.[21]

While the army halted in Plaisance a detachment took and burnt the fortress of Galiax.[22] There are said to be vestiges of the moat of the castle of Galiax, but they are not evident. Local tradition has it that the town of Aignan, seven miles north-north-east of Plaisance, was also taken by assault, pillaged and burnt by the prince.[23] It is possible that this also took place on Sunday, but it may have occurred during either the approach to Plaisance or the onward march.

Plaisance had been founded as a *bastide* by Jean d'Armagnac in 1322. It had a difficult start to its history with its foundation and early years coming at a time of depressed population, no doubt in part due to the ravages of the Black Death, and it did not initially fill its allotted space. Its troubles continued with the prince's army setting fire to the castle in the town on the Sunday and to the town itself before they left the following day. The destruction was so complete that it was said that it was 'left devastated and destroyed, simply surrounded by its ditches and only the foundations of the church and the bell-tower remaining'. With the church were destroyed books, sacred articles and the church furnishings, all consumed by the flames.[24] Its reconstruction was delayed for at least forty years until the late fourteenth or early fifteenth century, when the scale was much reduced with the new town walls surrounding an area only one quarter that of the original town. Even now Plaisance covers only twice the area it did at the time of its foundation. Not surprisingly, little remains of the early town, and of the original fourteenth-century defences only one tower still stands.

On Monday 19 October the army set off for Bassoues, twelve miles to the east, leaving, according to Baker, the town of Beaumarchés to their right. However, there is evidence that the army was, as usual, moving on a broad front since the Premonstratensian abbey of Case-Dieu, five miles south-east of Plaisance, and two miles beyond Beaumarchés, was pillaged and burnt.[25]

If the prince's division did leave Beaumarchés to the right, then the most likely route would initially have been along the course of the modern D37 to climb 300 feet out of the valley of the Arros, descend into the valley of the Midour, and then climb steeply 250 feet out of this valley to the hamlet of Mondebat with its twelfth-century church. The route then follows the ridge line along the modern D126 and D155 roads between the rivers Midour and Riberette. The ridge is narrow: on the modern road two cars can pass only with difficulty, with steep ground falling away to both sides. The nature of the terrain and the absence of alternative routes would channel vehicles along this ridge. As a consequence the baggage train would have been strung out here over a considerable distance.

The final few miles to Bassoues are over undulating ground, and the keep of the castle, standing 150 feet above the surrounding countryside, comes in and out of view as you approach the town. This is not a view which would have greeted the prince, however, since the castle was not built until 1368. Nevertheless, this small *bastide* town, surrounded by its earlier walls and towers, and with its population of a few hundred, would still be readily recognisable to those who passed this way all those years ago. There are numerous medieval buildings and substantial remains of the original walls and towers, and more than 600 years later very few buildings have been constructed outside the medieval walls.

The army reached Bassoues on the Monday evening and lodged outside the town. On the same day Sir Richard Stafford, the prince's steward, was promoted to banneret and raised his banner for the first time.[26] This banner would have been square, as opposed to the triangular pennant of a knight. It may be that, as with Sir John Chandos on the eve of the Battle of Nájera in 1367, this was achieved by simply cutting off the end of the pennant. In military terms a banneret was senior to a knight bachelor and would normally have responsibility for organising cavalry. However, the rank could also be a mark of social status. Whether this promotion was for military purposes or as recognition of Sir Richard's years of service to the prince, for his service to the crown at Crécy and Calais, or as a justice and commissioner for oyer and terminer, 'to hear and determine' legal cases, we do not know.[27] Whatever the reason, Sir Richard was an important member of the household and would go on to exercise stewardship of Gascony as the Black Prince's seneschal in 1360.[28]

On the following day Bassoues surrendered, but all save victualling officers were required to remain outside the town since it belonged to the archbishop of Auch and, as church property, was to be respected.

On Wednesday 21 October the army set out from Bassoues. The prince's division left the town of Montesquiou on their left. It was only four miles off their route, but it seems that it escaped the attentions of the army. The general line of march taken by the prince signalled to anyone who cared to watch that he was not heading for the major town of Auch, but continuing to move southeast through the territory of the count of Armagnac towards Mirande in the county of Astarac. The route descends slightly from Bassoues into the valley of the Guiroue before rising steeply on to high ground once more. The road then descends again to cross the Baradée, climbs again for two miles, and then descends into the valley of the Osse. The climb out of this valley takes the route past the château of Monclar-sur-Losse, clearly much modified over the years but with hints of its medieval past. The lord of Monclar-sur-Losse was a vassal of Montesquiou, but we do not know anything of the fate of his castle.

The army was now approaching the boundary of the county of Armagnac. It had done so at a relatively leisurely pace covering sixty miles in ten days, but it had left a wide trail of destruction throughout the 'noble, beautiful, and rich' lands of the count of Armagnac. Many, including perhaps the count himself, may have expected the prince to turn back from here, having inflicted retribution on the count for his hostility to the English crown. But this was not to be, and by nightfall, after crossing the fourth river on this day's march, the Lizet, the army had reached Mirande, the chief town of the county of Astarac, and the prince was installed in the twelfth-century Cistercian abbey of Berdoues, where, Baker tells us, 'no living thing was found', two miles south of the town close to the banks of the river Baïse. Although this march was only eleven miles, the four river crossings, notwithstanding the dry summer, would have made for a hard day's work for the baggage train even if the crossings were made at fords. This may explain why the army took a further rest day here, only a day after having rested at Bassoues, before moving on once again. Despite lingering near the town, no attempt was taken to attack the 'noble town of Mirande, belonging to the count of Comminges'.[29] The possession of Mirande by the count of Comminges, Pierre Raymond IV, at first sight seems inconsistent, since it was the chief town of the county of Astarac. However, this is probably explained by the close alliance of the two families through marriage.

Mirande was certainly the most substantial town that the army had seen since Nogaro, and indeed was probably the most populous since they had entered Armagnac. Its charter dates from 1281, and by 1355 it was fortified. Baker reports that Mirande was 'full of men-at-arms', and as a consequence the prince and his advisors probably judged that an attack on the town would have entailed too many casualties and too much time. The charter for Mirande includes a penalty for those caught in adultery of either a fine of 100 Toulouse *sous* or running naked through the streets. Less sensationally, all strangers coming to dwell in the town were to be granted the same liberties as those already residing there. No doubt this hospitality did not extend to the prince and his men, and their departure on Friday 23 October when the army set out once more would have been greeted with considerable relief. The army would now continue on its way through Astarac and towards the great city of Toulouse, leaving the abbey of Berdoues undamaged.[30]

4

Toulouse

Mirande to Montgiscard
Friday 23 to Thursday 29 October 1355

Appear at points which the enemy must hasten to defend, march swiftly
to places where you are not expected.

Sun Tzu, *The Art of War*, 500 BC[1]

From Mirande the army had a march of only eleven miles to reach the next halt,
Seissan on the river Gers. Baker refers to the army marching near the mountains
of 'Aragon', the Pyrenees, for this and the three following days, and describes the
passage to Seissan on Friday 23 October as 'difficult, hard and mountainous'.
Today's roads cannot be said to be difficult and to describe the countryside as
mountainous is an exaggeration. However, anyone on foot would sympathise
with Baker's overall judgement that it was a hard day's march. Indeed, the next
two days were going to be hard going, with eight rivers running north from the
Pyrenees to flow into the river Garonne to be crossed in a distance of a little
over twenty miles. The route first crosses the river Grande Baïse with a steep
climb of 300 feet up the escarpment on the eastern side, then down a gentle,
almost imperceptible descent to the Petite Baïse. The same pattern is repeated,
with a steep climb before descending gently to the Sousson, up again and then
down into the valley of the Cédon, before a final, slightly lower, escarpment, and
the last descent of the day into the Gers valley and the town of Seissan. None
of the rivers crossed on this day could be described as major obstacles, and the
Soussan and the Cédon are little more than wide streams. However, they run
in ravines with steep sides, and vehicles and horses would need to cross at fords
or bridges. It may be that there were multiple crossing points and that choke
points could be avoided, but even so several river crossings would have added to
the labours of the day.

Seissan is another *bastide* town, founded in 1288. There is little now to indicate its pedigree other than the characteristic rectangular pattern of streets, and
the only vestige of the thirteenth-century defences is a single tower. The prince,

for reasons we do not know, gave strict orders that Seissan was to be spared.[2] His orders were disobeyed and the town was burnt before the departure of the army.

On Saturday 24 October the army set out from Seissan. The march was again a short one, with only ten miles covered. The pattern was similar to the day before with the route running east to west across a series of river valleys running north to south. The march starts with a steep climb of 400 feet out of the valley of the Gers. The route then descends into the valley of the Arrats, goes up and over another ridge and down into the Lauze, and then up once more to come down to Simorre on the river Gimone. Again as, on the previous day, the minor rivers Arrats and the Lauze both run in ravines with steep banks. However, there are numerous fords, and these would have enabled the army to cross at multiple points. On 24 October, unusually, we know the location of all three battles of the army. The rearguard lodged in the abandoned Dominican monastery in Simorre itself, the middle guard at Villefranche, two miles to the south, and the vanguard at Tournan, three miles to the south-east. All are reported as having been wealthy towns full of supplies and abandoned by their inhabitants.[3]

Simorre was an ancient village predating the foundation of *bastides*; it had been destroyed by fire but had been reconstructed under a charter dated 1141. The new village was a *sauveté*, a type of fortified village offering protection for its inhabitants and constructed around a church or abbey. Today only the church survives from the original Dominican abbey which was destroyed at the time of the Revolution. It is of unusual construction with a central bell-tower in the form of a keep, and it dominates the skyline from every direction as it would have done in the fourteenth century. Some of the exterior walls are of stone, but much of the building is built in the regional gothic style using brick, similar to the more famous cathedral in Albi. It has the appearance of a fortified church, but some at least of the fortified aspects were added by the architect Viollet le Duc, who was also responsible for the controversial restoration of Carcassonne, in the nineteenth century.

We can assume that the town was defended since the charter required the villagers to construct defences consisting of a moat, a bank and earth ramparts. A regional construction technique, still much in evidence in the town today, is the use of *colombages*, half-timbered frames in-filled with *torchis* made from a mix of earth and straw and then covered with an earth or sand render. The use of either *terre cuite*, baked bricks, or *terre crue*, bricks dried in the sun, due in large part to the poor quality of the local stone, is also common in the area. There is also evidence in the Lauraugais, south-east of Toulouse, of town walls constructed of a mixture of straw, sand, and earth (see Chapter 5). It may well be that the earth ramparts here, as in other towns in the region, were constructed using some of these techniques rather than simply mounds of earth. Two gates were authorised in 1301, and they survived until demolished for reasons of *salubrité et sécurité* in 1806, an early example of the spreading tentacles of health and safety. The gates served symbolic and ceremonial as well as defensive purposes. These included a

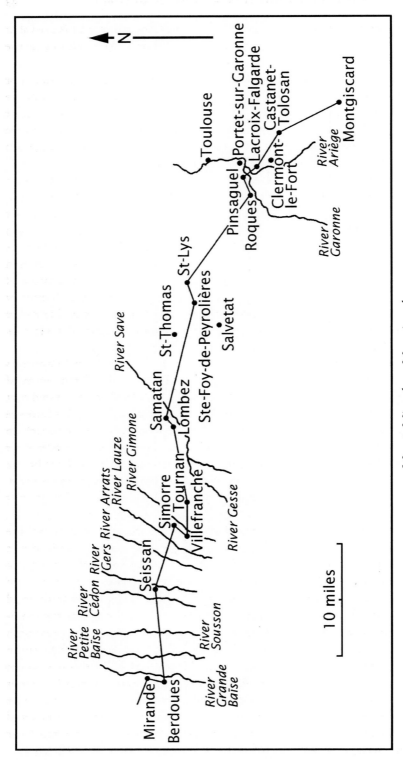

Map 6 Mirande to Montgiscard.

ritual requiring the baron de Boissède to meet each new abbot on his arrival at the gates with his head bared, one leg bare and the other booted, and to take the bridle of the abbot's horse or mule and lead him to the church.

Presumably the appraisal of the local inhabitants was that neither they nor the modest defences were likely to be able to resist the prince's army and hence the abandoned town. Baker does not specifically refer to the destruction of Simorre, but it is likely that it was burnt. However, the abbey church must have survived, since there is a record of four stained glass windows having been given by one Bernard de Lafitte in 1357.[4]

Villefranche and Tournan, where the middle and vanguards had stayed on the night of 24 October, were also probably destroyed. Villefranche had been founded as a *bastide* in 1293 by Centule III, count of Astarac, ostensibly to act as a counter to the expansion of Simorre under the tutelage of the Church. On the outskirts of the village is a motte which is all that remains of an early castle, probably constructed of wood, superseded by a stone castle. This was occupied by Centulle III, but it has disappeared without trace. The extent of the medieval defences is not clear, but there were gates, demolished in the nineteenth century to allow Napoleon's artillery to pass through the village, and it is likely that there would also have been walls, probably of earth or brick. Nothing remains to indicate the medieval past of the village of Tournan.

On Sunday 25 October the army moved on twelve miles from Simorre to Samatan. After leaving Simorre, they entered into the lands of the count of Comminges spreading destruction with fire and sword. It has been suggested that they forded the Save, but this is both illogical and unlikely. On leaving Simorre it is the Gimone that must be crossed immediately, and the best approach to Samatan is to keep to the north of the river Gesse and the river Save after their confluence seven miles to the south-west of Samatan. Crossing the Save before reaching Samatan would require the army to recross the river to enter the town, which is on its north bank. Recrossing at Samatan itself would entail two river crossings since here the river runs in two courses, 300 yards apart.[5]

Climbing 300 feet out of the valley of the Gimone on the way to Samatan, the army left the town of Sauveterre on the left, and passed Lombez, described as a strong town. Lombez housed a Benedictine community from the eighth century. Curiously Baker states that Pope John XXII chased out the Benedictines when he created Lombez a diocese in 1317, whereas the monastery had been transferred to the Augustinians in the twelfth century.[6] A good deal remains of the medieval town, including the unusual cathedral church, built largely of brick with an octagonal belfry, whose construction began in 1346. Unfortunately, however, nothing remains of the medieval defences, and it is not possible to say why the town was considered strong, other than that perhaps its construction in a series of concentric arcs may have aided the defence. The Italian scholar and writer Petrarch was a friend of the second bishop of Lombez, Jacques Colonna, and passed the summer of 1330 in Lombez, before the clouds of the Hundred Years War spread over France. Petrarch was later to say after the Battle of Poitiers:

In my youth, those Britons called English were taken as the most timid of barbarians. Today they are a very bellicose people. They have beaten the ancient military glory of France, in victories so numerous and unheard of that these people formerly inferior to the wretched Scots, in addition to the deplorable catastrophe of a great king [Jean] that I cannot recall without sighing, have crushed the realm by fire and steel, and are barely recognisable.[7]

Having bypassed Lombez, the army lodged at the 'great and rich town called Samatan', about two miles further downstream, on the night of Sunday 25 October.[8] Sixty years later to the day their successors, in another English army under the leadership of Henry V, won the famous Battle of Agincourt on this feast day of Sts Crispin and Crispinian. The prince's army had an altogether much easier day, travelling twelve miles with a relatively easy march. Sir John Wingfield, writing to the bishop of Winchester after the return to Bordeaux, described Samatan as being as large a town as Norwich, while the prince, also writing to the bishop of Winchester a few days later, reported that Samatan 'was the best town of the said county [Comminges] of which those which were within, deserted at the coming of our people'.[9] According to local tradition 'the population, terrified and dispersed by the approach of the most terrible of the enemies of France, who left behind him only ruins, blood and ashes, went in large part to Lombez' for protection, circumstantial evidence perhaps that Lombez was indeed a strong town.[10]

Samatan was burnt before the departure of the army, and amongst the buildings destroyed were the Minorite convent and the castle. It is curious to note from Henxteworth's records that the prince ordered £5 to be given to the Minorite friars as alms. Perhaps the destruction of the convent had been contrary to his wishes. While at Samatan the prince also authorised a payment of 10s, to be delivered by the hands of Sir Thomas de Rasen, to one of his grooms 'tarrying sick' at Bordeaux. Clearly, even though the army was now well into enemy territory, communications with base were being maintained. Nothing remains of the castle now in Samatan but street names and what looks to be a motte in the north-west of the town. The destruction was such that it took twenty years for the town to begin to re-establish itself.[11]

The next day, Monday 26 October, the army set out again, still heading east towards Toulouse and, having passed by Ste-Foy-de-Peyrolières, reached St-Lys after a march of fourteen miles. Baker describes the countryside as 'spacious, flat, and beautiful'. This is not entirely accurate since the land is undulating until Ste-Foy, and it is only then that the land flattens out towards St-Lys and beyond to Toulouse and the Garonne river.

There is nothing at either Ste-Foy or St-Lys to indicate their medieval past, or that the army passed by these towns. However, a history of Ste-Foy shows how total the devastation brought by the army could be. It refers to the probable passage of the prince's army, but records that after 1355 the nearby village of Salvetat, two and a half miles to the south-west of Ste-Foy, disappears from both consular lists and archives for the area. The author's conclusion is that,

after the ravages of the Black Death, the *chevauchée* of 1355 finally and irrevo-
cably reduced Salvetat to nothing more than the current hamlet of a handful of
houses.[12]

At St-Lys the army now stood only fifteen miles to the west of Toulouse. Sir
John Wingfield summarised the tactical position as follows:

> our enemies had broken down all the bridges on the one side of Toulouse and
> the other, save only the bridges in Toulouse, for the river goeth through the midst
> of the city. And the constable of France, the marshal Clermont, the count of
> Armagnac, were, with a great power, in the said city at that same time. And the
> city of Toulouse is very great and strong and fair and well fenced.[13]

Sir John was correct in describing Toulouse as well fenced. It straddled the river,
but both parts were walled, the ramparts having been rebuilt in 1347, and the
bridges connecting the two parts of the city were protected by the walls at both
ends.[14] Jean le Bel tells us that the army of the count of Armagnac, the constable
of France, Jacques de Bourbon, and Marshal Clermont had four times as many
men-at-arms as the prince. He also had some mercenary troops and local militia.
The reported numbers may well have been inflated, and many of Armagnac's
men are likely to have been inexperienced and poorly trained. They may not have
been a match for the Anglo-Gascon army in the field, but they could be expected
to give a better account of themselves in defence of the ramparts.[15] In addition to
the bridges in the vicinity of Toulouse having been broken, other major crossings
for 100 miles downstream as far as Tonneins were in enemy hands.[16]

Against this tactical background the prince's options were: to attempt to take
the city by assault; to lay siege; to try to draw the French into battle; to strike
in a different direction without crossing the Garonne and Ariège; to turn for
home; or to force a crossing of the Garonne and Ariège rivers near Toulouse and
continue to advance into French territory.

Toulouse, as the regional capital of Languedoc and owing allegiance to the
French crown, was a very important commercial and political city. Froissart
compared it to Paris in terms of population. This was certainly an exaggeration,
but nevertheless Toulouse was one of the great medieval cities of France, probably with a population in excess of 30,000.[17] To take the city would be a great
triumph. However, a successful assault would have been a very risky enterprise
which would almost certainly have resulted in heavy casualties. A siege would
have been even less attractive. The prince's army did not have siege equipment,
and an army such as this, living predominantly off the land, had to keep moving.
Spending more than a few days in any one place would lead to serious logistic
problems. At its height, the army of Edward III besieging Calais, a city with
perhaps a quarter of the population of Toulouse, had reached around 32,000
men.[18] The Anglo-Gascon army would not have been adequate to ensure a tight
blockade of a city the size of Toulouse. With the prince stationary, the French
would have time to marshal greater forces, and the Anglo-Gascon army would
reduce in strength and effectiveness through the inevitable toll taken by disease,

desertion and battle casualties associated with medieval sieges. The approach of winter would only exacerbate these problems.

What of the next option, to attempt to draw the enemy into battle outside the city? The prince and his advisors would not have been overly concerned about the odds. They had an army that had been together on campaign now for three weeks, and many had been present when they had defeated the French at Crécy when heavily outnumbered. If the right circumstances could be found then they would have no need to fear battle.

The next option, of striking in a different direction, was not a practical choice. The only way to turn was to the south towards the Pyrenees, but they would quickly enter the territory of the count of Foix, who was an ally. Turning for home would not have been an unreasonable course to take. They had already achieved a great deal in laying waste the territory of Armagnac and Astarac, and no doubt they had already collected a good deal of booty. They could be home comfortably by mid-November before the winter set in.

To take the final option and cross the rivers would be risky, particularly if the French opposed the crossings. However, many present had made opposed river crossings before at Poissy and Blanchetaque during the Crécy campaign, and to take the campaign beyond the Garonne would be to break new ground. Lancaster had been as far as Toulouse in 1349, but an English army had never before penetrated beyond the river Garonne. Although risky, this course of action had the advantage of being likely to be unexpected. It had the potential, through its audacity, to throw the French into disarray and change the strategic situation overnight, and the inhabitants to the east of the rivers Garonne and Ariège would be feeling secure behind these great rivers and would be ill-prepared to meet an invading army.[19]

There is an adage attributed to the Prussian Field Marshal Helmuth von Moltke the Elder, the architect of the Prussian victory over France in 1871, that 'you will usually find that the enemy has three courses open to him, and of these he will adopt the fourth'.[20] The prince, in choosing to cross the rivers and continue to move east, did precisely this. The French commanders in Toulouse were guilty of failing to expect the unexpected, and allowed his army to cross unopposed.

One area of uncertainty, however, is whether or not the prince sought battle before crossing the rivers. There are differing accounts from Baker and Jean Froissart of what happened over the next few days, with Froissart giving us two differing versions. However, we also have the letters of Sir John Wingfield and the prince written shortly after the *chevauchée*.

According to Baker, the army, having arrived at St-Lys on Monday 26 October, paused in the vicinity of the town on Tuesday, and on Wednesday crossed the Garonne and Ariège rivers. He goes on to relate that they stopped near Lacroix-Falgarde, on the far bank of the Ariège, on the Wednesday night and moved on to Montgiscard on Thursday 29 October.

Froissart's first account has it that the prince's army crossed the Garonne at

Port-Ste-Marie. He may have meant Portet-sur-Garonne which is at the confluence of the Garonne and the Ariège, but Port-Ste-Marie cannot be right since
this town is eighty-five miles downstream from Toulouse. Froissart talks of one
river crossing. He is alone in this. He may have believed that the crossing was
north of the confluence of the Ariège and the Garonne, but there is no reason
to doubt Baker, the prince and Sir John Wingfield in this matter. Froissart then
goes on to say that there was skirmishing between the two armies, and that the
prince's army set fire to some suburbs before moving on.

   Froissart's second account has been somewhat embellished. In this version, he
refers to skirmishing on the day after the river crossing. He goes on to say that
the French destroyed 3,000 dwellings outside the city walls to deny their use
to the prince and to prevent them being set on fire by the Anglo-Gascon army.
Then on the next day the Anglo-Gascon army was drawn up in battle order
with banners flying in anticipation of battle with the French. According to this
account the inhabitants of the city were apparently only too ready to do battle,
but were forbidden from doing so by Jean, count of Armagnac, on the grounds
that they were less experienced than the seasoned forces they faced and that in
sallying forth to fight they risked losing everything. He advised them that they
would do better to stay and defend their city. According to this account, when
the French declined to give battle the prince's army moved on to Montgiscard.
Froissart does not date these events, and they do not tally exactly with Baker's
itinerary, since they would have required a crossing of the rivers on Tuesday and
not Wednesday, with the troops arrayed and awaiting battle on Thursday 29
October, before moving on to Montgiscard that day.

   Neither the prince nor Wingfield mentions in their letters the stand-off of
the arrayed troops waiting for battle with the French, and the prince is quite
specific that

> we came to a league's distance of Toulouse, where the said count of Armagnac and
> other great men of our enemies were gathered; and there we tarried two days. And
> from thence we took our march and crossed in one day the two rivers of Garonne
> and Ariège.[21]

Thus there appears to be a difference between the prince's account and that of
Baker to the extent that the former implies that, instead of stopping at St-Lys
on 26 and 27 October, the army in fact moved forward to within three miles
of Toulouse. However, it is quite likely that the locations of the three divisions
over these days were dispersed, and these two accounts are broadly compatible.

   The two secondary accounts that deal with this period in most detail are
those of H. J. Hewitt and Clifford J. Rogers. Hewitt keeps to Baker's itinerary
but draws on Froissart to conclude that 'some slight demonstration (probably a
reconnaissance in force) within view of the city walls was apparently made, and
there was pillaging and skirmishing in the locality'. Rogers also adopts Baker's
itinerary, but states that the prince drew up his army for battle on 27 October
before crossing the rivers and not after the crossing as Froissart states. He argues

that to have crossed the rivers first and then drawn up his troops for battle would not have made sense. This judgement seems sound since, if the river crossings were opposed as the prince would have every reason to think that they would be, the risks of serious losses before battle could be joined would be great. In addition, the generally flat terrain to the west of the rivers would have been much more suitable for battle than the hilly ground beyond the crossings.[22]

Nevertheless, elements of Froissart's account ring true. The destruction by defenders of buildings outside the walls was a common practice, and some skirmishing or raiding in the suburbs is also plausible. The account of Armagnac's unwillingness to fight and his advice to the inhabitants of the city are consistent with his cautious approach to date, particularly as several companies of Genoese and Lombard mercenaries had recently defected from his service.[23] Also, there were other occasions later during the *chevauchée* when the prince arrayed his army because he believed that there was a possibility that the French might be tempted to join battle, and it is likely that he would have taken the opportunity near Toulouse. It is somewhat perplexing that Baker, the prince and Sir John Wingfield make no mention of these events, but that does not mean that the substance of Froissart's account is inaccurate. The prince and Wingfield were writing summary reports and not everything would or could be mentioned. Baker was writing only a year or so after the events, which gave him the advantage of being relatively close to them, but Froissart, who was writing some years later, probably had access to more witnesses than Baker.

In sum, there is no reason to doubt Baker's account and itinerary, subject to there having been some dispersal of the three divisions before crossing the rivers Garonne and Ariège. In addition it is likely that there was some skirmishing outside Toulouse, that Armagnac had destroyed some suburbs to counter a siege, and that the prince did array his army for battle, but that the count of Armagnac was not tempted to join him in battle and discouraged the citizens from doing so.

Whatever the sequence of events may have been, the army crossed the Garonne and Ariège rivers on Wednesday 28 October and halted in the vicinity of Lacroix-Falgarde. Sir John Wingfield, in reporting that the crossing of the Garonne was made at a ford, gives an indication that this was not a straightforward operation: 'And there was never a man in our host that knew the ford there, yet, by the grace of God they found it.' Baker reinforces this by describing the crossings as follows: 'the army crossed the river Garonne, swift, rocky, and very frightening; and on the same day they also crossed the Ariège, even more dangerous than the Garonne, and went downstream to Toulouse. No horse had previously crossed these rivers.'[24] The prince attested to the difficulty of these crossings when he reported, in a somewhat understated way, that 'we took our march and crossed in one day the two rivers of Garonne and Ariège, one league above Toulouse, which are very stiff and strong to pass, without losing scarce any of our people; and we lodged the night a league the other side of Toulouse.' Sir John Wingfield also describes the crossings as having been made a league from

Plate 1 The Garonne at Pinsaguel. The islands in the Garonne near Pinsaguel, and the white water in the background, show the relatively shallow waters on this stretch of river. The easy exit from the far bank, in contrast to the steep banks further upstream, can also be seen.

Toulouse, and Baker states that the night's halt at Lacroix-Falgarde was one mile from Toulouse.[25]

These distances do not help us find the likely crossing points since they are plainly incorrect. The crossings could not have been closer to Toulouse than the confluence of the two rivers, since otherwise only the Garonne would have needed to be crossed. This means, unless the courses of the rivers have changed a great deal, which is unlikely in view of the topography and the location of settlements on the river such as Portet-sur-Garonne, that the crossings were made at least seven miles from Toulouse, or just over two leagues. Similarly, Baker is woefully inaccurate since Lacroix-Falgard is eight miles and not one mile from Toulouse.

The most likely place for the crossing of the Garonne is about a mile upstream from the confluence with the Ariège near Pinsaguel.[26] Eight hundred yards upstream from Pinsaguel, from Roques onwards, the river flows between banks fifty or sixty feet high, and access to the river is very difficult. However, conditions for crossing rapidly improve as the Garonne flows towards Pinsaguel; the banks have less pronounced slopes and the water is shallower with rocks breaking the surface. The view from the west bank opposite Pinsaguel is of small

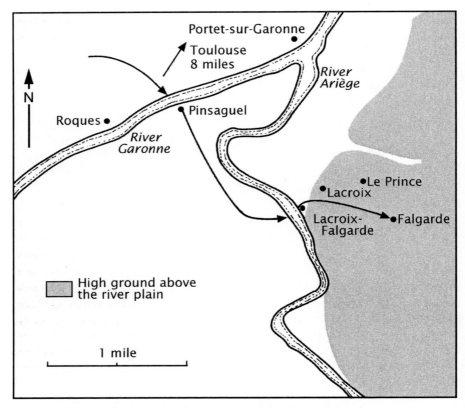

Map 7 Crossing the Garonne and the Ariège, 28 October 1355.

islands standing out of the water in mid-river, and this looks a likely place for a ford, albeit that the water can still be fast flowing here. However, the river was low because of a fine, dry season, and no doubt this would have reduced the speed of flow and depth of the water at the ford.[27] The case for Pinsaguel is reinforced by its name and early maps. Locally it is thought that the name of the village derived from a progressive deformation of *Passage à Guet* indicating a crossing at a ford.[28] Furthermore, the eighteenth-century Cassini map of the area shows the road arriving at the Garonne opposite Pinsaguel and starting again over the river. There is no sign of a bridge, and this probably indicated a ford.[29] The river is about 140 yards wide here and it is not difficult to imagine the crossing being 'swift, rocky, and very frightening'.

 The crossing of the Ariège almost certainly took place somewhere on the two-mile stretch of river between the confluence and Lacroix-Falgarde. There are signs of rocks and shallower water along much of this stretch of the Ariège, which is about eighty yards wide, which indicate a number of places where there could have been a ford, or at least a reasonable point to cross, and it may be that the crossing was made along a broad reach. The crossing of the Ariège is not

Plate 2 The Ariège at Lacroix-Falgarde. One of a number of suitable crossing points of the Ariège downstream of Lacroix-Falgarde. The higher ground behind the river can be seen in the background.

much more than a mile from the ford at Pinsaguel, and in effect the crossing of the two rivers should be seen as one operation, with leading elements having crossed the Ariège while some troops were still waiting to cross the Garonne.

On the far side of the Ariège on this stretch there is a large flat area, and access to and exit from the river look reasonable along most of this reach of the river from the modern village of Lacroix-Falgarde to the confluence. In addition, exit from the flood-plain is relatively easy, with several minor roads leading over the escarpment, about 250 feet high, towards Castanet and Montgiscard. Further upstream the ground is much less suitable, with high escarpments which in places abut the river; such flat areas of land as exist are restricted in size and dominated by high ground. In sum, Pinsaguel and a reach of the river downstream of Lacroix-Falgarde are the most likely crossing places of the Garonne and Ariège rivers.

The fact that at least one of the passages seems to have been made at a ford makes the absence of defensive forces even more surprising. Perhaps, if 'no horse had ever previously crossed these rivers' Armagnac just did not consider the crossings to be possible.[30] However, even if unopposed, the passage of two major rivers in close proximity to a large French army was a remarkable feat. The move undoubtedly caught Armagnac by surprise.

The crossings were judged by H. J. Hewitt to have been 'audacious to the point of foolhardy', leaving a powerful hostile army to his rear. Clifford Rogers, however, believes that Hewitt exaggerated the risks posed to the prince by Armagnac and makes the point that, as opposed to later times, the prince had no lines of communication to be cut.[31] The issue of logistics was, of course, a serious one, but not in the modern sense of supply lines for distribution of fuels, rations, spare parts and munitions. There were times when medieval armies would require resupply through lines of communication, but with a *chevauchée* the army would largely live off the land. However, the demands for food and water were considerable, and that meant that they had to keep moving if they were not to exhaust local supplies.

The diet of the medieval soldier would ideally include bread, which could be baked by the army on campaign, meat, salted fish and pottage, the staple diet of the medieval peasant, made from oats or beans cooked in water, seasoned with herbs and with meat, salted fish or bacon added when possible. Yuval Noah Harari refers to various calculations of the daily calorific requirements of the soldiers of the period, with figures ranging from 2,750 to 5,000 calories. He also cites work on how much grain or meat was needed to provide the required energy. For the sake of argument, if we take a figure of 1.25 kg of food per day per person as the norm, then for the men of the prince's army there was a daily requirement of around 12.5 tonnes. Horses of course compounded the problem. Each animal required some 25 kg of green fodder or 10 kg of dry fodder per day. Thus, the prince's army would need to find 350 tonnes of green fodder or 140 tonnes of dry fodder each day.

As this *chevauchée* was conducted in the autumn, supplies should have been relatively plentiful in the countryside, with stocks having been built up for the winter months after the recent harvest. There would have been occasions when fleeing populations either took as much with them as they could or destroyed supplies. As we shall see later, water was another matter, but overall the army does not seem to have had problems with foodstuffs, and on occasion Baker makes specific reference to supplies having been plentiful. It has been calculated that a village with a population of 200 people with 100 days of supplies would provide sufficient food for an army of 15,000 men for a day. Thus, meeting the needs of the army as they moved would not be too demanding, but if the army remained stationary for more than a few days it would start to run into difficulties. For the horses, the same historian has calculated that 150 square metres of pasture would meet the needs of one horse. Thus, the prince's 14,000 horses would need 210 hectares or about 500 acres of pasture each day. With the army spread out in three divisions, this should not generally have been a problem, even given that by no means all the land would be used for pasture and that the quality and nutritional value would vary. In the forests of the Landes, after leaving Castelnau, the army might well have experienced problems in finding sufficient pasture, and this could in part explain the long march on 11 October on the approach to Arouille where the countryside was more arable. Villages could be expected to provide dry fodder. There was one important difference between the needs of the men and horses. The supply train would almost certainly be carrying a contingency supply for the men but, in view of the quantities required, it would make no sense to carry fodder for horses. The need for either pasture or dry fodder would keep the army on the move. The horses, of course, would need to be watered as well as fed. The daily requirement was around four gallons for each horse, so plentiful sources of water were vital. The men would drink ale or wine, and this, as with the food, would generally be plundered from villages.[32]

The twentieth-century strategic thinker Basil Liddell Hart wrote that 'calculated risk guided by skill is the right way to interpret the motto, 'l'audace, l'audace, toujours l'audace'.[33] The prince and his advisors were prepared to take the calculated risk and demonstrated consummate skill in crossing the rivers. The army was across, Toulouse had been bypassed, and Armagnac had been caught off guard.

With the passages of the Garonne and the Ariège, fourteen miles covered since leaving St-Lys and some men lost in crossing the rivers, it had been a hard day. Baker tells us that after the labour of fording the rivers the army rested near Falgarde overnight on Wednesday 28 October.[34] The modern village of Lacroix-Falgarde on low-lying land hard up against the Ariège is a union of two separate, and still existing, settlements: Lacroix and Falgarde. The older settlements are on the high ground above and to the east of the river. Stopping for the night on the higher ground, rather than on the plain close to the river with the risk of the French taking the high ground during the night and penning the prince's army against the Ariège, would have been sensible. The hamlet of Falgarde is therefore a more likely place for the night's halt than the modern village. Whether or not the lieux-dit Le Prince, half a mile north-west of Falgarde, or Les Anglès one and a half miles east, owe their names to the prince's halt can only be a matter of speculation but they may have some long-forgotten link to the sites of the prince's quarters and the army's camp.

The army moved on the next day, Thursday 29 October, twelve miles to Montgiscard. It is possible that they spread out on a broad front immediately they were across the Ariège, with one local source suggesting that the castle at Clermont-le-Fort, some three miles south of Lacroix-Falgarde on the east bank of the river, may have been destroyed by the prince's army.[35] Certainly, some elements at least passed through and pillaged and burnt Castanet, which lies astride the Roman road to the Mediterranean and was a pilgrim staging-post on the way to Santiago de Compostela.[36] Castanet has a château but there is doubt over its age and it may date from a later period. There was an earth-walled fort protecting the road, which is unlikely to have offered much resistance, and from Castanet the way lay open to Montgiscard and the rich country and cities of the Languedoc.

Carcassonne

Montgiscard to Canet
Thursday 29 October to Saturday
7 November 1355

If the enemy country is rather loosely knit, if its people are soft and have forgotten what war is like, a triumphant invader will have no great difficulty in leaving a wide swathe of country safely in his rear.

Carl von Clausewitz[1]

Having crossed the Garonne and Ariège rivers and passed to the south of Toulouse, the army now had an open route to Narbonne and beyond to the Mediterranean, or the Greek Sea as it was known to the English at the time. The route would be along the axis of the Roman Via Aquitania, called the King's Highway by Baker, built in 118 BC to link the Via Domitia at Narbonne with Toulouse and Bordeaux. For the prince and his army the march to Carcassonne would be generally easy, along a flat valley with gentle hills rising on both sides. In one place the valley narrows to little more than half a mile but in other places it is several miles wide. The route of the Roman road is still in use today as the N113 and D33 roads.

The villages and small towns in the area were poorly defended, soft targets in today's parlance. It was a wealthy trading area and the most productive grain-producing area in France. In addition, some land was used for raising cattle and sheep, and near Castelnaudary a start had been made to the cultivation of woad which would one day bring wealth through the production of dyes. The consequence of this agriculture was that off-road movement, particularly in the autumn across harvested fields and before the winter ploughing, would have been easy going. In such a wealthy area the pickings would be rich for the army, and the economic and psychological impact of the army's transit on the Languedoc would prove to be profound.

Montgiscard, which the army had reached on Thursday 29 October, was once a fief of Amanieu de Fossat. Considered a rebel by the French, in March 1356 he forfeited his goods held in the *sénéchausée* of Toulouse to Pierre-Raymond Rabastens, seneschal of Agen. Amanieu was now a member of the prince's entourage and his advice, based on local knowledge, must have been of considerable value in the vicinity of Toulouse.[2]

Baker tells us that Montgiscard was rich and beautiful, and that twelve windmills in the vicinity were burned. Jean Froissart gives us a more vivid account of events. It seems that the townspeople had an inflated idea of their ability to defend themselves and elected to resist the prince's army. The lesson must have been a salutary one for those living in other towns anxiously waiting to see how events unfolded. The townspeople defended Montgiscard vigorously, wounding several of the attackers with stones and arrows. However, neither the defenders nor their fortifications were any match for the troops assaulting the town. The earth walls and thatched gates were breached and the infantry entered Montgiscard, the prince and the upper echelons having elected to stay outside rather than engage in hand-to-hand fighting in the streets. It was the norm at the time that those who surrendered a town could expect clemency, but that those who resisted could not hope for mercy. Nevertheless, unusually for him, Froissart displays pity for the inhabitants as he recounts that men, women and children were slaughtered indiscriminately. Perhaps the account he heard was of violence that was extreme even by the standards of the day. The attackers pillaged the wealth of Montgiscard before setting fire to the town and destroying the church. The destruction was extensive and exemptions from taxes were granted to encourage reconstruction. That these exemptions were not confirmed until July 1357 is perhaps an indication that a slow start had been made to rebuilding and the authorities needed to give an incentive to accelerate reconstruction of the town.[3] It is impossible to say how many of the inhabitants fell victim to the violence of the attack. However, the conventional assessment in the region is that a mill could support a population of around 200 people, and thus the destruction of twelve mills near Montgiscard is a good indication of a population of around 2,500 in the immediate area.

Two French scouts were taken prisoner and stated that Armagnac was in Toulouse and the constable of France was four leagues from Toulouse at Montauban anticipating that the prince would besiege Toulouse. This account raises two discrepancies. Montauban is thirty-five miles to the north of Toulouse, and as we saw in the last chapter the constable was already in Toulouse, although it is possible that some of his troops had been left in Montauban.[4]

In his account Froissart explains that earth walls were built because of the great difficulty of finding suitable stone in the region, which is consistent with the widespread use of brick in much of the country around Toulouse. Based on evidence found in the nearby village of Ayguesvives the walls, although described as earth, would have been constructed of a mixture of straw, sand, and earth. They would have been about 3 metres high tapering to a width of around 1.5 metres.[5]

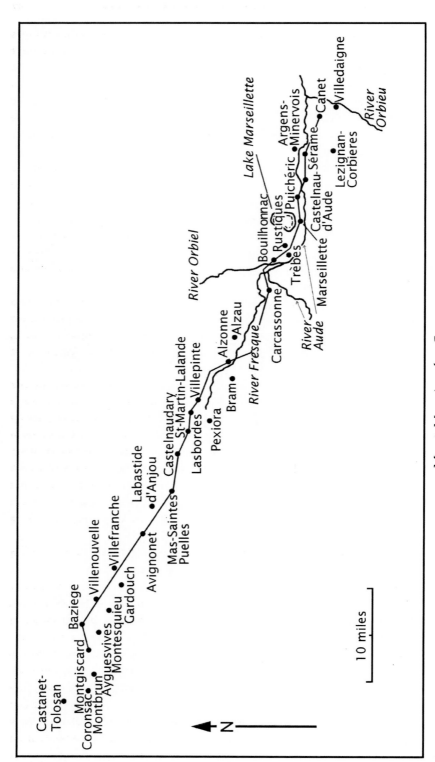

Map 8 Montgiscard to Canet.

Perhaps because fortifications of this type were weak, underground refuges were widespread in the area. One example, at Corronsac five miles to the west of Montgiscard, had three rooms, with a total surface area of 24 square metres, joined by tunnels. Provision had been made to enable the entrance to be secured and concealed, and ventilation shafts were incorporated. Thus, short-term shelter could be provided for a small number of people, perhaps while others took cattle to hiding-places in nearby woods. Part of a similar system has been found at Montalbiau, not much more than a mile from Montgiscard. There were similar refuges in other parts of France, sometimes on a much larger scale, which are believed to date from the period after the Battle of Poitiers. However, these shelters near Montgiscard, and similar examples elsewhere in the Languedoc, are believed to have been constructed during the twelfth and thirteenth centuries for protection during the Albigensian Crusade and the Inquisition into Catharism. Thus, they would have been available for use at the time of the *chevauchée*, and it may be that some of the more prudent local inhabitants used them to escape the ravages of the prince's army.[6]

Montbrun-Lauragais, two and a half miles to the west of Montgiscard, also seems to have been destroyed, presumably on 29 October. In the nineteenth century carbonised remains of burnt grain could still be found below old ruins, although whether or not these remains relate to the *chevauchée* of 1355 cannot be certain.[7]

The events of the *chevauchée* left a deep impression on the people of the region. Local historian Jean Odol recounts that until only a few years ago the *chevauchée* remained strong in the oral tradition with a local peasant relating stories of a legendary figure, known as *L'Homme Noir*, who had passed by with an army in the Middle Ages. There is a field adjacent to the village of Baziège, known as the English Cemetery, which to this day has remained uncultivated out of respect to those believed to lie there. There is some local speculation that it dates from the Middle Ages, but it is much more likely that, in common with other similar cemeteries in the region, it is the resting place of men killed during the duke of Wellington's pursuit of Marshal Soult in 1814.

The prince's army passed through Baziège on Friday 30 October, and on through Villefranche to Avignonet, a march of fourteen miles. Baziège was destroyed, including its church, as at Montgiscard; the existing church was built later in the fourteenth century. In Villefranche the church, built in 1271 by Jeanne, countess of Toulouse, and Alphonse de Poitiers, brother of St Louis, King Louis IX, was more fortunate and survived either by design or because its brick construction was sufficiently robust to withstand the surrounding conflagration. In addition twenty windmills in the vicinity of Avignonet were destroyed, as, according to local tradition, were the towns and villages of Ayguesvives, Ville-nouvelle, Montesquieu, and Gardouch. It is recorded for Montesquieu that 'due to the English war, the number of taxable households in Montesquieu was only forty after the year 1378'. Although this does not tell us the size of the population in 1355, the fact that this was worthy of mention is probably an indication that the reduction was significant. All the settlements above are within two and a half miles of the Roman road which the army followed that day. Only ten miles to the right of the line of march lay the territory of the prince's ally, the count of Foix, which would tend to narrow the breadth of the army as it advanced. All the army was lodged in Avignonet and its suburbs on the Friday night, which indeed implies that it was moving on a narrower front than usual.[8]

Avignonet was a large and rich merchant town with 1,500 houses. Froissart reports that the town 'was not closed', implying that it was not fortified. However, this is not consistent with the other evidence. The town has substantial remains of stone ramparts which are believed to date from the twelfth century, and it may also have been defended by a ditch to the west. The fact that Baker discriminates between the town and the suburbs when describing where the army was lodged also implies that Avignonet was fortified, and the prince in his post-campaign letter is explicit that it 'was great and strong, and it was taken by storm'. Whatever the case may have been, the town had been evacuated and the rich inhabitants had fled to a nearby hill fort protected by earth ramparts. Perhaps they judged that they did not have sufficient men to defend the town but that the fort offered a better prospect. They may also have hoped that the army would be content to leave them alone since the town rather than the fort would be the best source for plunder. If that was so then they were sadly mistaken, and they had either not heard the news of events at Montgiscard the day before or had not drawn the appropriate lessons. The defences of the fort were inadequate, and those who had fled there were captured. In a familiar pattern, before leaving on the Saturday the army pillaged and destroyed Avignonet, although the church (which dates from the first half of the fourteenth century) seems to have escaped the worst of the destruction.[9] However, damage in the rest of the town was clearly extensive, and on 28 August 1356 Jean II authorised a range of measures to stimulate reconstruction. Inhabitants were granted tax exemptions for three years, and if they rebuilt within the walls they could take wood from the king's forests at a fair price payable over fifteen years. If, as a measure to encourage rapid reconstruction, they built within the year they would be exempt from all war taxes for seven years. The order struck a cautious note, however, in permitting transport of materials without the need for specific authorisation provided that they were not taken from neighbouring fortifications! Having granted some concessions by way of a carrot, the stick was also threatened. The consuls were authorised to compel labour at fair wages, and the message to those who wanted to live in Avignonet was that they had the choice of either building a house to a value of four marks within one year or paying a fine of two marks to contribute to the reconstruction of the walls. The consuls were also obliged to rebuild the Château Royal (presumably the hill fort) but could take wood free of charge for this task.[10]

On Saturday 31 October the march continued along the Via Aquitania to Castelnaudary via Mas-Stes-Puelles. Mas-Stes-Puelles, with two windmills standing to the west of the village as evidence of the grain-producing heritage of the area, lies two miles south of the Roman road and is now a small village with a population of around 700. In 1355 it was home to an Augustinian convent which was destroyed with the rest of the village. In a similar manner to Avignonet, the village then benefited from tax exemptions to encourage rebuilding.[11]

More significant than either Avignonet or Mas-Saintes-Puelles was the town of Castelnaudary, sitting astride the Via Aquitania. Castelnaudary is the home of *cassoulet*, the famous dish of Languedoc with its rich mixture of sausage, pork, ham, bacon, duck and beans. There are two similar local legends for the origin of the dish. One has it that Castelnaudary had been besieged by the Black Prince and that as supplies ran low all the remaining food was put into a cauldron and *cassoulet* was born. The variation on the legend is that the dish was produced during a siege by the English at an unspecified date during the Hundred Years War. The effectiveness of the recipe was such that the defenders were filled with the strength and courage to chase the English back to the Channel! The flaw in both variations of the story is that the army stayed only two nights in Castelnaudary and took and destroyed the town without need of a siege.

More prosaically, the town was described by Froissart as being very large, with a good castle, full of people and goods. He goes on to say that the town was not closed, but that there were earthen walls around the castle in the local manner. Froissart is, however, ambiguous over the defences; having told us that the town was open he then recounts that the town was surrounded and taken by assault. English archers had a fearsome reputation for accuracy, with many instances being recorded of shots to the face as a counter to armour. Indeed, the future Henry V received a wound in the face from just such a shot at the Battle of Shrewsbury. Archers were also used to shooting in training and competition at butts up to 260 yards distant. In the assault on Castelnaudary the archers fired so strongly that it was impossible for defenders to stand at the walls.[12] Roger Maguer, a local historian who has researched the history of the town in great depth, states that the town was fortified in the fourteenth century, but that the walls were of poor quality, made of a mix of wooden beams, stones and earth. They were totally inadequate to resist the attack of an army such as that of the Black Prince. The château, which was probably of a similar construction to the town walls, was in the south-east of the town near the Porte de Narbonne.

Froissart gives us a vivid account of the events when a town such as Castelnaudary was still occupied and fell to the attacker. Citizens and soldiers were killed, with the assailants running through the town pillaging and robbing, taking all that was of value, including clothing, silverware and money, and when they captured a peasant or a bourgeois they ransomed him or 'did him some mischief' if he would not pay. The army remained at Castelnaudary on Sunday 1 November, All Saints Day, but before leaving burned the town, the castle, the church of St-Michel together with collegial church archives, the Minorite and Carmelite convents and the hospital of St-Antoine, reputed according to Roger Maguer to be famous for its treatment of burns, and destroyed the earth walls of both town and castle.

Some of the inhabitants had fled to seek safety in the church and one can only speculate as to whether or not they escaped before it was set alight, but some inkling of the impact of the destruction of Castelnaudary is given us through surviving archives.[13] It was necessary for the count of Armagnac to reinstate the privileges of the town because the archives had been destroyed in the fire. The consuls of Castelnaudary were authorised to take a third of any fines levied on inhabitants to put towards repairs, and all persons in the vicinity, whether or not living in the town, were encouraged to contribute according to their means to the rebuilding of the walls. Clearly this was not enough and in August 1356, much evidently remaining to be done, a royal charter for the reconstruction was issued. The consuls were authorised to dispossess and indemnify those property owners who had not started work on reconstruction within a year. The land was to be made available to those disposed to construct new buildings without delay. An indication of the protracted nature of the work is given by the confirmation recorded in July 1357 of tax exemptions to encourage reconstruction.[14] It was going to be some years before the work was completed and, with the opportunity being taken to increase the area of the town enclosed by walls, the work continued until about 1380. The castle was also repaired after the burning of the town, but in the sixteenth century its place was taken by the *présidial* to house the new *sénéchaussée*, created on the insistence of Catherine de Medici, to govern the Lauragais. The impact of the destruction went beyond simple reconstruction. The Carmelite convent burnt by the prince's forces was situated outside the walls in 1355. The Carmelites appealed for exemption from the rules governing the separation distance of their convent from that of the Minorites. Pope Urban V gave approval in 1363 and a new convent was built within the walls.[15]

Some of the prince's men decided not to rest on Sunday but rather to go in search of further plunder, taking an anonymous town and receiving 10,000 gold florins (£1,420) for sparing it and its goods. This place may have been Pexiora, a rich seat of the order of St John of Jerusalem, which could perhaps afford this sum, about five miles along the Roman road towards Carcassonne from Castelnaudary There are no other villages which stand out as obvious contenders within a similar range of Castelnaudary for the dubious honour of this away-day for some of the more eager troops.[16]

On Monday 2 November the army left the ruins of Castelnaudary behind them, passing three villages about two miles north of the Roman road, St-Martin-Lalande, Lasbordes and Villepinte, en route to Alzonne.[17] Lasbordes is an example of a number of towns in the Languedoc known as *circulades*. These towns are built in a series of concentric circles, usually with a church or castle at the centre. It has been suggested that the circular construction resulted from the symbolism of the circle representing pure form, the infinite and strength. However, there were more practical advantages with the circular form. The defensive perimeter wall would have no dead corners, could follow contour lines more closely than a rectangular construction, and was the most economic for enclosing a given area of land. The circular plan also appears to have been used to delineate parcels of land, with a spike at the end of a cord anchored at the other end used to describe circles. Diametric lines could then be drawn across the concentric circles to establish segments of land.[18] Lasbordes is a *circulade* of only 170 metres diameter, but, other than a string of recently built houses on the road leading into the village, there are few buildings outside the original curtilage.

It is widely held that the prince lodged at Alzonne, but Baker writes that he stayed at a 'small village called Alse'.[19] Baker normally uses the word *villam* to describe places of comparable size to Alzonne such as Bazіège, and it seems unlikely that he would describe Alzonne, with a church and a hospital, as a *viculum* or small village. Two and a half miles to the east of Alzonne is the hamlet of Alzau, and, with the prince's preference for sleeping outside towns after the near disaster at Montclar, Alzau is a credible location for Alse.[20]

Whether the prince lodged at Alzonne or Alzau, there can be no doubt that the town of Alzonne was burnt with the destruction of the church and the twenty-four-bed hospital. Once again we see evidence of both the severity of the destruction and the determination of the authorities to reconstruct the town. In August 1356 the inhabitants received a letter of privileges and immunities as a consequence of the town having been *brûlée par les Anglais*. The letter gave exemptions from recently imposed subsidies, suspended debt repayments and taxes for three years, and allowed wood to be taken from the king's forest to the value of 300 *livres*, free of all charges and taxes, to help in the rebuilding of the church and hospital. It went on to say that the inhabitants would always be under the protection of the king. This must have seemed a little hollow in the circumstances, particularly with the capture of the king at Poitiers the month after he sent this letter. The tax exemptions were confirmed in a royal ordinance in 1357.[21]

The prince moved on to Carcassonne the next day, Tuesday 3 November, covering nine miles over flat, open countryside along the route of the Roman road. Carcassonne then, as now, consisted of two parts: the *bourg* built on flat ground to the west of the river Aude and the *cité* on a hill on the far side of the river. The *bourg* was poorly defended with earth walls, while the *cité* was strongly fortified with a double curtain wall built of stone, much as it is today. Towering over the surrounding countryside, it would have been an impressive sight for the approaching army.

The still existing stone Pont Vieux was the only connection between the two parts. At first sight the bridge appears to be about 200 metres in length, but some of the fourteen arches are now hidden. The original bridge was 270 metres long, but a section of this was lost when the present embankment gardens on the *cité* side of the river were constructed in the nineteenth century to provide a cargo quay. Furthermore, much more water is now taken from the river than in the fourteenth century and dams have been built upstream to control the flow. Even so, floods are not infrequent, and in the fourteenth century the river would often have been subject to unpredictable and dangerous variations in depth, width and speed of flow.[22] The eastern end of the bridge is only about

250 metres from the walls of the *cité* and troops crossing the bridge would be exposed to missiles projected from the walls. In view of the river, the location of the bridge and the strength of the fortifications it is no wonder that the prince left the *cité* well alone and concentrated his efforts on the *bourg*.

Baker describes Carcassonne as extremely wealthy, well built and larger within its walls than London. Sir John Wingfield was closer to the mark in describing it as being bigger, stronger and fairer than York. However, with the exception of stone ecclesiastical buildings many of the buildings in the *bourg* were of poor construction. Baker tells us that there was a fine hospital in the *bourg* at the foot of the bridge, the Chapelle Notre Dame de la Santé (which still exists), and convents belonging to four orders of friars who sat tight while everyone else fled to the *cité*.[23]

The whole army was accommodated in just three-quarters of the *bourg*, and there was a plentiful supply of provisions, delicacies and muscat wine. On this first day the army was drawn up in good order for a ceremony to bestow knighthood on a number of men including the sons of the Gascon lord of Albret and Lord Basset of Drayton, who was also promoted to banneret, and Rouland Daneys. The army rested on the Wednesday and Thursday, a truce was arranged, and envoys were sent to the city to arrange peace. The townspeople are said by Baker to have offered the enormous sum of 250,000 gold *écus*, around £35,000 sterling, to spare the *bourg*, to which the prince replied that he 'did not come for gold, but for justice, not to sell but to take cities'. Baker describes the outcome:

> Since the citizens continued to fear the French usurper [King Jean], did not wish to obey their natural lord, or indeed did not dare to because they expected the usurper to take his revenge, the prince therefore ordered the *bourg* to be burnt, but the religious houses were to be spared.

Baker's account ends by reporting that the town was set on fire on Friday 6 November and that the army then left, with the prince receiving reports later that the *bourg* had been burnt to ashes. The letters of the prince and Sir John Wingfield to the bishop of Winchester are consistent with Baker in all major respects, with some minor variations of detail. The prince reports that:

> great chieftains were within and men-at-arms and commons in great number; for all the greater part of the people of the land of Toulouse, were fled thither, but at the sight of us they forsook the city [the *bourg*] and fled to the old city, which was a very strong castle.

He says that the army stayed two whole days and spent the third day burning the town. Sir John is briefer and to the point, simply saying that they came to Carcassonne, burnt it and left.[24]

As we have come to expect, Froissart gives us an altogether more colourful account, telling us that the townspeople sent their goods to the *cité* with the women and children and then defended the *bourg* as best they could. The town consisted of 7,000 houses and, in addition to the earth walls, was defended with chains drawn across the streets, as many as ten or twelve on each street, to slow movement and prevent horses from passing. Seeing the defences and the townsmen drawn up to fight, the prince's army dismounted and fought its way in, men-at-arms as well as infantry, with the archers driving the defenders back. Eventually the attackers prevailed, with Sir Eustace Daubriggecourt at the forefront, driving the defenders out of the *bourg*, some managing to cross the river and reach safety in the *cité*, but some rich bourgeois being taken and ransomed.[25]

We are, therefore, left with two very different accounts of events. There are local accounts of the defence of the *bourg*, even attributing a key role to a Consul Davilla dying heroically defending a breach in the defences. Unfortunately the records for Carcassonne have a gap in the list of consuls between 1318 and 1383, and there is no evidence to support this legend.[26] If there had been significant resistance that had been overcome it is strange, in view of the importance attached by them to Carcassonne, that neither Baker nor the writers of the post-campaign letters refer to fighting. One also has to ask why, in view of the experience of other towns in the days and weeks before, the townsmen would opt to fight when a safe refuge was close at hand and they could be reasonably confident that the prince would pass on in a matter of days. There is also the question of such a huge ransom. It has been calculated that 250,000 gold *écus* would have been sufficient to pay 2,000 skilled craftsmen for a year. One local historian, writing in the eighteenth century, refers to a sum of 25,000 gold *écus*, but there is no evidence to gainsay Baker's figure.[27] If the larger sum is accurate then it could imply that the townspeople went to enormous lengths to save their town and that, when the offer was rejected, they opted to fight. Alternatively, it may be that the consuls felt the very large sum offered was necessary to tempt the prince and that they would worry about when and if it would be paid later.

However, Baker's account is that envoys were sent to the city to negotiate, and that then the offer was made. This implies that the citizens had already taken refuge in the *cité* and that the money was the last desperate throw of the dice to save their houses and businesses. The clergy of the city sent a letter to the prince pleading for the *bourg* to be spared, and the words of the letter perhaps give us a further clue, 'that the Bourg is not burnt or that another new damage be added to that which it has already suffered'. Perhaps there had been some fighting but this may have been a relatively minor incident embellished by Froissart rather than a full-blooded assault. The letter from the clergy is a remarkable document. It was sent on behalf of the senior representatives of an impressive range of religious bodies: the orders of the Dominicans, the Franciscans, the Carmelites, and the Hermits of St Augustin; the churches of St Michel and St Vincent; the Commanders of St Eulalie and St Antoine; the Sisters of Ste Clare and of St Augustin; and the Penitent Sisters of Ste Marie Madeleine. The letter appeals to the prince's charity and gentleness, his nobility and religious sentiments, his sense of justice, his support for the church and above all his mercy. It finishes with a call for the prince to respond favourably to the offer of the citizens of the *bourg*:

If your Excellency refuses us this grace, by necessity the houses will be burnt, the churches abandoned and divine services cease. We do not believe that a heart as noble and as religious as yours could consent to this. Poor wretches that we are, we dare to make this humble plea to your Excellency, because we are persuaded of your clemency, that you love Jesus Christ and his servants, that you and yours seek only to defend and support the Church and to search for justice. [28]

Their plea may have touched his heart but had no practical effect. The prince, or at least members of his army, had not been averse to taking ransoms in the past. However, here was a different situation. Carcassonne as a large and rich city gave the prince an excellent opportunity to send a powerful message to the inhabitants of Languedoc: they were deluded in continuing to be loyal to King Jean, he was a usurper and not their rightful lord, and what is more he was powerless to exercise his duty of kingship to defend them.

The churches of St Michel and St Vincent, the Chapel of Notre Dame, and the seneschal's house all survived the flames, although archaeological excavations have shown traces of fire damage from the period at the Chapel of Notre Dame as well as at the sites of the Dominican and Franciscan convents.[29] While all this was going on the prince's officials could still find time for day-to-day administration, with Henxteworth recording payment for the purchase of 'wax bought at Caracassonne by the hands of Thomas the oven keeper'.[30]

Having set the *bourg* ablaze the prince's army took its leave of Carcassonne on Friday 6 November. Froissart talks of the prince reviewing the possibility of taking the *cité* but concluding that there was more to lose than to gain. A nineteenth-century description of the defences shows what a formidable challenge it would have represented:

Wall on wall, and tower on tower rise in imposing strength and forms to frowning heights along the side and summit of the ridge-like hill. A party that attacked and even gained a lodgement near the outer gate must first have crossed a wide, wet fosse around the barbican, while under double raking fires. It must then penetrate a long and narrow passage stretching up the hillside and enclosed between strong walls, joined to alternate sides of which, at right angles, are cross walls. Advance through these would be like threading wards inside a lock. If any party gained the top of this long passage, it must then turn sharply to the right, and, in an oblong court surrounded by strong walls and swept by raking and by downward fires, next storm a parapet to gain the outside of the lowest of three gates, and those no farther than the outer line of the main defences. Then, in even more confined and dangerous positions it must carry the other two gates.[31]

The architect Viollet-le-Duc carried out widespread restoration of the *cité* in the nineteenth century. His work is controversial, with some considering that he has not restored the edifice but rather created something of a fairy-tale castle with its turreted, tiled, and slated roofs. However, he has also preserved in its form a most magnificent fortress town.

Not content with the inherent strength of the *cite*, the French had recently paid close attention to the defence of Carcassonne. A royal order had been issued in 1336 for the maintenance of a professional company of crossbow men and another in early 1355 required that the state of defences throughout the Carcassonne *sénéchaussée* must be attended to.[32]

There is an account of the seneschal, Thibaud de Barbasan, repelling attacks, and it may be that there were some probing attacks to test the defences, but if so these could only have reinforced the view of the formidable nature of the fortifications. It has been suggested that there was a shortage of water due to the hot dry summer and that, with all the extra people now seeking refuge inside the *cité*, 'if he [the prince] had prolonged the siege, it would certainly have surrendered'. One account supports this view, saying that all fountains and wells were dry due both to the large number of refugees and a long hard drought.[33] This is plausible since the dependence of the *cité* on deep wells for its water supply was a known weakness which had been a major factor in its fall in similar circumstances in just a fortnight in 1209 during the Albigensian Crusade.[34] However, for the prince to have settled down for a siege of even relatively short duration would have handed the initiative to the French, and would have been inconsistent with the approach adopted throughout the *chevauchée*. His decision to move on and leave the *cité* could not have been a difficult one to take.

Froissart says that before departing the prince heard mass and then led his troops under the walls of the *cité* to progress towards Trèbes, presumably to pick up the Via Aquitania which runs through the *cité* and continues to the east towards Narbonne. He acknowledges that the *cité* was well provided with cannons and springalds, capable of projecting stones and large crossbow-like bolts, and states that the prince suffered casualties in passing. This account seems most improbable. The prince would be well aware of the risks of passing near defended walls having seen the use of a masking force to protect the army passing close to Vernon during the Crécy campaign while staying out of bow range. Similarly, he had taken pains to cross the Garonne and the Ariège well to the south of Toulouse. As French historians have acknowledged, he was far too good a tactician to take such an unnecessary risk.[35] Any masking force here would be a sitting target for a considerable time. To expose his army to this fire, let alone to attacks from bows and crossbows and to sorties from the city, with it strung out as it passed the walls, would have been foolhardy in the extreme. Furthermore, there was no tactical advantage to be gained from taking such a risk.

Baker says that they passed by the castle of Bouilhonnac on the way to Rustiques, and that the roads were difficult and rocky, and crossed by rivers. If they had picked up the Roman road, which would have necessitated passing under the walls of the *cité*, they would not have experienced these difficulties. However, if they did not cross the Aude at Carcassonne but followed the left bank of the river then they would have had to cross the rivers Fresquel and Orbiel, as well as several other streams feeding into the Aude, and have passed close to Bouilhonnac.[36] Baker's description of the terrain and the proximity of the castle at Bouilhonnac fits the route proposed above much better than does Froissart's account, as well as being much more prudent militarily.

On 22 November, only two weeks after the destruction of the *bourg*, King Jean wrote to the people of Carcassonne. His letter is as remarkable as that of the clergy to the prince, but for entirely different reasons. He explains at length why he had been detained in the north to counter a threat from Edward III, says how deeply affected he has been by the events at Carcassonne, expresses his desire for nothing more than to avenge the wrongs done to the people of the town, and promises to send his son with a great army. He wisely gives himself some leeway with this promise, adding the caveat that the despatch of the prince and his army will be 'God willing'. He finishes with an appeal for the continuing loyalty of the people. The tone of the letter gives a strong impression that the king was deeply concerned by the possible impact of the *chevauchée* on the cohesion of his realm and the loyalty of his subjects in the Languedoc. This letter was, first and foremost, an attempt to stiffen their resolve. He ordered Armagnac to restore the defences of the *bourg* with 'walls of stone and great ditches'. To assist in this project taxes were deferred a year, and permission was given to levy taxes on all foodstuffs sold within the city for two years. The cost of the work was evidently significant and Armagnac's successor, Jean, count of Poitiers, had to extend the tax provision for a further year. Nevertheless, by April 1359 the *bourg* was entirely enclosed and measures were being taken to re-establish the tax base throughout the *sénéchaussé*, with orders given for preparation of a new list of households. Authorisation was also given for the appointment of six royal sergeants charged with tax collection. Clearly lessons had also been learned from the *chevauchée*, with authorisation given in 1361 for the construction of two new windmills, stipulating that they should be built within the walls.[37]

From Carcassonne the route follows a wide northern loop of the Aude, crossing the river Fresquel two miles after leaving the *bourg*, and then turning east once more. The castle of Bouilhonnac would soon come into view, standing in a small village on a hill about 200 feet above the valley, half a mile to the east of the river Orbiel. A good part of the castle keep remains, and judging by the nature of the village it is probable that it consisted solely of a donjon without a curtain wall. It is small, about 40 metres square, and although it may have been useful for controlling the crossing of the river in normal times it would not have posed a threat to an army the size of the prince's. If there were a garrison they would have had a clear view of Carcassonne burning five miles to the west, and since the army was also burning all in its path, they would no doubt have been happy to keep their heads down and grateful that the army passed them by, crossing the minor river Orbiel en route to Rustiques two miles south-east of Bouilhonnac.

Two miles south of the castle is the town of Trèbes on the confluence of the Orbiel and Aude rivers, with open approaches from the north and east. There is confusion over the fate of this town. Baker makes no mention of it, but some secondary sources say that it was burnt. Froisssart, however, states that the town, which was defended with earth walls and gates, was ransomed. There is also a story that while the army was at Trèbes a woman gave birth to a son and begged the Gascon Lord d'Albret to allow the baby's baptism and to stand as his godfather. D'Albret is said to have duly obliged and to have spared the town as a consequence. However, there is evidence that a nearby hamlet called Millan (no longer on maps and probably long since absorbed into the town) was burned since, in 1372, Géraud de Barbairan claimed that, because all his papers had been lost at the time of the passage of the prince, he could not verify the taxes demanded of him for land that he held. This suggests that Trèbes too was burned.[38]

Less than two miles further east from Trèbes is Rustiques. Although this small town has remnants of stone ramparts it may be that these date from a later period. Any defences for this village in 1355 would probably have been the usual earth walls and would have offered little protection. We are not told where the army stopped for the night of Friday 6 November, but it was certainly somewhere in the vicinity of Rustiques, since on the Saturday, during a tiring day with wind and dust, they passed on their left a freshwater lake called Esebon which is only four miles beyond Rustiques. The lake is marked on the modern map as the dried-up lake of Marseillette. Baker was exaggerating considerably, when he described the lake as being sixty miles in circumference, and fifteen miles is a better approximation.

There is some confusion over the army's itinerary on Saturday 7 and Sunday 8 November and where and when they crossed the Aude. Baker says that on Saturday they came to 'Syloine' which surrendered to the prince but was left unharmed because it belonged to Isodo de Bretagne, a friend of the prince. Baker goes on to say that the prince lodged at Canet, and on Sunday the army crossed the Aude partly at a ford called Chastel de Terre and partly over a new and incomplete bridge.

Syloine has been interpreted as being either Lézignan, a substantial town, or Sérame which is now only a hamlet but at the time was a fief of the crown and stood at an important crossroads.[39] The march from the lake at Marseillette to the crossing points of the Orbieu, probably at or near Villedaigne, through Sérame is more direct and over easy terrain, while Lézignan lies three miles to the south of the best route behind a spur of higher ground. The chronicler Jean le Bel, records that en route to Narbonne the army passed through 'Lesignen', and it is feasible that the army, particularly if it were spread out across the line of march, passed through both places.[40] Whichever of these places was Baker's Syloine, the army would have had to cross the Aude beforehand, that is on 7 November. The crossing that Baker refers to on the Sunday was that of the Orbieu. We know that the army also passed through and burned Marseillette and Puichéric. Included in their destruction was the castle at Puichéric, the current castle having been rebuilt from the stones.[41]

The latter town stands on the Aude and would have been a logical place to cross since it could be expected to control either a ford or a bridge, but Castelnau-d'Aude, two miles to the east of Puichéric and a few hundred yards beyond the current course of the meandering river, could be Baker's Chastel de

Terre. The likely route for Saturday 7 November is via Puchéric and Castelnau-d'Aude, crossing the Aude that day, with some of the army passing by Lezignan-Corbières, to lodge at Canet for the night. They had had a longer than usual march, covering twenty-one miles in the day, but now the large and prosperous city of Narbonne stood only ten miles further east.[42]

6

Turning for Home

Canet to Pennautier
Sunday 8 to Saturday 14 November 1355

War without fire is as worthless as sausages without mustard.

Henry V[1]

Lodged at Canet, the prince was poised to cross the Orbieu and move on to Narbonne, little more than half a day's march away, on Sunday 8 November. Narbonne was a wealthy town and, being built on low, flat ground, potentially a softer target than Carcassonne. It promised rich rewards for the army. However, it was also close to the Mediterranean coast and a decision would soon be needed whether to turn for home or strike in another direction.

We cannot be sure of the location of the crossings of the Orbieu, but there are two likely places. The first of these is at La Rougeante near Ornaisons, five miles south of Canet, where the Roman road from Narbonne to Carcassonne is believed to have crossed the Orbieu. It seems that there was a bridge here from Roman times which at first sight brings this location into conflict with Baker's report that a bridge was under construction. However, the Orbieu is prone to very heavy flooding with even modern bridges being carried away, a recent case being in 1999, and it is possible that a bridge was being constructed to replace an earlier structure destroyed by floods. The second option is at Villedaigne, a mile to the south-east of Canet and the closest crossing point to the overnight halt. At some period the preferred route from Narbonne to Carcassonne, shown on the eighteenth-century Cassini map, switched from the Roman road to the route of the modern N113 through Villedaigne.[2] It is possible that it was here that Baker's partially built bridge was to be found, with the ford that he mentions as the other crossing point being Le Gué de l'Homme, three miles north-east of Villedaigne near Raissac d'Aude.

If the crossing was made at Villedaigne then the onward route would have been along the modern N113 which passes between hills rising 300 feet on both sides of the road on the approach to Narbonne.

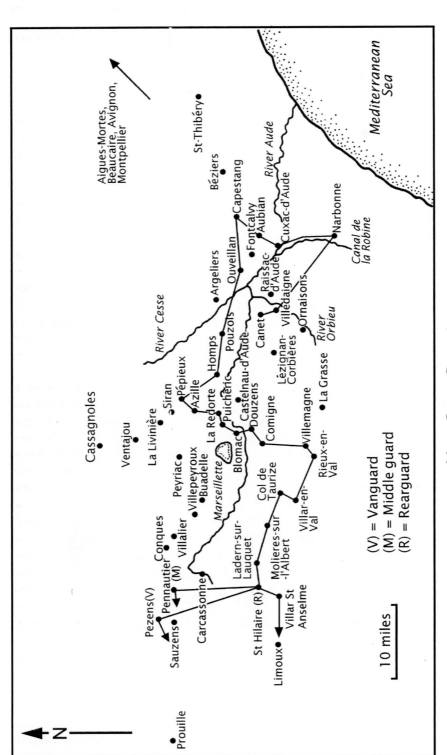

Map 9 Canet to Pennautier.

Narbonne was similar to Carcassonne in so far as it consisted of a *cité* and a *bourg* separated by a river, now the Canal de la Robine but in the fourteenth century a branch of the Aude.[3] Both parts were walled and the walls of the *cité* surrounded the cathedral, a castle for the bishop and a strong tower for the viscount. There were three bridges between the *cité* and the *bourg*, two of stone and one of wood. Only the central bridge, le Pont Vieux or Pont des Marchands, passed directly between gates in the walls of the *bourg* and the *cité*. The *bourg* was larger and better built than the *bourg* at Carcassonne, and it housed four convents. Sir John Wingfield described the town as only a little smaller than London, but the prince was more realistic, writing that it was 'a noble city, of fair size, greater than Carcassonne'. Narbonne was indeed a large town for the time, with 30,000 inhabitants and according to Froissart the *bourg* had more than 3,000 fine houses.[4]

Once again the inhabitants, or at least the women and children, had fled to the *cité*, and no doubt taken as many of their moveable riches with them as they could. The defence was in the hands of Viscount Aimeri of Narbonne with 500 men-at-arms and presumably a significant number of local levies. The army took lodgings in the empty *bourg*, with the prince himself being accommodated in the Carmelite convent. His stay is recorded with a plaque on the site of the convent in the Placette des Carmes, commemorating the energetic resistance of Aimeri and the townspeople in the face of the prince's assaults on the *cité*.

The choice of this convent for the prince's accommodation was risky. It was within easy range of siege engines, which were firing from within the *cité* throughout the night and the following day, contributing to the many wounded reported on both sides. The prince escaped unscathed, but the Gascon Sir Jean de Pommiers is named among the wounded in his company, although one source, which also records the death of a French knight Erathe de Tournel struck by an arrow, claims that Pommiers was killed among a total of around ten Anglo-Gascon soldiers. However, the death of Sir Jean is directly contradicted by Sir John Wingfield in his letter after the return to Bordeaux where he clearly records the death of only one knight or squire in the prince's service on the *chevauchée*, Sir John de Lisle at Estang. Similarly, Baker recounts that many were wounded on both sides but no one was killed. Nevertheless, the defence of the *cité* was vigorous and effective, and on Tuesday 10 November the prince's army withdrew from Narbonne, setting the *bourg* alight as they departed. They left in some disorder and the townsmen were sufficiently confident to sally forth and plunder and destroy two of the prince's carts, falling upon the Anglo-Gascon army at a vulnerable time as they crossed the river in a number of places. Since the army withdrew to the north, it is likely that these river crossings were made to the east of the *cité*.[5]

As the people of Narbonne watched the departure of the army they might well have reflected upon, and given thanks for, the wisdom and resolution of their consuls a few years before. Construction of the cathedral of St Just and St Pasteur had started in 1272 and came to a halt in 1344. Completion of the tran-

sept and the nave would have required part of the walls of the *cité* to be demolished. The consuls, seizing on instructions from King Philippe IV in 1344 to put
the defences of the province in order, were adamant that they would not permit
this demolition, and protracted discussions between the town government and
the clergy ensued. The consuls petitioned the *viguier royal de Béziers* and, despite
an appeal from the archbishop of Narbonne, their case was upheld. The result
was that the transept and nave were never completed and, most importantly for
the people of Narbonne, the city walls were intact in November 1355.[6]

There are differing accounts and interpretations of events and the route on 10,
11 and 12 November. Baker simply reports that the prince lodged on Tuesday 10
November at the town and castle of 'Ambian', almost certainly the tiny hamlet
of Aubian six miles north of Narbonne, that on Wednesday 11 November they
had a long and difficult march, and that on Thursday 12 November they passed
'Ulmes', modern Homps, with the middle guard lodging at 'Aryle', believed to be
Azille. However, much more was happening than is recorded in Baker's brief
account.

On the way north from Narbonne the army had to cross the Aude once again,
and this probably happened near Cuxac-d'Aude, four miles north of Narbonne.
There does not seem to have been a bridge at Cuxac in the fourteenth century,
and even in the eighteenth century the crossing is shown on the map as being
by ferry, so it is likely that the river had to be forded.[7] Cuxac was fortified and
escaped destruction, but it was the scene of one of the less savoury episodes, at
least by modern standards, during the *chevauchée*. Prisoners taken at Narbonne
either found the means to pay ransoms or were put to death under the town
walls in view of the inhabitants, perhaps in part to serve as a lesson to the local
people of the power of the invader and of the consequences of resistance.

Nothing remains of either a medieval castle or a town at the small settlement of Aubian, two miles north-east of Cuxac, where the prince lodged for the
night of 10 November, and it looks an unlikely place for a town and castle. It is
almost at sea level and in medieval times it would have been close to the shore
of a saltwater lagoon and prone to flooding. However, the Roman Via Domitia
ran close to the site and a castle here would have been well positioned to control
traffic on the road. Two miles to the west of Aubian are the ruins of the fortified abbey grange of Fontcalvy, looking more like a fortress than a store-house
with its four corner towers and tall central tower. Fontcalvy was once one of
twenty-five such remote granges supporting the Cistercian abbey of Fontfroide.
It survived unscathed when the army passed by, but was very likely to have been
a source of supplies for the army.

Two miles further on is Ouveillan, which was visited by at least part of
the army and destroyed. It is an example of the impact of the *chevauchée* on
a small town normally well beyond the reaches of the English army. Ouveillan
had been protected by castles for some centuries before the events of 1355, and
by the fourteenth century there were two of them. Below the town was the
Castel Bas, protecting the original village, and on the hill, where more recent

development had taken place, the Castel Naou which also enclosed the church within its walls. The destruction of Ouveillan by the prince's army spurred the consuls to construct defences for the town itself, and later in the fourteenth and fifteenth centuries the village was surrounded by new ramparts, incorporating the Castel Naou in the perimeter wall but with the Castel Bas being abandoned. However, the village itself, spreading out from the Castel Naou, was unprotected in November 1355. Between 1297 and 1370 the population of the village reduced from 210 to eighty households, or from a little over 1,000 people to 400. Some of this depopulation would have been due to the plague in 1348, but some was probably due to the *chevauchée*. The result was a much-reduced capacity for raising taxes and funding the building of new fortifications. The impact was still being felt many years later when Guillaume Bérenger d'Ouveillan reported in 1402 the burning of documents relating to liberties and privileges at the time of the village's destruction in 1355. Ouveillan also gives an example of how deeply these events of more than 600 years ago remained seared into the local culture until very recent times. The local historian Julien Aussenac related how, in the 1930s, his grandfather would say to him if he were complaining: 'Mon petit: ne te plains pas. Tu verras quand la machine de guerre Anglaise passer.' ('Don't complain little chap, you'll see how bad it gets when the English army comes through.')[8]

The army was now close to its furthest point of penetration into Languedoc. There is some evidence that elements of the army penetrated as far as Béziers, fifteen miles beyond Ouveillan, and St-Thibéry, fifteen miles further still. However, the evidence for this is not substantial. Also, we know that on 12 November the army had reached Azille on its return journey. This was a march, using the most direct route from Narbonne via Capestang, of around thirty-three miles. If they had travelled via Béziers this would have been a distance of forty-eight miles, or an average of sixteen miles each day. This would by no means be impossible, but to sustain this over three days would have been exceptional for the *chevauchée* to date and there seems no logical reason for the army to have pushed to the north at such a pace when a decision to turn for home had already been made. It is possible that mounted elements, without the encumbrances of foot-soldiers and the baggage train, ranged as far as Béziers and St-Thibéry, but it is probable that Capestang, five miles north-east of Ouveillan, was the furthest point reached at least for the main body of the army.[9]

Capestang stands at the northern end of the lake which bears its name. Today the lake is marshy for much of the year, covered in water in winter, and can be almost dry in summer, but in medieval times it was part of a saltwater lagoon. The production of the precious commodity salt from the lagoon had made Capestang a rich town, and with 4,000 inhabitants it was more populous than today. This wealth enabled the town authorities to enter into negotiations with representatives of the Anglo-Gascon army for a ransom, perhaps as much as 40,000 *écus*, approximately £5,700, to save the town which was protected by walls and a substantial castle.[10] The first perimeter wall dated from the twelfth century and a second larger wall was added in the fourteenth century. Whether this second wall was in existence in 1355 is not clear, but in view of the pattern elsewhere it is probable that the defences were extended as a reaction to the *chevauchée*. Even if the defences were those of the twelfth century they were presumably enough to encourage the army to negotiate a ransom in preference to an immediate assault. Whether the consuls were negotiating in good faith is open to doubt. They may only have been stalling for time on the assumption that the prince would move on if he could not take the town quickly, and they broke off the negotiations when it became known that a militia army raised from the *sénéchausée* of Beaucaire was approaching from Avignon. They may also have been aware that at long last the count of Armagnac, albeit with some timidity, had emerged from cover and was close by with his army. Certainly the prince had heard of Armagnac's movements from prisoners.[11]

Hewitt considers that the withdrawal from Narbonne was a check for the prince's army.[12] It is true that they withdrew after only two days and had not taken the *cité*. However, that was no different from the pattern elsewhere where sieges were avoided and attempts at assault broken off if they looked unlikely to succeed quickly and at reasonable cost. The move north towards Capestang still left the prince and his advisors with options. Even with the news of the advancing army from Beaucaire they could have continued to move north-east towards Montpellier and face the French army. However, they needed to consider the strategic situation, the goals to be achieved by continuing to advance further, and the advancing season.

From a strategic point of view, with the evident caution of Armagnac, they might have been able to meet and destroy the army from Beaucaire separately. However, they would have had to consider that there was the possibility that they would be trapped in an unfavourable tactical position between numerically superior forces. Jean le Bel claims that the total French forces were three times as numerous as those of the prince, while one source puts the strength at the incredible figure of 11,000 men-at-arms and 115,000 men raised from the common people.[13] Whatever the figures, it would be better to avoid meeting the French as a combined force. It may well have been that the militia from Beaucaire would have been raised for a limited period and only for local defence. If this were so, then turning to move away from Montpellier and Avignon to face Armagnac, as the prince did, would neutralise their contribution without the need for battle. It would also allow him to concentrate his forces on the more important target of Armagnac, the constable, and the marshal.

What was to be achieved by going further north-east? More of the same, of course, but a great deal had already been accomplished and the message given to the people of the Languedoc had been a powerful one. The inhabitants of Montpellier had already destroyed suburbs outside the city walls in anticipation of the arrival of the prince's army, and had sent much of their wealth to Avignon, Aigues-Mortes and Beaucaire for safekeeping. The pope had also taken fright and sent two bishops to try to head off the prince near Narbonne and encourage him to negotiate with the French.[14] There was nothing to be gained for the prince in doing so and he declined.

Finally, to continue towards Montpellier and Avignon would have taken the army further away from Gascony when it was already late in the year for campaigning. At Capestang they were three weeks march from home, and by the time they got to Avignon, still a week's march away, they would be doing well to get back by Christmas. In the meantime, autumnal rains could make many rivers which were minor obstacles in October much more challenging on the return and turn roads into mud. In sum, consideration of the strategic situation, what remained to be achieved, and the impact of the likely deterioration in weather all pointed in the same direction. It was time to turn for home. However, this was a change of direction, not of method. Burning, looting and destruction continued as the order of the day. In addition there was still the possibility of bringing Armagnac, the constable and the marshal to battle and victory in such an encounter would add another dimension to the success of the *chevauchée*. In the meantime, operations outside Capestang were broken off and the army turned to the west.

Baker's description of the route on Wednesday 11 November is that it was long and difficult, over rocky terrain, without water or other supplies, requiring wine to be used both as a substitute drink for the horses and for cooking food. He does not give place-names again until Thursday 12 November when he mentions the army passing through Homps. Presumably they stopped in open country short of the town for the Wednesday night. Their march would have been somewhere between ten and fifteen miles. This was not an exceptionally long distance. However, time would be a more meaningful measure for them than distance and the terrain to the west of Ouveillan becomes harder going. It begins to undulate, is uneven, and is criss-crossed with many minor streams, which were probably still dry after the summer. They would offer no succour but would hold up movement, resulting in a long day's march.

The only river of any size between Ouveillan and Homps is the Cesse, which is reached about three miles after leaving Ouveillan. Most of the march was still to come and even if the river did have a reasonable flow in November 1355, this would not have solved the problem of water when the day's march finished further west. Overall, Baker's account of the march on Wednesday fits well enough with the terrain. It is likely that the axis of advance was along an old Roman road, the Chemin Romieu, which ran from Béziers to Homps close to Argeliers and Pouzols-Minervois.

On Thursday 12 November when they passed Homps they discovered that officers of the count of Armagnac had intended to stay there the night before.[15] The French army was evidently close at hand, but there was no major contact between the two armies, although with prisoners having been taken there must have been contact of sorts between scouts or foraging parties. Froissart tells us in one of his accounts that Homps was ransomed for 12,000 *écus* (£1,700). However, his sequence of events is suspect, with this supposedly taking place en route from

Carcassonne to Narbonne via Capestang, rather than in the sequence Narbonne, Capestang, Homps. Nevertheless, his story does show us something of the state of mind of the people in the area, with scouts being accosted by bourgeois from Homps who anxiously asked if the prince was coming towards their town. They could perhaps have taken some comfort when the scouts replied, 'Not at all, why do you ask?' They are said to have replied: 'Because we want to enter into a treaty, if he wishes to hear us.'[16] There is no record of the destruction of Homps, so there may be some truth in the story even if the timing is wrong.

From Homps the prince's division continued west to Azille, where he was to stay for the night. Other elements of the army destroyed the town of Pépieux, two miles to the north, and the castle at La Redorte two miles to the south. Captured French scouts revealed that Armagnac and the constable of France had intended to spend the night in the same towns used as lodging by the prince's forces. It is possible that while the prince lodged at Azille the other divisions rested at Pépieux and La Redorte and destroyed them the next day before moving on.[17]

At Pépieux little remains of the medieval heritage of the village, but there is an account in the church of St Etienne of the destruction of the thirteenth-century church by the prince's army and its reconstruction in 1379. The twelfth-century castle at La Redorte, which is believed to have stood on high ground in the northern part of the village, has long since disappeared.[18]

Azille, however, has much more to show of its past. Vestiges of the ramparts, towers and gates remain, and the line of the ramparts can be clearly seen. Azille had been fortified from the eleventh century but most of the remaining fortifications, which originally included a ditch, were built after 1355. The church of St Julien and St Balisses was built in the fourteenth century. The earliest documentary date recorded for the church is 1351; it was either under construction or in existence in 1355, and it was either spared or survived the destruction. There were also two convents. One belonging to the Cordeliers in a suburb outside the walls to the north of the town, and a second for the Poor Clares within the town in the north-west corner. The prince stayed in one of the convents which held a great store of muscat wine for the countess de l'Isle, whose husband held the lordship of the town. The wine was reported as being wasted, but not, one assumes, before the prince and his companions had enjoyed at least a tasting.[19]

On 12 November, while the prince lodged at Azille, the two armies were in close proximity, and it has been suggested that the French were to the south of the prince and La Redorte on the southern bank of the Aude.[20] A local guide of the constable of France had been taken prisoner and examined, and it is likely that the prince had sound intelligence on the location of the French.[21] On the same day Tiderick van Dale, an usher of the prince's chamber, described as an 'Almain', was dubbed as a knight. Sir Tiderick was to go on to serve with the prince for a number of years and was rewarded in due course with annuities for his services.[22] This dubbing may indicate, since it was common practice for

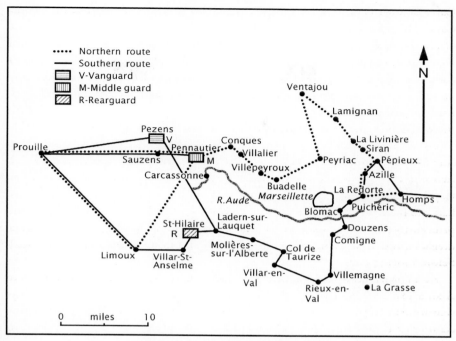

Map 10   13 to 15 November 1355.

knights to be created on the eve of battle, that, with the French close at hand, there was some anticipation of combat.

The itinerary from leaving Azille on Friday 13 until Sunday 15 November has been subject to two significantly different interpretations.[23] The essence of the controversy is whether the army passed either south or north of Carcassonne. The route chosen is fundamental to the question of whether or not the prince was seeking battle with the French, and this is a matter which has divided historians. Hewitt's view is that the prince was trying to avoid the French army: 'from now onwards, the ultimate objective is quite clear: it is to reach the marchland near Bordeaux with as much of the accumulated booty as can be convoyed without endangering the column.' Rogers takes the opposite view and refers to a general battle-seeking strategy underpinning the *chevauchée*: 'the desire for a decisive battle on favourable terms which always characterized the English approach to strategy in this period … guided the Prince of Wales in the conduct of his first independent campaign.'[24]

The determination of the most likely route will give an indication as to whether the prince was either pursuing or seeking to avoid Armagnac.[25] With the French army to the south of the Anglo-Gascon army on 12 November, the clear implication of the northern route would be that the prince was trying to avoid contact and battle with Armagnac. This is the essence of the case of Henry Mullot and Joseph Poux (the chief exponents of the northern route) and of J. F.

Jeanjean, who draws widely on their work.[26] The southerly route would imply
pursuit of the French in quest of battle.

As for the French, although we know that they were close at hand we do not
know their intentions. It may be that they were looking for set-piece battle if
the circumstances were right, although their conduct of operations to date, and
indeed later in the *chevauchée*, indicates a reluctance to confront the full Anglo-
Gascon army.

As Clifford Rogers wrote concerning the itinerary for these dates:

> Since the account in le Baker, clearly based on a campaign diary written during the
> *chevauchée*, provides by far the most detailed and accurate narrative we have of this
> expedition we should not accept any proposed route which directly contradicts its
> statements.[27]

Nevertheless, an argument has been constructed by Mullot and Poux for a
northern route, based in part on local archives, and has been accepted by H. J.
Hewitt amongst others.[28]

Baker's account is detailed but peppered with names which are obscure:

> On Friday the army lodged at 'Lamyane', a poor place with few houses and little
> water, after a long and waterless march. On Saturday they turned back towards
> Gascony, leaving to the right the lake of 'Esebon' and 'Carkasonam' and the whole
> of the previous journey, and the rearguard lodged at a good town called 'Alieir' and
> the centre at 'Puchsiaucier', where a fortified tower was captured; but the prince lay
> beyond the bridge on a pleasant river bank. From there the countryside on both
> sides was burnt, including 'Pezence', where the vanguard had lodged. On Sunday,
> St Machutus' day, they entered fair open country, and made a long march, the
> army pressing on because the prince was to lodge at the great abbey of the Blessed
> Virgin at 'Prolian' ... That day the army burnt among others the town of 'Lemoyns'
> ... and a fine town called 'Falanges', which had twenty-one windmills, and the
> towns of 'Vularde' and 'Serre'.[29]

Advocates of the northern route suggest that Lamyane was Lamignan. In a
near contemporary act, dated 1316, Lamignan was recorded as La Méjane and a
corruption from La Méjane to Lamyane is certainly feasible.[30] Two suggestions
for Lamyane to the south have been made. The first, Comigne, can be quickly
dismissed. It is only two miles from the Aude and ten miles from the starting
point for the day. It cannot fit Baker's description of a long and waterless march,
and the Latin name of Cominiano in use at the time is not a convincing Lamyane.
Rogers has suggested that Lamyane was Villemagne, south of Azille across the
Montagne d'Alaric. Records from the thirteenth and fourteenth centuries show
Villemagne variously as Villamagnha, Villa Magna, De Villamanha, and Villare
de Villa Magno, and a corruption to Lamyane is again feasible.[31] Both Lamignan
and Villemagne fit the bill as being poor places with few houses and little water,
assuming that the minor tributary of the Orbieu near to Villemagne had suffered
from the unusually dry summer of 1355.[32] As for the day's journey, Lamignan is
only seven miles from the starting point: not a convincing long march. Ville-

magne, on the other hand, is twenty miles from Azille. With a climb of 800 feet to cross the Montagne d'Alaric this would be a long day's march. The route to Villemagne does cross the Aude, which at first sight does not sit easily with a 'waterless march,' but it would have been behind the army early in the day and from then on the route is certainly without significant sources of water.

If, as Baker says, they left lake Esebon, now the dry lake of Marseillette, Carcassonne, and the outbound route to the right then they must have moved south on the Friday.[33] The proponents of the northern route explain this by saying that the prince's army would have seen the lake as a river and the northern shore as the right bank of the river.[34] Given Baker's clear description of Esebon during the outbound march as a freshwater lake into and out of which no water flowed, this stretches credulity. Furthermore, the lake, even in its current dried-up state, is clearly visible from higher ground, and is less than a mile from the Aude. It is difficult to conceive that the prince and his senior companions would not have known where they were in relation to both the lake and the Aude.

In his letter to the bishop of Winchester, written after the return to Bordeaux, the prince wrote:

> and by reason that we had news from prisoners and others that our enemies were gathered together and were coming after us to fight us, we turned again to meet them, and thought to have had the battle in the three days next following. And on our turning back towards them, they turned again towards Toulouse. So we pursued them in long marches towards Toulouse.[35]

Sir John Wingfield, in his letter written after the return to Bordeaux, tells us that: 'they drew away and disappeared towards the mountains and the strong places, and went by long marches towards Toulouse'.[36]

With the French south of the Aude the prince's words 'turning back towards them' imply the southerly route. It is implausible that the French moved towards the hills of the Minervois with both the Aude and the prince's army in between if they were withdrawing from contact with the Anglo-Gascons. The mountains in question in Sir John's letter must have been those of the Montagne d'Alaric.

Henry Mullot and Joseph Poux, in their advocacy of the northern route, have referred to the destruction of Peyriac-Minervois, Buadelle, Villepeyroux and Conques to support their case.[37] For Peyriac, a royal order of 1364 which authorised the inhabitants to rebuild the walls of their church after the passage of the prince's companies is cited. However, tax exemptions to encourage repairs after the 1355 chevauchée were granted for Limoux by the count of Armagnac in February 1356, and King Jean II made similar concessions for Alzonne and Castelnaudary in August 1356.[38] A nine-year delay for Peyriac is improbable. Furthermore, there had been incursions by the Great Company in the Languedoc in the early 1360s, with the castle of Peyriac occupied by them from 11 November 1363 until mid-June 1364. It is more likely that the authority for repairs related to this period.[39] No sources are quoted for Buadelle, and that given for Villepeyroux is erroneous.[40] As for Conques, there is nothing more substantive than a

.ocal tradition that the town was sacked by the English.[41] Even if
again it could easily relate to the period after Poitiers when the
is ravaged by the companies. Siran, La Livinière, and Ventajou
s locations that were sacked by the prince's army. Both Siran and
e within three miles of Pépieux, and their destruction would be
consistent with them being sacked by outriders from the prince's army on 12
November as suggested by Rogers.[42] The only Ventajou to be found now is a
hilltop hamlet seven miles north-west of Pépieux. One source relates that this
village, having survived the ravages of the Albigensian Crusade in 1210, was oblit-
erated forever in 1355. This may be so, and it may be that the existing hamlet is
an old town of that name, but again this could well have been the work of the
prince's army as they moved through Pépieux. Furthermore, the archival reference to the destruction of Ventajou is in an order in 1390 to fortify Cassagnoles,
six miles north of La Livinière, in the light of the destruction of Ventajou. It
is unlikely that this relates to the *chevauchée* of 1355, thirty-five years earlier.
Indeed, one local historian makes an explicit link between the fortification of
Cassagnoles and the later activities of the Great Company, and by inference the
destruction of Ventajou.[43]

Unusually, Baker records the locations of all divisions on the Saturday night,
14 November. The middle guard was at Puchsiaucier, probably Pennautier about
three miles north-west of Carcassonne, and the vanguard at Pezence, almost
certainly Pezens, three miles to the north-west of Pennautier.[44] Both Pezens
and Pennautier are feasible locations for marches from either Lamignan or Villemagne. For the vanguard, Villemagne to Pezens, twenty-six miles, would have
been a long day's march, but not unique for this *chevauchée*. The positions of the
middle- and vanguards do not, therefore, help in deciding between the northern
and southern routes.

The position of the rearguard at Alieir, however, is of more interest. It has
been interpreted by those who favour the southerly route as St-Hilaire, eight
miles north-east of Limoux, and as Villalier, five miles to the north-east of
Carcassonne by those who argue for the route to the north.[45] Archival evidence
is lacking, and toponymy does not solve the problem.[46] However, there is no
reason to doubt that in Baker's account of Sunday's events the abbey of Prolian
was the Dominican abbey of Prouille, and Lemoyns, Falanges, Vularde and Serre
were Limoux, Fanjeaux, Villar-St-Anselme and Lasserre-de-Prouille. Of these
Prouille, Fanjeaux, and Lasserre-de-Prouille are all in close proximity. Limoux,
however, is fifteen miles south-west of Carcassonne and Villar-St-Anselme is
between Limoux and St-Hilaire. The destruction of Limoux is not in dispute,
and it seems probable that this task was undertaken by the rearguard starting
from St-Hilaire and routing via Villar-St-Anselme. Assuming that they then
lodged in the vicinity of the rest of the army near Prouille that night, they
would have had a march of twenty miles. This is feasible even with the activities at Limoux and Villar. Given that the prince's middle division went directly
to Prouille from Pennautier, the same operations conducted by the vanguard at

Pezens or the rearguard from Villalier would have entailed a march of at least thirty-four miles. This would have been quite exceptional and is unlikely.

On the only other occasions when Baker records the overnight dispositions of all three divisions, in the vicinity of Simorre on 24 October and at Avignonet on 30 October, the army was closed up in an area less than three miles across. Thus, it could be argued that the wide dispersal of forces on the night of 14 November, with the rearguard thirteen miles to the south of the other divisions, would be tactically unusual and casts doubt on St-Hilaire as the location of the rearguard. However, the following year there is an instance when the rearguard was lodged thirty miles from the rest of the army. Furthermore, Armagnac still showed a reluctance to do battle, and the initiative was with the prince. It is likely that he had both sufficient intelligence of the disposition of the French forces, and the confidence, to detach one division to destroy Limoux.

A final consideration is the practicality of the route over the Montagne d'Alaric to Villemagne and then on to Pezens, Pennautier and St-Hilaire. The Montagne d'Alaric is a series of hills in a ridge running east to west. The highest point is 2,000 feet above sea level, 1,800 feet above the river valley, and the hills are rugged and steep. From Azille to Villemagne the only practical route without a wide detour is south-west to Comigne and over a pass 1,000 feet above sea level, a climb of 800 feet from the valley. The pass is generally flat and wide, but at one point has a significant choke point where it narrows to little more than the width of the road. After the pass there is a gentle descent into a broad valley, with two points where it narrows to about half a mile. Villemagne sits in an extensive flat area, with a road running west along a wide valley to Villar-en-Val where the climb over the western edge of the ridge begins.

The road twists and turns as it climbs towards the pass at the Col de Taurize, 1,600 feet above sea level. To both sides the ground is steep and movement would have been restricted to the width of the road, which, once across the pass, descends to Ladern-sur-Lauquet where the terrain opens out. A distance of less than six miles in a straight line has taken ten miles by road. This road existed in the Middle Ages, linking several ancient settlements, and there is reference to it connecting St-Hilaire with La Grasse a few miles to the east of Villemagne.[47] There is a second route out of the valley to the west. Both roads converge before Ladern, and although the way over the Col de Taurize is the easiest of the routes, the use of both roads would have eased the movement of the army. There is no reason to suppose that the army could not have followed this route as suggested by Rogers.[48]

Using modern maps to trace a route across Montagne d'Alaric is straight-forward, but gives a totally misleading impression of the problems of navigation faced by the prince. There are very few maps of European countries from medieval times, and the best that the prince might have seen would have been Ptolemy's map of Gaul, which although giving a reasonable representation of the shape of France, has little detail. There may have been campaign itineraries from earlier expeditions and itineraries of trading routes, showing in a straight-line sequence the route to be followed with names of towns on the route and distances between them. However, for the most part reliance had to be placed upon guides and local knowledge of members of his army, which for parts of the route in Gascony would have been considerable. Christine de Pizan, writing her treatise on the art of warfare in the early fifteenth century, summarises the importance of knowledge of routes within the army and the use of guides:

> The commander and other leaders should know the routes and passes, mountains, woods, bodies of water, streams and narrows that they will encounter. And yet, in addition to being well informed, the wise commander, for fear of failure, will take along, if need be, guides chosen from those who know the way. These people used as guides should be so well guarded that they cannot escape and will not have an opportunity to betray the army or do any sort of harm. He will give them money and promise great rewards if they lead loyally, but will also threaten them with great harm if they do otherwise.[49]

In his journal of receipts and payments John Henxteworth records a payment of 22s 6d for two varlets who showed the prince the way for the seventeen miles from Castets-en-Dorthe to Bazas. Later in the *chevauchée* Arnold Bernard received 40 gold leopards, or £9, for his services as a guide in parts of Gascony, and two varlets were paid 9s for leading the prince in the right way for the twenty-eight miles from Casteljaloux to Meilhan-sur-Garonne. Clearly those who had the skills and knowledge as guides could on occasion command considerable sums compared with the daily wage of 3d for an archer.[50]

If the prince's primary objective at this stage of the campaign was to return home, then the most obvious route would have been west along the valley of the Aude, leaving the lake at Marseillette and Carcassonne on his right and the Montagne d'Alaric on the left, and not the route to the north of Carcassonne. This would not, however, have been a 'long and waterless march' and it would not have entailed pursuit of the French 'towards the mountains'. Furthermore, there are no place-names along the valley which correlate with those in Baker's account. The choice is between north and south. The prince's and Sir John Wingfield's letters, Baker's account, a review of the archival evidence, the topography, toponymy and an assessment of time and distance all point to the prince crossing the Montagne d'Alaric in pursuit of Armagnac with the rearguard at St-Hilaire, the middle at Pennautier, and the vanguard at Pezens on 14 November, the whole army having spent the previous night in the vicinity of Villemagne.

Having decided to head for home it was important to get across the Garonne, the only major obstacle between them and Gascony, before autumn rains made the river impassable at fords. The army had now been on the move for five days continuously, the longest period during the *chevauchée* to date without taking a halt. They would continue without rest until they had crossed the Garonne on 18 November, a further four days' march.

Recrossing the Garonne

Pennautier to Carbonne
Sunday 15 to Wednesday 18 November 1355

> ... done all those things which a man can and ought to do in a just war,
> as taking Frenchmen and putting them to ransom, living on the country
> and despoiling it, and leading the company under his command about
> the realm of France and burning and firing places in it.
>
> A fourteenth-century English mercenary captain[1]

On the night of Sunday 15 November the prince was due to lodge with the brothers at the Dominican abbey of Prouille, and on their way from Pennautier, according to Baker, the prince's division entered 'fair, open country'. They probably followed the Via Aquitania before turning south-west towards Montréal and then west to Prouille, a journey of sixteen miles.[2]

As the prince was readying himself for the journey to Prouille, the other divisions were preparing to continue with the usual routine of destruction. Considerable havoc was wreaked that day with Villar-St-Anselme, Limoux, Routier, Montréal, Fanjeaux, Lasserre-de-Prouille and perhaps Villasavary all falling victim to the marauding army.[3] The rearguard carried out a left hook from St-Hilaire by way of Villar-St-Anselme, Limoux and Routier before halting in the region of Prouille and Fanjeaux, a march of twenty-five miles. The vanguard would have taken a more northerly route and had a slightly easier day of it with about twenty miles to cover from Pezens through Montréal to Fanjeaux, taking in Villasavary and Lasserre-de-Prouille as they went.

Limoux was the jewel in the crown of the day's activities. Its importance no doubt lay behind the decision to deploy the rearguard well out on the left flank on the night of 14 November. It was a more heavily populated town in the fourteenth century than it is today. With a population of 15,000 it was more populous than Carcassonne and approximately half the size of Bordeaux and London. It was also wealthy due to cloth manufacture, dressing of furs, tanning, viticulture, and the cultivation and milling of wheat, barley, rye and oats. It held

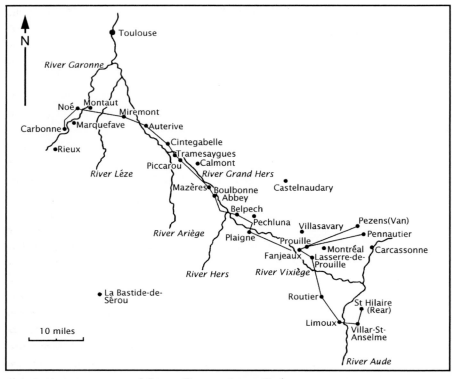

Map 11 Pennautier to Carbonne.

a substantial fair each year spread over fifteen days either side, somewhat ironi-
cally in the circumstances, of St George's Day.[4] The town straddled the river
Aude, as it does today, with the fortified, greater part of the town to the west
of the river. To the east of the river were suburbs which were not fortified. The
two parts were linked by two bridges. The Pont Vieux in the south-east corner
of the town was washed away in floods and rebuilt in the nineteenth century,
while the Pont Neuf, constructed originally of wood and rebuilt in stone in the
early part of the fourteenth century, still exists. There were Augustinian and
Franciscan monasteries outside the town and a Dominican monastery inside the
walls. At least one, and possibly both, of the monasteries outside the walls was
to the east of the river.[5]

The suburbs and religious house to the east of the river would have been
reached first by the army approaching from St-Hilaire and Villar-St-Anselme.
They would have been quickly pillaged and set on fire since, on this occasion,
religious property did not escape the destruction wrought on the rest of the
town. Beyond the suburbs was the town itself. In a letter written in 1350, King
Philippe VI stated that Limoux, 'even though situated on the frontiers and limits
of the realm, is neither defended nor fortified, nor surrounded by ramparts,
walls, or ditches'. Taking this evidence alone, we would assume that Limoux was

unprotected. However, writing in October 1356 Jean d'Armagnac talks of the walls having been destroyed by the Anglo-Gascon army, and there is a papal letter relating to reconstruction of a monastery within the walls, clearly implying that the town was fortified.[6] It is, therefore, very likely that the town was fortified but, irrespective of the state of the defences, when news of the approach of the army reached the townspeople they fled into the surrounding hills. Without a determined garrison the walls would have served little purpose, and the result was widespread destruction.

The population remained dispersed in the hills through the following winter. It was not until February 1356 that the consuls of the town were able to obtain from the count of Armagnac the means that they needed to encourage the townspeople to return and begin the task of reconstruction. The extent of the destruction can be judged by the measures authorised. These were similar to those for Castelnaudary, but at Limoux, in view of the size of the town and the scale of destruction, the cost implications of the measures were much greater. The powers were also more far-reaching. The inhabitants were exempted from taxes and personal service for a year, and authorised to take wood from royal forests for reconstruction of houses against a payment of two *livres*. To encourage an early start to the work, and in view of a lack of manpower, the consuls were permitted to require masons, carpenters, workers and inhabitants of neighbouring villages to work on the reconstruction in return for a salary which could be determined by the consuls. Debtors were given a period of grace to repay debts in return for a deposit as a sign of good-will. Merchants were allowed to export, either abroad or within France, 1,000 loads of wheat and 100 loads of cloth each year free of all taxes for six years. *La leude*, a tax imposed on merchandise sold at fairs and markets, was abolished and replaced by the *gabelle*, a tax normally levied on salt and sometimes other goods such as cloth, at a rate of 4 *deniers* in the *livre*, or about 1.7 per cent. Every mounted visitor would be required to pay a toll of a penny and every pedestrian visitor a halfpenny. Rafts carrying goods on the river were liable to a substantial toll of 5 *sous*, and other rights were given to the consuls to raise taxes on transport of wood by cart and on cattle sold in, or passing through, the town. The consuls were also authorised to rebuild two mills belonging to the town located near the Pont Vieux. Finally, lawyers were instructed, by all means possible, to reproduce the archive records which had gone up in flames. As for the religious houses, the convents of the Augustins and Franciscans were rebuilt inside the walls. Rebuilding the fortifications was a high priority. New ramparts and ditches, seven gates, each forming a tower, and eleven other interval towers were constructed. These defences were strong enough to resist a siege two centuries later during the Wars of Religion. Clearly the lessons of the *chevauchée* had not been lost on the consuls.[7]

Leaving Limoux behind, the rearguard would first have climbed 200 feet out of the valley of the Aude. The prince might well have been in a fair and open country, but the rearguard was not. For the rest of the day they would be moving across steeply undulating terrain. The changes in elevation are not great, but they are frequent and make for hard travelling. The area is now given over predominantly to vines, but the many ruined mills are testimony to the earlier history of grain production. The countryside is peppered with small hilltop villages, many of which, although they have long since lost their curtain walls, have preserved their shape and size over the centuries with a circular or oval centre indicating their defensive construction. One or more of these villages is almost always in sight, and, although the names of these settlements may not have merited mention in the chronicles of the time, many must surely have been burnt by the passing troops.

Routier, seven miles north-west of Limoux, is an example of one of these small hilltop villages. At one time walls and a ditch enclosed about five acres, and at some date there was a modest castle in the centre. By the fourteenth century a fort, perhaps as small as 50 by 30 metres, and a fortified church were built in the eastern part of the village and took on the role of the old castle in the defence of Routier. However, they are thought to have been built in the second half of the century as a result of the ravages of the war, caused by either the *chevauchée* or routiers in the 1360s. Presumably the defences in 1355 were both primitive and inadequate. Beyond the oval shape of the village perimeter road, which follows the line of the surrounding ditch, the only reminder of the fortifications in the Middle Ages is the street name rue du Fort.[8]

Five miles to the right of the rearguard's route is Montréal which was pillaged and its Carmelite convent burned down by the vanguard. The following year the ecclesiastics of Montréal tried to avoid obeying a general order given for reconstruction in the diocese of Carcassonne, arguing that their existing privileges exempted them from contributions to municipal expenses. Their efforts were to no avail, and the future Charles V, regent of France in the absence of his father King Jean, ordered that all should contribute regardless of existing exemptions.[9]

Lasserre-de-Prouille is a classic example of a *circulade* village. The central circle of buildings is complete, forming a defensive perimeter with a single entrance through an arched gateway. It is thought that there was once a keep in the centre but this has long since been replaced by a group of other buildings.[10]

The monastery at Prouille is on the road from Montréal to Fanjeaux. Nothing remains of the thirteenth-century abbey founded by St Dominic, which was destroyed during the Revolution. In 1355 there were 100 male and 140 female Dominicans housed in separate cloisters. During his stay the prince was admitted to the brotherhood of the house, and no doubt in recognition of this honour the prince gave the abbey the substantial sum of £32 in alms. This was delivered by Richard of Leominster, also a Dominican brother, who accompanied the prince. Richard was to receive his own reward after his return to England when the prince granted him an annuity of £20 in 1358.[11]

Fanjeaux stands on a hill only a mile from the abbey and 450 feet above Prouille. It was surrounded by ramparts, and it had two castles, the first to the north of the village and the second south of the church, although in 1355 it is likely that only the southern of the two castles existed. As had been the case in so many places, the fortifications were insufficient and the village was fired, as were twenty-one windmills. The required rebuilding was clearly extensive with exemptions from taxes, similar to those granted elsewhere, to encourage reconstruction.[12] The medieval part of the village includes a thirteenth-century church, the house where by tradition Dominic is said to have lived, and a viewpoint called the Seignadou, or sign of God. It is from here that Dominic is said to have watched a ball of fire fall to earth on Prouille. He took this as a sign that this was where he should build a monastery and found the order of Friar Preachers. On 15 November 1355 it was the fires in the village that would be clearly seen from St Dominic's foundation at Prouille, and on the same day the Dominican monastery at Limoux was also destroyed. News of events at Limoux might not yet have reached the brothers at Prouille, but one can only wonder what was going through the minds of those present as the village burned while the prince was admitted to the brotherhood, although Hewitt surmises: 'That the "Flower of Chivalry" should spend a Sunday with a devout brotherhood at Prouille while their men only a few miles away were burning down the homes of the burgesses of Limoux, was not incongruous to the mind of 1355.'[13]

There is no discernible pattern to account for the escape of some and the destruction of other church property during the *chevauchée*. We have already seen examples where the prince's orders for religious premises to be spared were obeyed, but equally there were many cases of church property being destroyed. The prince's use of Prouille for his lodgings no doubt ensured that it was spared, but we have no information to indicate why this monastery was singled out for use by the prince's party. Does the large gift signify some special relationship or connection? We simply do not know.

From Prouille on Monday 16 November the prince's division set off to a town that Baker calls 'Ayollpuhbone'. It has been suggested that this was either Pech-Luna or Belpech. The latter is more likely. To reach Pech-Luna would require movement across hilly ground from Prouille, while the seventeen-mile march to Belpech would initially be across a gently rolling plain and then along the valley of the river Vixiège. Belpech also fits better with the onward march to Boulbonne Abbey and the next night's halt at Miremont. In addition, Belpech is consistent with Baker's description of a castle outside the town.[14]

Belpech castle consisted of a tall square tower surrounded by a curtain wall. The village itself was encompassed by a wall about a kilometre long. It ran from the river to the south of the village, climbed along the side of the rue du Castelas, and skirted the castle. It then turned back to the river at the most northerly of the three bridges which now cross the river, and then ran along the river to complete the circuit. Part of the wall was made up of the outer walls of houses. There were two gates towards the land, one giving access to the present day D102 to the east, and one to the north to allow access to the castle. A further gate with a drawbridge allowed access to the bridge across the river on the present D102. It is likely that there were three bridges across the river in 1355, in the positions of the current bridges. The oldest, furthest upstream to the south of the village, dates back to around 200 BC. In addition, there were two fords over the river in the immediate vicinity of the village, one of which was still in use in the 1960s. The only vestige of the ramparts is a small part of a garden retaining wall facing the river. A good part of the castle tower and some traces of the outer wall remain.[15]

Clearly the village was readily approached across the river, and the obvious approach would be along the valley of the Vixiège. The fortifications should not have presented much of a challenge to an attacking army of the size and experience of the prince's, but Baker tells us that Belpech was taken by assault after a long defence. The occupants of the castle, perched 150 feet above and only 250 yards from the village, would have had a grandstand view of the capture of the village. Little wonder that they surrendered when their turn came. Baker recounts that neither the town nor the castle was burnt since they belonged to the count of Foix. This is not strictly accurate. Since the early thirteenth century the lord of Belpech owed his allegiance to the archbishop of Toulouse.[16] However, the count of Foix was always ready to defend neighbours in return for a financial consideration and this may have been what happened on this occasion. Why it was felt necessary to take the village by assault and secure the surrender of the castle if it was thought to belong to the count of Foix is not clear. Perhaps, in anticipation of the meeting planned with the count for the following day, the prince wished to send a signal of the capability of his army. Alternatively the allegiance of the town to the archbishop of Toulouse may have been known, and in that case the prince would not have wished the archbishop, who was very much in the French camp, to have escaped unscathed.

On Tuesday 17 November the prince met Gaston Phoebus, the count of Foix, at the Cistercian Abbey of Boulbonne, five miles beyond Belpech. The bridge over the river Hers at Marty, about a mile west of Belpech, was not built until the early fifteenth century, and it is likely that the crossing was made at the Gué de Mourgail, 150 yards upstream from the junction of the Hers with the Vixiège.[17]

The monastery of Boulbonne was founded in 1129 and became the spiritual home of the counts of Foix, much as St-Denis in Paris was for the kings of France. It was, therefore, a natural place for Gaston Phoebus to meet the prince. All that remains now are traces of the ruins of the abbey burnt down in 1567 during the Wars of Religion.[18]

From Boulbonne the prince rode on in the company of the count of Foix, who had just returned to his lands after two years' captivity in Paris and was a natural ally for the English. They rode through Mazères, a *bastide* town founded jointly through a sharing of rights of lordship between the Abbey of Boulbonne and the count of Foix in 1253. It was the principal residence of Gaston Phoebus. The town was fortified at the time, but since an accord had been reached at Boulbonne between Phoebus and the prince it was in any case safe from attack. It seems one young man from Mazères, Raymond Sans, was seized by the spirit of adventure and departed with the prince. We do not know what became of him, but four years later another inhabitant of the town, Raymond de Pisseloup, bought Raymond Sans' property in Mazères. He gave the purchase price of 12 gold florins to Sans' sister who promised to give the money to her brother if he returned to the town.[19]

It is said that the count of Foix gave the prince permission to cross his territory by way of La Bastide-de-Sérou. If so, it appears that the prince paid it scant regard, since the town was twenty-five miles to the south-west of Mazères and instead the army moved on towards Calmont, four miles beyond Mazères, which also belonged to Phoebus who was still in the company of the prince. Baker tells us that at Calmont on the far side of the river were the ruins of a castle.[20] The high ground immediately behind the town is the obvious place for a castle, and the implication is that from Mazères they left the river, which from the confluence with the Vixiège near Belpech becomes the Grand Hers, on the right. There had been a bridge at Mazères since at least 1259, and there were numerous fords over the Grand Hers to allow them to pass over the river and through Calmont. However, the terrain makes the going much easier if the river is kept on the right and it seems likely that they passed by without entering Calmont.[21]

Gaston Phoebus rode with the prince as far as the hamlet of Tramesaygues, just before the confluence of the Ariège and Grand Hers, two miles short of Cintegabelle. Although the prince had spared the lands of the count from destruction, he was probably under no illusions about the nature of Gaston Phoebus' support as they parted. The counts of Foix and Armagnac had a long-standing feud, and the appointment of Armagnac as King Jean's lieutenant in Languedoc had very much displeased Phoebus. In addition, although it is possible that he had fought on the French side at Crécy, relations between Phoebus and the king of France were strained. This was largely over homage for Béarn, which the count argued that he held independently of the king of France in much the same way that Edward III considered Aquitaine. In view of the enmity between the king of France and Phoebus, the alliance with the prince was built on the basis that 'my enemy's enemy is my friend'. However, the alliance between the English and the count was only likely to last as long as it served the count's interests.

Baker states that nothing was burnt on 17 November out of respect for the property of the count of Foix. That is not so. Certainly Calmont and Mazères were spared, and so also presumably were farms and small settlements in the vicinity. However, Cintegabelle and Auterive, neither of which belonged to the count of Foix, did not escape unscathed.

Cintegabelle had been in the possession of the counts of Foix in the twelfth century, but by 1271 it had passed through the hands of the counts of Toulouse to become a royal domain. Thus, there was no incentive for Phoebus to try to protect Cintegabelle; indeed four years later he was back to attack the town himself having quarrelled with the dauphin over the issue of homage.[22] There was no reason why the prince should not attack Cintegabelle. It would have been an attractive target, with a population, according to various witnesses at an enquiry seventy years later, of some 1,200 households. Cintegabelle was wealthy,

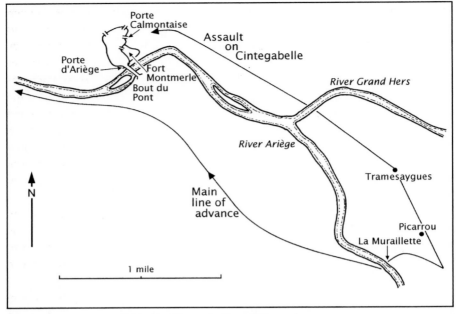

Map 12 Cintegabelle, 17 November 1355

largely due to the income from weekly markets and two annual fairs, all of which were free of taxes for the town. The resulting income was sufficient to pay for the upkeep of the fortifications and the bridge at a cost of 100 *livres* per annum.

Baker relates that after Calmont the army left Cintegabelle and Auterive on their right and then crossed the Ariège. This does not work geographically. The approach to Cintegabelle from Calmont is between the Grand Hers and the Ariège which converge about a mile before Cintegabelle. Both Cintegabelle and Auterive are on the right bank of the river Ariège, to the east, and are hard up against the river. To leave these towns on the right the Ariège must be crossed before reaching Cintegabelle. The most likely place for the crossing is a ford called La Muraillette, near the village of Picarrou, one mile south of the confluence of the Ariège and the Grand Hers, possibly also used a century earlier by Simon de Montfort during the Albigensian Crusade.[23]

Once across the river the army could attack Cintagabelle by crossing back towards the town using the bridge over the Ariège. However, the bridge was narrow and dominated by the Fort Montmerle standing 150 feet above the river. The entrance through the Porte d'Ariège was also protected by a drawbridge. Thus, an attack from the other side of the river would have been less hazardous, and it seems that elements of the army remained on the town side of the river, rather than crossing at La Muraillette, and attacked through the Porte Calmontaise, on the current D35 from Calmont.

There was resistance, particularly from the castle, Fort Montmerle, to the east of the town, but the town was at least in part fired and the crops harvested from the area destroyed. Houses in the suburb of Bout du Pont, outside the walls and across the Ariège from the main part of the village, would have been particularly vulnerable. A lord from Cintegabelle, Pierre de Campellis, was taken prisoner and presumably ransomed. The account of damage to the town is corroborated by an inquiry conducted in 1423 to investigate the case for re-establishing markets and fairs lost during successive misfortunes of the town. The inquiry, led by Raymond de Senesses, a lawyer from the town acting as a lieutenant of the judge for the Lauragais, took evidence from a number of witnesses, including a centenarian Pierre Besian. One witness, B. de Villario, said that he had seen the town taken by the prince's troops. All affirmed that the town was captured by the Anglo-Gascon army and a large part destroyed.[24]

There has been some urban sprawl in Cintagabelle over the years, but the medieval footprint of the village is easily recognisable. The line of the walls and the ditches can be traced along the edge of streets in the village, and the internal street pattern is precisely as it was. Similarly the positions of the five gates, although most of the original works have long since been demolished, can readily be seen. One of the gates, Pourtasse, gave, and still gives, access to Fort Montmerle which was attached to the walls of the town. The fort consisted of an outer bailey of irregular quadrangular shape with the village walls forming two sides. There was a keep on a hill to the eastern side of the enclosure. The church in the village is close up against the wall of the fort, and it is thought probable that the lower part of the present bell tower was originally part of the fort. There are also substantial remains of one of the guard towers protecting the drawbridge that gave access to the main bridge over the Ariège. The fort was too much of a threat to royal power to be allowed to continue in existence and in 1630 it was demolished on the instructions of Cardinal Richelieu.[25]

Five miles further downstream from Cintegabelle is Auterive. In places between the two towns the river runs tight up against a steep escarpment with hills rising 300 feet above the valley. Leaving the town and the river on the right as described by Baker would be the most practicable route.

Auterive has spread considerably over the years, but the medieval town, with the main fortified part on the right bank and a smaller undefended suburb on the left bank, is readily identifiable. Baker describes Auterive as a powerful castle, and makes no mention of the town itself. In the twelfth century an eleventh-century wooden castle of motte and bailey design to the north of the town had been abandoned, and the town itself was then fortified with brick walls with a new castle integrated into the north-west corner of the town, possibly giving the impression of the town as a whole being a large castle. At the end of the Albigensian Crusade the consuls of Auterive were obliged by the Treaty of Paris of 1229 to demolish the town's fortifications. It is not at all clear if they did so, but it in any case it is probable that the fortifications would have been rebuilt by the mid-fourteenth century. In 1355 there were two suburbs outside the walls, one to the south-east towards Cintegabelle and another across the river at the bridgehead. There were two monasteries, both outside the walls on the right bank. To the west of the town between the ramparts and the river was a religious house devoted to the Clares, and on the southern side of the town was a monastery belonging to the Pères de la Merci, a religious order for the redemption of Christian captives held by Barbary pirates operating from the north African coast.

The suburb on the left bank was linked to the main town by a substantial twelfth-century bridge with eleven spans crossing both the river and a canal built to take water through a mill. The bridge fell into disrepair from the sixteenth century, but one span still stands just to the south of the modern bridge. The town ramparts stood about 150 yards back from the river and thus the suburbs on both sides of the river and both monasteries were vulnerable to attack without the need to tackle the town or the castle. This may have been the assessment of the army's leaders also, for the castle and the walled town seem to have escaped attention, while the suburbs and the two monasteries were destroyed.[26] From Auterive the army pressed on west across the flood-plain of the Ariège towards the Garonne, with the prince's middle guard stopping for the night at Miremont.

Wednesday 18 November was to be an eventful day with the crossing of the Garonne in prospect, but the day's work started with the burning of the 'great town' and castle of Miremont.[27] The village stands on ground rising from the valley floor of the Ariège, and the castle, of motte and bailey design, formed an integral part of the fortified part of Miremont. The castle keep stood on the highest point to the west of the church, giving a dominant view over the surrounding countryside out towards the Ariège and Toulouse sixteen miles to the north. From this vantage point the approach of the prince's division could have been observed for some distance. The walled part of the village covered about seven acres, with two suburbs and the village windmill outside the walls. The walls, constructed of brick, were 1.6 metres thick and of an unknown height. They were surrounded by a ditch, some of which was fed with water to form a moat. As an indication of the strength of these brick walls, a local story has it that in the 1930s it took three men four days to demolish a hole large enough for a garage door. Parts of underground passages have been found leading from the castle out into the valley. These are thought to have allowed secret egress from the castle rather than to have been refuges. The church was originally the chapel for the castle, but has been modified over the centuries, mainly to increase its height. The crypt, dating from the twelfth century, has a niche built into the wall, with evidence of strong points for a grill, and is thought to have been used to secrete relics, valuable items and archives. Whether or not the crypt was discovered by the prince's pillagers is unknown.

Archaeological research is under way in the village to investigate its medieval past, and three grain silos have been revealed in a house in the village within the perimeter of the walls. These had been hollowed out of the clay subsoil and were in a rough barrel shape. To prevent damage to grain from damp, the sides were lined with rye straw held in place by flexible sticks which followed the curve of the walls. The grain would still be vulnerable to some dampness but a crust would form over the top to protect the grain below, keeping the rest of the supply edible. The silos are thought to date from slightly different periods, but the earliest has been dated to the twelfth century by the type and irregular shape of the bricks. Bricks with signs of fire damage were found with the rubble, but these have been dated as belonging to the period of the Wars of Religion rather than to the passage of the Black Prince.[28]

The silos are not uniform, but are approximately 2.5 metres high and 1.6 metres across, giving a total capacity of 15 cubic metres, or enough space to store about 11 tonnes of wheat. When supplies allowed, typical consumption of bread would be between 1 and 1.5 kg per day per person, often cut in thick slices and used first as a plate to eat other food such as cheese, salted meat and bacon. These silos, therefore, were much larger than required solely for the occupants of the building, and indeed smaller silos for domestic storage have been found in other houses. Because of their size these are thought to have been for use either by the miller or as a communal store.[29]

Extrapolation from a study of grain production in the Cintegabelle area in the Middle Ages shows that about 100 acres would be needed to supply enough grain to fill the silos discovered in Miremont. However, around 250 acres of arable land would be needed to provide this stock to allow for rotation, and some overproduction for tithes and levies. One tenth or one twelfth of the crop would typically go to the church as a tithe, and a fifth to the local lord. Control of the tithe was seen as so important that harvested crops had to remain in the fields, whatever the weather, for twenty-four hours to allow it to be assessed. The lord would also hold a monopoly on the mills and communal bread ovens. Charges were levied in kind. For example, one loaf in twelve had to be given up in return for the compulsory use of the ovens for baking bread. Similarly, a tax might be levied in the form of a measure of grain for the use of the communal forge to sharpen blades. In addition, of course, seed would need to be put aside for next year's crop. Taking into account all these demands it has been estimated that a yield of four to one would allow a sustainable supply. With bread being an essential part of the diet and grain production central to the life and economy of medieval villages such as Miremont, the loss of the stock of such silos would have been very serious. Concealment of supplies for long enough for the prince's army to pass by would have been a high priority for the villagers.[30]

Setting off from Miremont on the morning of 18 November the prince's division faced a steady climb of 400 feet out of the valley of the Ariège, followed by a descent into the valley of the river Lèze. There is a further climb of 300 feet out of the valley of the Lèze to an escarpment overlooking the Garonne. Standing on the escarpment is the tiny village of Montaut. There is no trace of the castle belonging to the count of Foix which Baker tells us once stood here.[31]

The last significant barrier before the return to friendly territory was the Garonne. The crossing of the river gives us a glimpse of the tactical employment of the prince's troops. Baker tells us that they made this crossing on Wednesday

Plate 3 The Garonne at Noé. This photograph of the crossing point of the Garonne was taken after a dry winter. It gives perhaps a deceptively benign view of the point where the crossing of the Anglo-Gascon army aroused such astonishment among local inhabitants.

18 November near Noé. Although the river here is only about half the width that it is further downstream at Pinsaguel where they crossed on their way east, it remains a formidable obstacle. Baker recounts that the boats that were normally kept here to ferry people across the river had been removed, and that the local inhabitants were astonished to see the cavalry cross the river in single file. Baker makes no mention of the infantry or the baggage train, and in contrast to his account of the earlier crossing of the Garonne, reference to the cavalry is explicit. The prince, however, states that the army 'pursued them [the French] in long marches near to Toulouse; where we took our road to pass the Garonne at a town called Carbonne'.[32]

Baker relates that, having taken the village of Noé and accepted the surrender of the castle, the rearguard stayed in the town overnight. The middle guard moved on up the river, and to the amazement of the local people crossed back over the river three miles upstream to take the village of Marquefave. They then crossed a third time to take Carbonne by assault from the river side, which was not walled, before the arrival of the prince.

In 1355 Carbonne was further south than the present town, on a promontory in an oxbow bend of the river. The town was to the west of the promontory, with

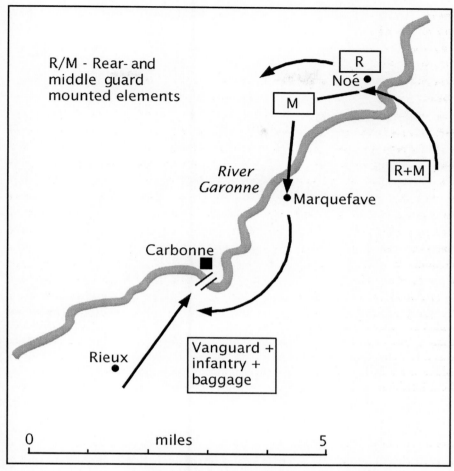

R/M - Rear- and
middle guard
mounted elements

R

Noé

M

River
Garonne

R+M

Marquefave

Carbonne

Rieux

Vanguard +
infantry +
baggage

0   miles   5

Map 13 Crossing the Garonne.

open ground to the east and south between the town and the river. It was fortified with ramparts of brick and stone. If any side were unprotected by ramparts
then it would be that to the west.

According to one source the town had been deserted by the inhabitants before
the arrival of the army. Another source states that the inhabitants, seeing that
they could not resist, abandoned their houses and withdrew with their families beyond a bridge to the right bank of the river. They resolved to defend the
bridgehead where they fortified themselves and repulsed with vigour the attacks
of the prince's army, having realised that they must either hold their ground or
perish with their families.[33] If there is truth in this account then the townspeople were foolish in the extreme and had failed to learn from the experiences
of others in the region. However, the account is interesting in that it refers to a
bridge over the Garonne which is not mentioned by either Baker or the prince.

Plate 4 The site of the bridge at Carbonne. A view back across the Garonne from the site of the town of Carbonne in the fourteenth century showing the surviving pillar of the ancient bridge. The stone foreshore shows the low state of the river when this photograph was taken, in contrast to the accounts of the difficulties posed by the river in 1355.

A bridge did exist in 1355, to the south of the town and three-quarters of a mile south of the present bridge, possibly of Roman construction or perhaps built in 1264 to provide access between the abbey of Bonnefont and the town. The bridge was constructed of wood supported by brick pillars, one of which still exists having survived the floods of 1436 which washed away the rest of the bridge.[34] The presence of the bridge over the Garonne at Carbonne may explain why the description of the crossing at Noé refers only to cavalry. If the conditions were so bad that the crossing of horsemen aroused such wonder then it is likely that the crossing by foot-soldiers and wagons would have been very hazardous if not impossible. One historian has claimed that elements of the army passed by the town of Rieux, about three miles south-west of Carbonne, approaching the ramparts, assessing the defences and then deciding to pass on since the ramparts were well guarded.[35] This would be consistent with an approach to Carbonne from the south rather than along the river.

The use of scouts would have revealed the river conditions at Noé and confirmed that the bridge at Carbonne was still standing and would afford a safe and easy passage for transport and infantry. Baker's comment that the middle guard, having moved up river, took Carbonne *before* the arrival of the prince could also imply that the cavalry of his division had been detached from the infantry and baggage train, and that the prince was with the latter body and the vanguard.

Late on Thursday 19 November news came to the prince that the French, having come out from Toulouse, were in camp about six miles from the Anglo-Gascon rearguard. It is likely that he would have been aware from scouts of the movement of the French in advance of this news. A prudent course of action would have been to get men-at-arms and mounted archers over the river at Noé. They could provide a covering force on the far bank and also a means to secure the bridge at Carbonne for the infantry and baggage train. The account of an initial crossing of the cavalry at Noé, the recrossing of the middle guard, and the rearguard remaining on the left bank is consistent with such tactics. The result was an uncontested crossing for the army. It is perhaps indicative of the importance that the prince and his council attached to ensuring a safe and unopposed crossing of the Garonne that they had marched for nine days without rest, covering 146 miles, since leaving Narbonne.

Home for Christmas

Carbonne to La Réole
Thursday 19 November to Wednesday
2 December 1355

And, forasmuch as we perceived that they would not have fighting, it was agreed that we ought to draw towards our marches.

Black Prince to the bishop of Winchester, Christmas Day 1355.[1]

On Thursday 19 November the army took advantage of fine weather to rest for the first time since leaving Narbonne. They now had no major obstacles between them and a return to friendly territory, and the march would regain a more measured pace interspersed with days of rest again. They lodged in Carbonne, with the prince, as was his habit, remaining outside. As they rested in welcome fine weather and contemplated the days ahead they must have wondered why yet again Armagnac had not taken the opportunity to oppose the crossings of the Garonne, particularly as scouts would have brought them news that the French army was gathering nearby. Indeed, sometime before midnight news came to the prince that Armagnac, the constable, Marshal Clermont, and the prince of Orange had come out from Toulouse and were camped about six miles from the Anglo-Gascon rearguard. It also seems from the prince's account to the bishop of Winchester that there may have been skirmishing at this stage, since he reports that the French 'lost some of their men and wagons at their camping'.[2]

On the Friday morning the prince's army moved out from camp and was drawn up in battle order to face the French army organised in five large divisions. Baker tells us that the army was drawn up about a mile away, the Anglo-Gascon rearguard, which had initially remained at Noé, having now presumably moved closer to Carbonne. However, it is not clear whether he means a mile away from their camp or from the French position. It is impossible to judge where the armies were positioned, but the land to the west of the Garonne in this area is flat and featureless until the ground starts to rise six or seven miles to the west of the river. We know that the French subsequently withdrew north-west towards Lombez, and it is probable that the stand-off between the armies took place to the north-west of Carbonne, downstream from the town and towards Toulouse. The prince reported that he sent forward a number of lords, including Chandos, Burghersh and Audley with thirty lances, which probably consisted of thirty men-at-arms with a number of supporting mounted archers, to reconnoitre the position of the French.[3] Riding towards the enemy they came to a town with 200 men-at-arms, thirty-five of whom were taken after fighting. If the French were downstream towards Toulouse, and six or seven miles from Carbonne, then either Bérat or Longages may have been the town in question. If this is so then Bérat would have given the French a strong position either on or with their backs to the ridge rising from the flood-plain of the Garonne. Nevertheless, even if they were in a good position, the prince relates that the French took fright and withdrew in haste towards Lombez and Sauveterre, twenty miles distant.

Baker gives an account which differs from that of the prince. He tells us that when the Anglo-Gascon army was drawn up one of their men called out on seeing a hare, and that the French sent forty lances to investigate. They promptly turned and fled when they saw the prince's army drawn up. Baker goes on to say that prisoners were subsequently taken who told their captors that the whole French army fled after this incident. He also recounts the scouting mission by Burghersh, Audley and Chandos but gives them a force of eighty lances. Baker implies that this incident followed the flight of the French army, with their rear-guard being engaged and thirty-two knights and squires captured, including the lord of Romery, many carters killed, and provisions destroyed. Given the number of prisoners reported as taken in both accounts, the figure of eighty lances seems more plausible than the prince's figure of thirty.

Although these accounts vary in detail, it is clear that once again the French had declined to give battle despite a significant numerical superiority, their army probably being around three times as large of that of the prince. Writing on 18 December 1355, shortly after the end of the *chevauchée*, King Jean acknowledged that the French army was several times greater than that of their opponents and expressed some frustration that the Anglo-Gascon army had not been brought to battle. It is of note that his dissatisfaction seems to have stemmed from his view, or at least that given to him, that the Anglo-Gascon army had been able to avoid battle, rather than that the French had withdrawn.[4] The confidence of the prince, and perhaps his frustration, must have grown with every such encounter.

Following the withdrawal of the French, the prince's army moved off in pursuit, but before leaving Carbonne they destroyed the town. In August the following year, at the request of the count of Armagnac, King Jean confirmed and extended the privileges of Carbonne, the archives, including the original charter of 1257, having also gone up in flames. The aim of the confirmation and extension of privileges was to rebuild houses and provide for protection of the town through the construction of walls and bastions. Buildings inside the ramparts, with an eye to the practicalities of defence, were to be at least 10 feet from the walls, and

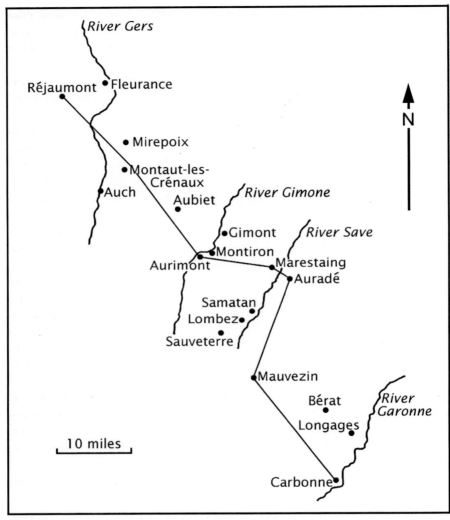

Map 14 Carbonne to Réjaumont.

those outside 300 feet from the walls. To aid the process of reconstruction the land of those who did not wish to rebuild their properties could be transferred to others who would build for a 'fair price'. The townspeople were authorised to bring in wood and tiles free of taxes for one year. The bridge seems to have been destroyed by the departing Anglo-Gascons, since there was specific provision for rebuilding it, with authority granted to tax boats crossing the river during rebuilding, provided the proceeds were used for the bridge. However, the king's letter makes no mention of the range of measures such as wider tax exemptions, deferred debt repayment, or authority to raise special taxes and tolls that had been granted in the cases of Castelnaudary and Limoux.[5] The original town had been so thoroughly destroyed that a fresh start was made. Rebuilding took place on the site of the present town centre, a little to the north of its position in 1355. The original site was abandoned since the new site was easier to fortify and free of the encumbrances of a multitude of manorial rights. The reconstruction, or at least that of the fortifications, was completed by 1362 at the latest since in that year the town walls, 7 metres high, were able to withstand an attack by a company of routiers.[6]

The pursuit on Friday 20 November took the army out of the valley of the Garonne and north-west over gently undulating hills nineteen miles to Mauvezin, six miles south of Lombez and Sauveterre where the French had fled. Mauvezin is now little more than a few scattered houses but with a substantial church in which four men-at-arms, fugitives from the prince's army, were cornered. They were allowed to go after surrendering their horses and armour.[7]

Armagnac had clearly either been anticipating withdrawing in front of the prince or preparing for the worst if engaged in battle since the prince reported that the French had broken down the bridges over the river Save during the night before the arrival of the Anglo-Gascon army. He also stated that the army camped within sight of the French camp-fires across the river.[8] Since there is high ground in the area between Mauvezin and the Save camp-fires beyond the river would not have been seen from Mauvezin itself. However, if the army were camped on the ridge two miles to the north of Mauvezin they would have had a clear view down into the valley of the Save and towards the French encampment near Sauveterre and Lombez.

The next morning, Saturday 21 November, the prince sent men forward to repair the bridges over the Save and the army pursued the French. The prince's army moved in rain along the eastern bank of the Save on a poor, narrow road to Auradé, about fifteen miles along the river. A castle at Auradé was burnt before the departure of the army on Sunday morning.

On the morning of Sunday 22 November the army initially moved west across the Save. The prince's report of bridges having been repaired could imply that the whole army crossed on bridges. However, the obvious place to cross the Save near Auradé is at a ford half a mile north-east of Marestaing which had been in use since ancient times.[9] It is possible that the prince's division crossed here, with other elements using repaired bridges elsewhere along the river. Baker's account of subsequent events that day is that:

> On Sunday, St Cecilia's day, having made a long march they realised that the enemy were on the far side of a large hill, near and below the town of Gimont, so that the English, delayed until midnight, sent in the meanwhile sixty lances with some archers to the right, to the town of Aurimont, where they found four hundred men-at-arms of the constable of France's company, and forced them to abandon the town, killing and capturing some of them as they pursued them towards Gimont.[10]

This account is puzzling. The direct route from Auradé to Gimont is only twelve miles, and, although the terrain is a little hilly, this would not have been a long march even in terms of time. Furthermore, if a direct route had been taken towards Gimont, troops sent to Aurimont would have been despatched to the left not to the right.

Hewitt's interpretation is that: 'Here [Gimont], however, on a hill outside the town, they [the French army] offered sufficient resistance to hold the English force at bay until midnight. During the delay some English troops were sent upstream and gained possession of Aurimont.'[11] This does not fit with the despatch of troops to the right to Aurimont, unless the Anglo-Gascon army had already moved beyond Aurimont in a north-westerly direction when they realised that the French were in the vicinity of Gimont. In this case, in turning back to face the French and the town of Gimont the army would have had Aurimont to their right. However, this does not explain the reported delay. Also, if there were a stand-off between the two armies somewhere near Gimont, it is difficult to see why there would be a French detachment at Aurimont and why the prince would despatch a force to deal with it, thus diverting troops from a confrontation with the main body.

A more plausible explanation is given by Clifford Rogers. He argues that the prince, having crossed the Save, initially turned south-west towards Lombez.[12] This is a reasonable supposition given the most recent known location of the French near Lombez and Sauveterre. This route also explains other aspects of Baker's passage. When news came to the prince that the French had moved away and towards Gimont he would, first of all, have wanted to confirm that this was accurate before changing the line of march of the whole army. Thus a halt, pending a report from the reconnaissance party, with a subsequent resumption of the march, but now towards Gimont, would explain the delay, the long march and the late arrival.

Following the engagement at Aurimont and the pursuit of the French towards Gimont, the middle guard lodged, none too well we are told, at Aurimont, which today is only a minor village with a population of a hundred or so with no signs of either fortifications or a castle. The vanguard lodged at 'Celimont', 'a small town a mile from the enemy'.[13] There is no obvious location for Celimont. The nearest approximation is the hamlet of Semont marked on the eighteenth-century Cassini map, a little over half a mile to the east of the village of Montiron, itself about a mile and a half upstream towards Gimont from Aurimont.[14] If Celimont were Semont, and the French were between the vanguard and Gimont, then the men of the vanguard would have been on high ground above the French, which would accord with the description that they were 'on the far side of a large hill'. Unfortunately, there is no obvious hill which stands out from the generally undulating terrain and meets the description of a 'large hill' to allow the likely position of the French army to be determined.

On Monday the baggage train and non-combatant personnel were instructed to remain in the vicinity of Aurimont, while the army was drawn up in battle order once again. Scouts were sent out and they discovered that the enemy had fled the field. Baker argues that this constituted a technical victory for the prince, in that after a persistent pursuit by the English with several opportunities for battle the French had consistently avoided combat with the Anglo-Gascon army.[15] One historian advances the theory that Armagnac avoided battle because he had suffered defections from his army as he had done some weeks earlier in Toulouse.[16] However, in view of the series of opportunities for battle over the previous few days, all of which had resulted in the withdrawal of the French, it is difficult to escape the conclusion that Armagnac either did not have the confidence to join battle or else considered that, with the Anglo-Gascon army already heading for home, the risks outweighed any potential advantage to be gained through battle.[17]

Gimont, a *bastide* founded by the Cistercian order in 1265, was well fortified with walls, ditches and an external perimeter road to give a clear area away from the walls. The French having withdrawn from the field, the prince had to decide whether to attempt to take Gimont with the French inside or to continue on the way home. He took counsel and the assessment was that the town was too large and too strong to attack, and the army moved off once more towards Gascony on Tuesday 24 November.[18] We know little about events on this day. The army had a long day and camped in the open. Lack of water was a problem and the horses were given wine to drink, with the result that on the Wednesday they were drunk and unsteady on their feet, resulting in the loss of many of them. The going from Aurimont is not as difficult as some of the terrain that they had crossed. However, it is hilly with small winding roads, and there is very little in the way of water. If we assume roughly equal lengths of march on the Tuesday and Wednesday and a fairly direct route from Aurimont, then it is likely that the army camped in the area between Mirepoix and Montaut-les-Crénaux, a twelfth-century *castelnau* village. If this is so they would have been only four miles or so short of the plentiful water supply from the Gers. It is unlikely that scouts would not have found the Gers, and it seems surprising that the army did not press on to reach the river. However, in late November the days are getting short. The French army was also presumably still within range, and an advance in the dark to the Gers might have been judged to be imprudent with the risk of harrying attacks on the baggage train.

The Anglo-Gascon army crossed the Gers on Wednesday, and left Fleurance, formerly in the possession of the English, on the right with the army spread out widely in the expectation of meeting the French. The encounter with the French army did not materialise and, the army having passed through what Baker calls the large town of 'Silarde', the prince's division lodged on the night of Wednesday 25 November at Réjaumont, ten miles south-west of Fleurance.[19] The location of Silarde, however, is not obvious. It has been variously interpreted as Ste-Radegonde, a small village three miles west of Fleurance, or St-Lary. With this latter name there are again two alternatives, one ten miles south of Réjaumont, and the other close by Ste-Radegonde. The presence of ruins of a castle dating from the thirteenth century at the southerly village lends some support to that having

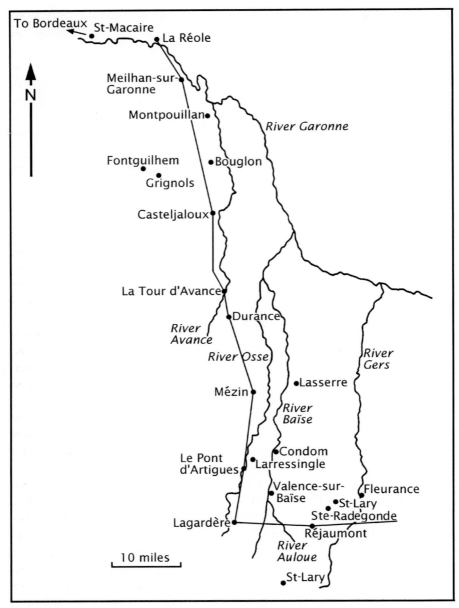

To Bordeaux St-Macaire

La Réole

N

Meilhan-sur-Garonne

Montpouillan

River Garonne

Fontguilhem

•Bouglon

Grignols

Casteljaloux

La Tour d'Avance

•Durance

River Avance

River Osse

River Gers

•Lasserre

Mézin

River Baïse

Le Pont d'Artigues

Condom

Larressingle

Valence-sur-Baïse

Fleurance

•St-Lary

Ste-Radegonde

Lagardère

Réjaumont

River Auloue

St-Lary

10 miles

Map 15 Réjaumont to La Réole.

been Silarde, but, with Baker's description relating to the passage of the prince's middle guard and their halt for the night at Réjaumont, the hamlet of St-Lary near Ste-Radegonde seems the more plausible location for Silarde.[20]

Today's small village of Réjaumont was in the medieval period a much more substantial town with a castle, protected with fortifications and ditches. In common with many towns in the area it had passed back and forth between English and French jurisdiction. Indeed, there is some doubt over whether the *bastide* was founded by the English or the French, with one source attributing its foundation in 1285 to Eustache de Beaumarchais, the seneschal of Toulouse, and another to John of Havering, seneschal of Gascony for Edward I in 1292. By 1355 it was back in French hands and suffered the consequences, being taken by assault and burned. There is one account from later in the Hundred Years War, that the town was besieged by the English in 1369, and that, when they seemed to be on the point of departure having abandoned the siege, one resident decided to show her backside to the English to demonstrate her contempt for them. Unfortunately, this insult had completely the reverse effect and the English surged into the town, destroying ramparts and town and putting the population to the sword. The moral drawn from this story locally is: 'Ladies, before showing your backside, check carefully that it is not to the English.'[21]

The army rested at Réjaumont on Thursday 26 November. Intelligence was gathered from a prisoner, a stray man-at-arms, who reported that there had been a quarrel between the constable and Armagnac over failure to engage the Anglo-Gascon army, with accusations of broken promises and blame for having avoided battle on several occasions.

On the Friday they moved on, with the terrain much as it had been for the previous days, gently undulating and punctuated by rivers running predominantly north to south. They crossed, in scattered groups, a great river and marched for the rest of the day between walled towns and strong castles.'[22] The river was the Baïse; the implication is that, with the army marching in dispersed contingents, the threat from the French was not considered to be great. It also seems to imply that there was now little interest in further pillage and destruction, and the priority was to return home. As they moved through this countryside an example of the walled towns that they passed by would have been Valence-sur-Baïse, a good-sized *bastide* founded in 1274 by the count of Armagnac. The town sits on high ground on the eastern bank of the river. It was well defended with walls 8 metres high pierced by four gates. One of these gates survives, as do some parts of the ramparts sitting on rock cliffs and adding to the height and effectiveness of the walls. An assault on the town would have been a difficult proposition, but the abbey of Floran, on low ground just outside the walls to the west of the town, would have been very vulnerable. Earlier in the expedition this town, belonging to Armagnac, would probably have attracted the attention of the army and have merited comment from Baker. Its escape at this stage of the *chevauchée* tends to confirm that the focus was now on returning safely home rather than further destruction and plunder.[23]

Having crossed the river the prince's middle guard moved on and lodged at 'le Serde'. The location of this town is unclear. It has been suggested that this is either Lagardère, ten miles south of Condom, or Lasserre, a similar distance to the north of that town. Both of these names could be corruptions of Le Serde, but neither is entirely satisfactory. Both are more than the one league from Condom stated by Baker. Also the march from Réjaumont to Lasserre would either not take them across the Baïse, or would require them to cross the river twice. It would also leave them ten miles to the east of Saturday's halt after a march of twenty-five miles from Réjaumont. Lagardère makes more sense since it is fourteen miles on from Réjaumont and there is a march of eighteen miles to the next destination at Mézin on Saturday. It also lies on a logical route west across the Baïse and then north to follow the remainder of the known route. An alternative could be the fortified village of Larressingle which is three miles, or one league, to the west of Condom as described by Baker. Thus, it fits geographically, is a logical point on the route, twenty miles from Réjaumont, with a crossing of the Baïse close to Valence-sur-Baïse, and a ten-mile march the next day to Mézin. Furthermore, it could be a corruption of le Serde. Although Baker tells us that the town and the castle at 'le Serde' had previously been destroyed by the duke of Lancaster, presumably during his *chevauchée* of 1349, we do not know whether Lancaster passed by any of the towns of Lasserre, Lagardère or Larressingle. However, the small fortified village of Larressingle, its thirteenth-century ramparts still intact, is said to have escaped the ravages of the Hundred Years War and, despite its favourable position is not, therefore, a likely candidate if Baker is correct that Le Serde had been destroyed by Lancaster. In view of the route and its position to the west of the Baïse, Lagardère is the most likely of the other proposals.[24]

The onward march on Saturday 28 November was to Mézin with the army crossing the minor river Osse, again in dispersed groups, and the prince's division marching on a narrow forest road. The crossing of the Osse would not have presented any problems, and it is possible that some may have crossed by the twelfth- or thirteenth-century bridge at Pont d'Artigues a mile south-west of Larressingle, built to help pilgrims on their way to Santiago de Compostela. Mézin, a fortified town, of which vestiges of the ramparts and one of the gates, La Porte Anglaise, remain, was wealthy with a flourishing trade in wine for England, including exports specifically for Westminster Abbey. It lay in the lands of the lords of Albret, who had for long been loyal to the English cause, and the army was now back in friendly territory. Banners were furled and many of the Gascon troops were allowed to disperse.

On Sunday the prince received the homage and oaths of loyalty of the townspeople and rested. While at Mézin, John Henxteworth took the opportunity to bring the accounts up to date with the first entries in his journal since leaving Carcassonne. There was some catching up to be done, with payment made to a guide, compensation for two horses taken from messengers at Carbonne, and settlement for two hauberks bought for the prince at Réjaumont. The payment to the monastery at Prouille was also now regularised. Somewhat intriguingly 54 shillings were given as a gift to Bernard Dassatz, a swineherd of the count of Foix. We also see life returning to the pattern we would expect in friendly territory with purchases of fodder, hay, bread, oats, wheat and firewood. Also a sign of a return to normality is an advance of wages of 3s 4d to Roger Geccombe, carpenter and tent-maker to the prince. Unfortunately, some of the troops do not seem to have adjusted to the return to peace, since we also see a payment of 18 shillings to Gerard de Rynaly of Mézin in compensation for the burning of his house.[25]

On the Monday, St Andrew's Day, the remaining elements of the army continued on their way home and lodged at Casteljaloux.[26] The march, still through the lands of Albret, was for twenty-two miles through the eastern reaches of the barren Landes, described by Baker as a long march *per vastam solitudinem*. Nowadays the view is obscured by pine forests. In the fourteenth century, however, the *bastide* town of Durance, founded by Edward I in 1320 alongside a now ruined thirteenth-century Premonstratensian monastery, and La Tour d'Avance, an imposing fortified tower once a commanderie of the Knights Hospitallers, or Knights of Malta, dating from the twelfth century, would have stood out sharply from the landscape as the army continued its march towards Casteljaloux.[27]

Baker describes Casteljaloux as having three castles, one of which stood in the marshes. Today there are no signs of these castles, beyond some traces within the sixteenth-century château in the town. Casteljaloux was a thriving town in medieval times, with forges, paper and glass industries, tanneries, mills and rope-making all benefiting from the abundance of water from the river Avance and its springs. It was also home to an abbey, Benedictine and Franciscan monasteries, and a Templar commanderie. It was surrounded by walls with three gates, but the only remaining monument that would have been extant in the fourteenth century is the bridge, which had been built by the Franciscans.[28]

The next day, Tuesday 1 December, brought the remaining elements of the army to 'Meulan' for the night. This must have been Meilhan-sur-Garonne, although it is six miles further on than the three leagues from Casteljaloux related by Baker. Some of the prince's household crossed desolate forest and passed near the monastery of 'Montguilliam', and moved on directly to La Réole without pausing for the night at Meilhan-sur-Garonne. Montguilliam, assumed by some to have been at Montpouillan, is believed by one French historian to have been the Cistercian abbey of Fontguilhem seven miles north-west of Casteljaloux.[29]

From Casteljaloux the ground starts to climb onto a ridge between the flat Landes and the valley of the river Garonne. On the top of the ridge is the small village of Bouglon which was still in French hands at the time along with a handful of other strongholds to the west of the Garonne which were to be taken by the English in early 1356.[30] Isolated from the main body of French towns and forces on the other side of the river, the garrisons of such places must have

experienced considerable relief as the prince's troops passed by and left them
unmolested.

A few miles north of Bouglon the land falls away towards Meilhan-sur-
Garonne and the wide flood-plain of the Garonne. The town stands on a steep
escarpment 150 feet above the river, giving it panoramic views and command
of the river. Meilhan had a long history as an English town, having been part
of the Angevin empire on the marriage of the future Henry II and Eleanor of
Aquitaine. Its strategic importance had been recognised by Edward I who had
taken it into his direct control from the Albret family, although they regained
control from Edward II through the intervention of Pope Clement V in 1306. By
1345 it was back in French hands, but the duke of Lancaster regained control by
assault in November of that year. The fortifications and the defenders were very
resilient, but Lancaster commandeered local labour to fill part of the ditches. He
then brought up 300 archers to provide covering fire for a further 200 men to
work with picks under cover of shields to force a breach in the wall. Once this
was sufficiently wide to allow ten men abreast to enter the town, Meilhan was
taken with a large part of the garrison being killed, only those having retreated
into the church before surrendering being spared. A footpath which climbs up
from the river to the town bears the name La Brèche des Anglais.[31]

On Wednesday 2 December the *chevauchée* reached its conclusion as the prince
entered La Réole after a short, final march of six miles. The town lies across the
Garonne from his route, and Baker tells us that the prince and his entourage
crossed the river at a place where none could remember a horse having crossed
before. The river is certainly daunting here, fast flowing and 150 yards wide.
However, it is probable that Baker was embellishing the story, since there was a
ford in the Middle Ages used by, amongst others, pilgrims going to Santiago de
Compostela. This ford was probably about a mile south-east of the town where
the modern road bridge carries the D9 across the river. La Réole, which to this
day has a statement on display near the Benedictine priory recording that the
town owed its prosperity to the English occupation, was a town which, after
many years under English jurisdiction, had passed under French control in the
prelude to the Hundred Years War. In 1345 it returned to the English camp, once
more due to the efforts of Henry of Lancaster. The townspeople were under no
doubt where their loyalty lay, and by a subterfuge opened the gates to the Anglo-
Gascon troops. Although the garrison had managed to take refuge in the strong
castle in the south-west of the town, the castle was susceptible to undermining.
The besieging forces set to the task of mining the walls. After three weeks the
garrison commander could see the way things were going and agreed a truce. If
he were not relieved in five weeks he would surrender and depart with his men
under safe-conduct. Relief was not forthcoming, and in January 1346 the fortress
was handed over to Lancaster. The strategic importance of La Réole was not
lost on him. To reward the townspeople he confirmed the customs and liberties
of the town, and granted a new tax exemption for customs dues on their wines
which they had hitherto paid at Bordeaux. He also granted them the right to

raise a new tax on goods passing the town on the Garonne, but with an eye to defence half of the money raised was to be spent on repairs of the castle. Finally, he made payment of 2,000 gold florins for provisions commandeered in the town.[32]

On reaching La Réole the prince would have seen an impressive town with its castle, of which part of the curtain wall and three of its four corner towers dating from the thirteenth century remain, and the town ramparts standing on the ridge above the river. Taking pride of place then, as it does now, would have been the town hall, built on the orders of Richard the Lionheart as a gift to the townspeople. On passing through the gates the prince's great *chevauchée* in the Languedoc came to a close. The prince had led his army on a march of more than 600 miles deep into French territory and back in less than two months. He had not brought the French to battle, but the effects of his campaign were profound and remain seared in the history of the region to this day. The prince left La Réole on or about 5 December, passing via St-Macaire to reach Bordeaux four days later where he remained for Christmas.[33] But before he left La Réole it was time to take stock and look ahead to the coming year.

PART III

INTERLUDE

9

Consolidation and Preparation

Wednesday 2 December 1355 to Wednesday 6 July 1356

And, by the help of God, if my lord had wherewithal to maintain this war and to do the king's profit and his own honour, he would easily enlarge the marches and would win many places; for our enemies are sore astonished.

Sir John Wingfield to the bishop of Winchester, 23 December 1355[1]

After his arrival at La Réole on Wednesday 2 December the prince held a council to take stock of events and plan for the coming months. The *chevauchée* of the last two months had laid waste the lands of Armagnac, and in going beyond Toulouse had brought fire, pillage and destruction to parts of France that had previously been spared the direct ravages of the war. From the Anglo-Gascon viewpoint the immediate benefits were evident in the form of considerable financial rewards. The booty was said to have been sufficient to fill around a thousand carts, and there were ransoms to be collected for prisoners taken.[2]

Of great importance was the financial impact on the French king's ability to wage war. The direct impact was the reduced tax base of the region as a result of the devastation caused during the *chevauchée*. In his letter to the bishop of Winchester at Christmas Sir John Wingfield gave his assessment that the devastated area normally accounted for more than half of the revenue raised in France for King Jean.[3] This may have been an exaggeration, but there can be no doubt that the impact was very considerable. In addition there were secondary effects, which although not apparent in December, would become so when King Jean tried to marshal his resources for the coming year's campaigning. In fact, as early as the end of October 1355 the first signs of what was to come had surfaced when the council in Millau, well away from the route of the *chevauchée*, resolved to allocate the major part of their tax resources to restoring the town's defences. Although it could not be foreseen in December, a similar pattern would emerge elsewhere in the Languedoc, with tax exemptions granted, often over several years, to allow for rebuilding.[4] When the Estates of Languedoc met in March and April 1356 to consider the king's request for raising taxes, things were to go from bad to worse for Jean. They agreed a subsidy, but it was conditional on the arrival of the dauphin to defend the Languedoc. It was only to be used for operations in the south-west, and collection would cease if the dauphin withdrew for operations elsewhere. Raids by the Anglo-Gascon lords into the Languedoc and the Rouergue in the spring of 1356 did nothing to improve the situation. Jonathan Sumption describes the overall effect as being that 'the work of tax collectors and recruiting officers was paralysed'. The financial situation was similarly unhappy for Jean in the north, with the Estates of Languedoil also deciding to retain subsidies for the defence of the areas in which the taxes had been raised.[5]

Raising money for restoring fortifications suffered from perennial problems. Memories could be short and self-interest could quickly return. Less than two years after the prince passed by Belpech, Thibaud de Lévis-Montbrun, lord of Lapenne, just four miles to the south, felt the need to appeal to the seneschal of Carcassonne for help to persuade the inhabitants to repair the walls and ditches of his château, on the grounds that it was there that they would take refuge with their families and possessions in the event of peril. The townspeople in turn appealed to Parlement in Paris which, somewhat surprisingly perhaps, did not summarily find in favour of Thibaud. Instead the seneschal was charged to arrange for expert inspection of the fortifications to verify the extent of the work required before Parlement concluded its deliberations.[6] With the risk of abuses by those raising money ostensibly for the benefit of the local community, such appeals were not unusual. An example of the kind of problem that could arise comes a few years later, in 1365, when the captain of the château of Loches was accused before Parlement of having raised taxes for the improvement of the fortifications but having refused access to the local inhabitants. His case was probably not helped by the report that he had been heard to say that he saw no great difference between the king of France and the king of England, and that they could both 'boil their pots for sixty years in front of the château before he would let either of them enter'.[7] There was also the problem of persuading the clergy to contribute, one notable case being that of Béziers where, after the *chevauchée* of 1355, the consuls had imposed a tax to raise funds for the repair of the fortifications. The Hospitallers had claimed exemption, but an appeal by the consuls to Parlement was upheld and they were required to contribute.[8]

Nevertheless, despite the heavy financial impact, the French forces in the south-west had not been brought to battle. The immediate objective of the prince was to counter any residual threat from these forces, and then to prepare for the next year's campaigning. Both of these goals could be achieved, and the initiative retained, by securing the frontier of the duchy and extending Anglo-Gascon influence by pushing the borders out and bringing more lords back into allegiance to Edward III. The majority of the Gascon forces had dispersed, but a few hundred of the Gascon troops under the command of leading Gascon lords remained active to supplement the prince's English and Welsh contingent. The available forces were divided and deployed into the marchlands. Warwick was to remain at La Réole, Salisbury to go to Ste-Foy, Suffolk to St-Emilion, and the prince marched to Libourne with Chandos and Audley. The next three weeks or so were quiet after the exertions in the Languedoc, and operations restarted in earnest shortly after Christmas. In the meantime the prince had left Chandos and Audley at Libourne and returned to Bordeaux to stay in the archbishop's palace for what appears to have been a relatively modest Christmas.[9]

The prince and his advisors probably took the view that overall they had had a most satisfactory two months, though it would have added the icing to the cake to have met and defeated the French in battle. Some historians, however, hold the view that the success was limited. Sumption acknowledges the economic impact of the operations, but considers that 'the military value of the enterprise was more questionable. No battles had been won, no territory conquered, and no castles garrisoned.'[10] The lack of concrete results in terms of conquered territory and garrisoned castles is undeniable. But this was the norm rather than the exception for a *chevauchée*, which was a key instrument of war for Edward III. The prince's operations of 1355 have been characterised by some as simply brigandage with little military purpose, but the *chevauchée* must be seen within the strategic context and the values of the time.[11]

When Edward III came to the throne, England had a population approximately one third of that of France. France was also wealthier than England, and the French king was potentially able to raise three or four times as much in taxation as the English king.[12] The English also had the disadvantage of external lines of communication. They needed to use the sea for reinforcement and logistic support from the home base, with all the challenges of finding shipping and the vagaries of the weather with which to contend, while the French enjoyed the inherent advantages of internal movement over land. Overall, the English did not have the capacity to wage a war of conquest and occupation, but they could carry the war to France through the *chevauchée* and, as a secondary but important consideration, keep the war away from home. As Christine de Pizan wrote, 'it is better to trample another country than to allow one's own to be trampled underfoot'.[13] The *chevauchée* allowed the English to exert the maximum of pressure from the available resources, and to choose the area of operations. Also, the French kingdom was more vulnerable than England to quarrels between the king and some of the great lords. The *chevauchée* could exploit such divisions.

In the right circumstances the *chevauchée* could entice the enemy to do battle and encourage allies, but a key aspect was, of course, pillaging. Some of this was necessary to supply the needs of the army, but in addition there would have been the looting of movable wealth by troops. Not only did this diminish the resources available for taxation of the French king's subjects, but it also offered the prince's army the prospect of considerable personal gain, despite the general principle reflected in indentures that half of the spoils would be surrendered to the retinue commander of the man concerned and half of that figure to the king, or in this case the prince. This was a powerful recruiting incentive for the English.[14] As was evident later in the war, troops engaged in garrison duty often raided their surrounding area, which was supposed to be friendly territory, precisely because of the lack of opportunity for personal enrichment provided by a *chevauchée*.

One of the critics of the prince's 1355 *chevauchée* unwittingly put his finger on the military objectives of such operations: 'They proposed above all to pillage and to ravage one of the richest parts of France, from where the king drew his greatest resources for waging war.'[15] In other words, the *chevauchée* was an instrument of economic warfare which reduced the potential of the enemy to wage war. There was also the psychological impact on the inhabitants of the Languedoc to be considered, which as H. J. Hewitt indicates was considerable and enduring:

> Mentally and morally unprepared to bear with fortitude the horror, misery, and grief inseparable from war, they had seen their great bridges broken down, their suburbs razed, their cities burnt, their valuables stolen and, in many instances, their fellows killed. The swift-moving, devastating power moved on un-resisted, irresistible, spreading havoc wherever it went. Winter found them mourning, bewildered and fearful for the morrow.[16]

The concept and strategic value of economic warfare was certainly not alien to the French in the period: Jean II, in relation to the war at sea, encouraged his subjects in 1355 'to take, capture, and pillage the enemy', for by enriching themselves by their prizes they would damage the enemy and weaken his military effort.[17] Christine de Pizan, also writing from the French perspective, acknowledges the role of non-combatants in supporting the war-fighting capacity of a nation, their inevitable vulnerability, and implicitly the legitimacy of the *chevauchée*:

> But if the subjects of that king ... be they poor or rich, farmers or anything else, give aid and comfort to maintain the war, according to military right the French may overrun the country and seize what they find ... occasionally the poor and simple folk, who do not bear arms, are injured – and it cannot be otherwise, for weeds cannot be separated from good plants.[18]

Within the values of the day, the burning and pillaging by armies on *chevauchée* do not stand out as unduly barbaric. As one French writer puts it, the acts of the army of the prince belonged to the customs of the period, a time when Jean II believed that he was demonstrating exceptional clemency in commuting a woman's sentence from being buried alive to being drowned in the Seine with a stone around her neck.[19]

Rogers measures the achievements of the prince in the closing months of 1355 against the aim of bringing the French to battle and the objectives of an Edwardian *chevauchée*, drawn from a letter of Edward III to King Philippe during the Crécy campaign: 'to punish rebels against us and to comfort our friends and those faithful to us ... to carry on the war as best we can, to our advantage and the loss of our enemies'. Even without battle with the French, the prince could judge the *chevauchée* a success against the other objectives.[20] The punishment of Jean d'Armagnac and the comfort to friends were evident for all to see, and the

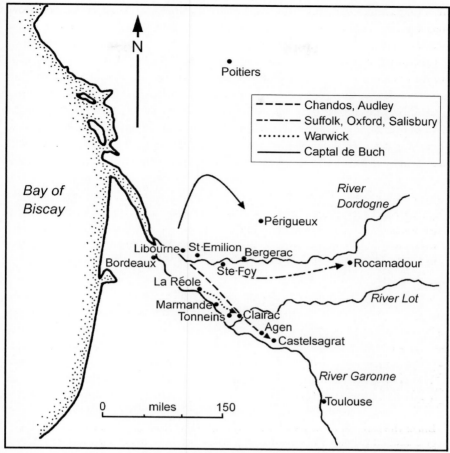

Map 16 Operations, Christmas 1355 to January 1356.

economic, psychological and military results short of a battle had, without question, been to the advantage of the king of England and to the loss of the king of
France. The lack of a set-piece battle was not for the want of trying on the part
of the prince. As we have seen, the return route taken past Carcassonne between
13 and 15 November 1355 favours the interpretation of a southerly route with
the prince in pursuit of the French and intent on battle. Similarly, the tactics at
the crossing of the Garonne at Noé and Carbonne show the prince prudently
protecting his crossing when in the proximity of the French army in preparation for an anticipated engagement, and again subsequently near Gimont he was
ready for battle until the French faded away.

    Looking forward to the summer of 1356, we know that Edward planned to
deploy three English armies to France with Lancaster operating from Brittany,
the prince from Aquitaine, and the king himself from Calais as he had done
the previous year. In preparation for the summer the prince set about securing

his borders and extending influence further into French-held territory. Progress came quickly, and by 22 January Sir John Wingfield was able to report to Sir Richard Stafford, by now back in England on the prince's business, the surrender of five towns and seventeen castles. Chandos and Audley had raided 100 miles along the Garonne and taken Castelsagrat by assault. They had then sallied out from there and raided up to the walls of Agen. Jean d'Armagnac was in Agen and again he had shown himself reluctant to come out and fight, Wingfield gleefully reporting that 'my lord Jean d'Armagnac and the seneschal of Agenois, that were within the town of Agen, would not once put out their heads nor any of their men'. Suffolk, Oxford and Salisbury were no less enterprising, pushing out to the east along the Dordogne, again for more than 100 miles, to the town of Roca-madour. Meanwhile Warwick had been operating along the Lot and Garonne rivers taking Clairac and Tonneins and destroying all about in the vicinity of Marmande. Finally, the captal de Buch had moved north into Saintonge and garrisoned a number of towns. At the time that Wingfield was writing he had news that the captal had gone out to raid towards Poitou and Anjou.[21] In fact the captal hooked right, captured the *cité* at Périgueux by escalade at night and handed it over to the lord of Mussidan.[22] Earlier the count of Périgord had, through the mediation of his brother the cardinal of Périgord and the pope, tried to ransom the town. This had drawn a similar response from the prince as to the offer from Carcassonne the previous autumn, to the effect that, by the grace of God, his father had gold and silver aplenty and that he had come to discipline those in rebellion against the king and bring them back to their rightful allegiance.[23] The message was clear and presumably had a salutary effect on those Gascon lords who had not so far shown themselves for King Edward. By the end of April a number of lords came across of their free will and others in response to either gifts of money or offers of land. Collectively they brought with them a further three dozen more walled towns and castles to be added to those captured in the early weeks of the year.[24]

With the security of the duchy much enhanced, the prince could now turn his attention to planning for the summer, and on 29 February orders were issued for 1,000 bows, 2,000 sheaves of arrows, and 400 gross of bowstrings to be procured in the prince's palatinate of Chester. This order was placed in Chester because the king had ordered all arrows elsewhere in England to be taken for his use. Two weeks afterwards, on 15 March, the king ordered 300 archers to be allotted to the prince as reinforcements, and ten days later this was increased to 600.[25] Of these, 500 were to be raised from Cheshire, with the remainder to come from Gloucestershire. Hewitt expresses doubts over the ability of Cheshire to furnish this number, particularly at relatively short notice since the troops were ordered to assemble at Plymouth by Palm Sunday, 17 April. However, the sailing of reinforcements was delayed by six weeks, a delay which must have aided those responsible for marshalling the additional troops.[26]

While the English and the Gascons were preparing for the forthcoming campaign, events were moving on apace in France. For some years Charles the

Bad, count of Evreux and king of Navarre, had been a thorn in the side of his father-in-law King Jean. Jean suspected Charles, not without reason, of plotting his overthrow. Things came to a head in April 1356 when Jean seized Charles at Rouen and imprisoned him. As Sumption points out, this coup may have been very satisfying for Jean, but it proved to be an act of great folly since Charles' younger brother Philippe promptly set about organising resistance in Normandy and solicited the help of the English.[27] Meanwhile, in May Jean had summoned his main army to assemble near Chartres, well placed to counter an English attack from the west. However, the dauphin was fully occupied attempting to restore order in Normandy in the face of continuing Navarrese resistance, and it was no longer possible for him to lead an army to Languedoc. Thus, Jean's fifteen-year-old son Jean, count of Poitiers, was appointed as the king's lieutenant south of the Loire. An army was ordered to assemble under his command at Bourges.

In England, in response to the Navarrese approach, Lancaster's plans were changed and he landed in Normandy early in June. Having assembled an army of 2,400, comprising the troops that he had brought with him, others from the English garrisons in Brittany, and the small band of Navarrese under Philippe, he set about conducting fast-moving operations in Normandy and then with-drew to Montebourg in the Cotentin. He had not achieved all that he might have hoped. He had not relieved Conches, and the Navarrese garrisons at Evreux and Tillières had been overwhelmed by the French besiegers. Nevertheless, he had disrupted French strategy, and he had delayed the despatch of the army due to go to the Languedoc. With the prospect of Edward also crossing the Channel with a third army, Jean was facing an increasing challenge.

Meanwhile, around 19 June, Sir Richard Stafford returned to Bordeaux with the reinforcements and additional horses, bows, bowstrings, arrows and vict-uals.[28] It is possible that he also brought orders for the prince on the conduct of the forthcoming campaign. On 6 July the prince left Bordeaux to join up with his army assembling at La Réole.

PART IV

THE POITIERS *CHEVAUCHÉE*,

AUGUST TO OCTOBER 1356

10

Advance to the Vienne

La Réole to Manot
Wednesday 6 July to Sunday 14 August 1356

... that it was our purpose to ride forth against the enemies in the parts of France, we took our road through the country of Périgord and Limousin, and straight on towards Bourges, where we expected to have found the King's son, the Count of Poitiers.

Black Prince to the City of London, 22 October 1356[1]

According to his own account, the prince left Bordeaux to join his army assembling at La Réole, probably some 8,000 to 10,000 strong, on the eve of the Feast of the Translation of St Thomas Becket, Wednesday 6 July 1356.[2] The obvious route from Bordeaux to La Réole would have been the reverse of that taken in December, along the river Garonne and through St-Macaire. He had forty-five miles to cover and he probably arrived on the Friday or Saturday.

The French seemed to have assumed from the assembly at La Réole that there would be a rerun of the previous autumn's *chevauchée*. Jean detached forces to reconstitute the count of Poitiers' army at Bourges for operations in the south, and measures were ordered to enhance the defence of towns in the Languedoc.

However, on or about 22 July the prince left La Réole and moved forty miles north-east to Bergerac.[3] Although we do not have an account of his route from La Réole to Bergerac, it would have taken him across low-lying land scattered with numerous castles and almost certainly through the *bastide* of Monségur. The town, granted its charter in 1265 by the wife of King Henry III of England, Aliénor de Provence, stands on a steep escarpment looking north over the river Dropt. Monségur's allegiance had passed back and forth over the years between the English and French, and it had most recently fallen to the earl of Derby in 1345, with the help of a siege engine transported from Bordeaux via Bergerac and used initially for the earl's assault on that town.[4]

The surviving records for Monségur give an unusually complete insight into the foundation of *bastides*. It was decreed that streets should be 24 feet wide,

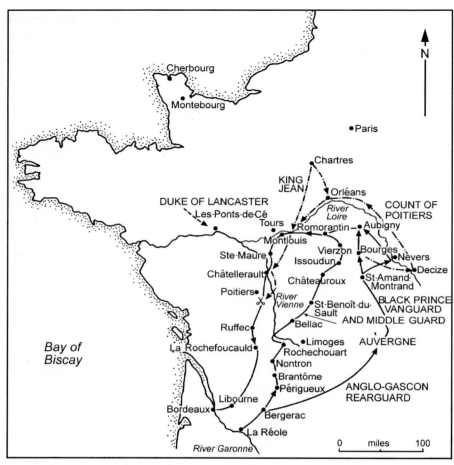

Map 17 The Poitiers *chevauchée*, August to October 1356.

houses were also to measure 24 feet wide and were to extend to a depth of 72 feet. A third of the houses were to be built in the first year, a further third in the next year, and the remainder when circumstances permitted. The king undertook to build stone walls around the *bastide*, subject to the inhabitants being responsible for their upkeep. The king also granted them as much land for agricultural cultivation as two oxen could plough in a day, and some further ground for a garden and some vines. Currency, weights and measures were to be those of La Réole. The town was to be governed by twelve jurors and the rights and privileges of the townspeople were defined in detail. Military service was restricted to one day's march from Monségur, including the return, and in the case of prosecution of townsmen royal officials could not seize the bed, clothes, armour, grain prepared for milling or wine from casks already opened for family use.[5]

From Monségur the prince's route would cross the Dropt to the town of Duras, just to the north of the river and again on high ground. Duras is dominated by its castle, built in 1308, and the town itself was fortified from the end of the thirteenth century.[6] Duras was in the hands of Gaillard de Durfort I. Gaillard was a minor Gascon noble, but he serves as an example of the frequent changes of loyalty on the part of the lords in the marchlands of Aquitaine and France and of the inducements to change sides. Gaillard had inherited his lands in 1345 at the age of forty-six. Up to this point he had been following a career as a canon lawyer and had been successively prebendary of Saintes, Agen and York as well as archdeacon of Périgueux. His inheritance changed all that. He now became enmeshed in seeking to steer a steady course in the ebb and flow of the fortunes of the parties to the quarrel over Aquitaine. In November 1345 he came across to the English following the success of Henry of Lancaster in defeating the French at the Battle of Auberoche and the capture of La Réole. He brought many other nobles with him together with a number of towns and castles, and in return he was granted an annuity. In 1352 he changed allegiance to the king of France, apparently in exchange for a financial consideration. In 1354 he forfeited his lands as a consequence, but Edward III, with an astute eye to the future, placed a condition that the transfer to the beneficiary of the forfeiture, the lord of Mussidan, could be reversed in return for compensation. Thus, when in April 1356 Gaillard came back to the English cause he regained possession of his lands. Gaillard was to die at Poitiers, five months after his latest change of side, fighting for the English cause.[7]

From Duras the prince's route to Bergerac was through undulating land with numerous small villages and castles, which often perch on small hills, until descending into the flood-plain of the Dordogne two miles from Bergerac. Bergerac had been taken for the English by the earl of Derby in 1345, with an assault across the bridge, which was protected by a barbican on the southern side of the river and a portcullis on the town side, between the village of La Madeleine, now the suburb of Bergerac of the same name, and Bergerac proper.[8] The acquisition of Bergerac had given the Anglo-Gascons a strong base in a good strategic position. It was well placed for the defence of Gascony and gave control of the Dordogne valley. Derby had arranged for it to be garrisoned by 100 men-at-arms and 200 foot-sergeants at the expense of the constable of Bordeaux.[9] Now, provided it were not left unguarded, it could serve as a launching base for the prince's operations beyond Aquitaine.

The deployment to Bergerac caused great concern to the French in the north, since it now seemed that the Anglo-Gascon army was more likely to strike either north towards the Loire or east towards the Massif Central, rather than into the Languedoc. It cannot have helped the French assess the prince's intention to learn that while this was happening some of the prince's men went as far north as the gates of Poitiers where the mayor was taken and ransomed in late July.[10] Shortly after receiving the news of the prince's move to Bergerac, Jean learnt that Edward had issued orders on 20 July for the assembly of an army for embarkation at Southampton by mid-August.

Then came better news for Jean, and perhaps events seemed to be turning

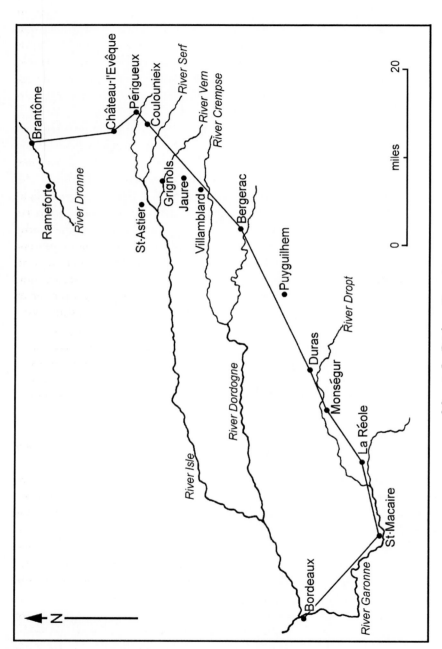

Map 18 La Réole to Brantôme.

in his favour. A fleet of Aragonese galleys, in the service of the French, arrived at the mouth of the Seine in the first week in August. This promised to thwart the despatch of King Edward's army to France, at least for the time being.[11] In addition, the duke of Lancaster had apparently been seen off, and Charles of Navarre was safely in custody. On the debit side, Lancaster's army, although not large enough to present a serious challenge to Jean in a set-piece battle, remained at large, and the prince had a fair-sized army on the move into the French heartland. The main threat was the prince, but Jean could not ignore Lancaster and the initiative still rested with his opponents.

But what was the English strategy for the summer of 1356? Some historians have taken the view that strategic planning was largely absent from English operations in the fourteenth century. Hewitt, writing of the 1355 chevauchée, commented: 'that this campaign lacked a strategic plan is largely true, but it is also a truism of all warfare in the fourteenth century'.[12] Tourneur-Aumont, reviewing assessments by a range of historians of the operations of Edward III and the Black Prince, refers to a view that the campaigns were never the execution of a strategic plan destined to obtain lasting results, and to the judgement of another French historian that the 1356 chevauchée leading to Poitiers had no other aim than the pillage and devastation of enemy territory. His conclusion was 'let us not talk of forces serving the English crown, it was just a matter of brigandage'.[13] Clifford Rogers summarises the conventional wisdom as follows:

> When his attempts to escape a pursuing French army and avoid battle failed, the argument runs, the prince was forced to fight, and once again the tactical prowess of the English soldiers rescued their leaders from a disaster nearly brought on by incompetent generalship. Prince Edward's words to the contrary, stating that during the campaign he had been seeking rather than avoiding battle, have been dismissed as the 'official version', designed to sway public opinion in England after the fact, and rather different from reality.

Rogers goes on to argue for a strategic plan for the prince that fulfilled objectives similar to those of the 1355 chevauchée, namely to bring harm to King Edward's enemies, the prospect of bringing at least the count of Poitiers to battle, and the opportunity of a strategic conjunction with Lancaster and King Edward.[14] This analysis rings true. It may be that often the direct evidence for strategic planning by Edward III is lacking, but that does not mean that it did not take place. It is difficult to believe that the extraordinary efforts and resources devoted to the despatch of expeditionary forces to France by Edward III were not based on a strategic view, even if not committed to paper. Certainly Andrew Ayton argues convincingly that there was a much stronger strategic basis for the Crécy campaign than many historians have thought in the past.[15] In the case of the English plans for France in 1356 we have clear statements from the prince of a plan to join with both the king and Lancaster. Writing after the Battle of Poitiers the prince stated that he had set out towards Bourges in the expectation of meeting the count of Poitiers. He was equally clear that 'the sovereign cause for our going towards these parts was that we expected to have had news of our said lord and father, the king, as to his passage' and that he was intent upon joining up with Lancaster, 'of whom we had certain news that he would make haste to draw towards us'.[16] To dismiss the prince's statements as self-justifying spin for public consumption after the battle is far-fetched. It is very difficult to see why, having just won a great and stunning victory which included the capture of the French king, he would need to conjure up such a justification.

The route and conduct of the *chevauchée* bear witness to his intent, and the despatch of 600 additional archers from England provides further evidence of his purpose. Casualties in the previous autumn's campaigning had been light. A campaign in the summer of 1356 with the accent on brigandage and avoidance of battle would presumably have been within the capacity of the existing forces. The additional archers, however, would give the prince's army more fire-power and was entirely consistent with the aim of drawing either the count of Poitiers or King Jean into battle. The prince was determined on battle if the right circumstances could be engineered.

Moving to the north as he did entailed the risk that Gascony would be exposed to an attack by the count of Armagnac. A substantial part of the army, thought to be 2,000 or 3,000 strong was, therefore, left at Bergerac under the command of the seneschal John de Chiverston, Bernard d'Albret and the mayor of Bordeaux to defend Gascony.[17] The remainder of the prince's army was about 6,000 strong and overall probably some 10,000 souls, including non-combatant personnel, set out from Bergerac on 4 August.[18]

The *Eulogium* gives us a detailed itinerary from the departure from Bergerac until the return to Bordeaux, but, as with Baker for the previous autumn, it deals largely with the prince's division with occasional reference to the location of the other divisions. At first sight the *Eulogium* seems to be in conflict with other sources, including that of Bartholomew Burghersh writing immediately after the campaign, which describe a more easterly route through the Rouergue, Agenais, Limousin, Auvergne and Berry. However, the likely explanation is not that we have a difference to resolve. It is most probably simply that one of the other divisions was following a more easterly route than that of the prince for the initial part of the *chevauchée*.[19]

As the route climbs out from the flood-plain the countryside changes in character. There are still the vineyards which formed such an important part of the economy of the area in the Middle Ages, but these gradually give way to dense woodland and more steeply undulating terrain, cut with minor rivers running across the route. The ascents and descents with the crossing of the Crempse, Vern and Cerf valleys are only of a few hundred feet, but the repeated nature of the climbing makes for tiring travelling on the way to Périgueux.

The prince's division entered Périgord on Saturday 6 August, where two unidentified fortified towns had already been taken by Bartholomew Burghersh and were being held by the lord of Marsan pending the arrival of the prince, and reached the city of Périgueux on Sunday. Although the captal de Buch had taken the walled *cité* in the south of the town earlier in the year, the walled *bourg* to the east of the *cité* around the cathedral of St Front remained in French hands. The extent of the *cité*, in the Middle Ages still surrounded by walls built in the year 275 and enclosing about thirteen acres, can be easily seen. The line of the ramparts of the *bourg*, with its eastern boundary backing onto the river Isle, is similarly evident in the existing street pattern.

There were several roads and bridges giving access to Périgueux from Bergerac in the Middle Ages. Two routes would have brought the traveller across the Pont de la Cité to the west of the town. There is thought to have been a third road, along or close to the line of the modern N21, which would have entered over the Pont de Pierre adjacent to the church of St Hilaire. In addition, access to the *bourg* from the south was possible by the Pont de Tournepiche, but since the prince's army remained outside the *bourg* a crossing of the Isle on this bridge can be ruled out, with the army gaining access across the other bridges.

There were extensive suburbs between and around the *cité* and the *bourg* which were completely exposed to attack. No doubt the townspeople in the *bourg* would have watched with considerable consternation, from the ramparts and its towers, the arrival of the prince's army, and its activities before its departure. The bishop is said to have threatened looters, presumably visibly active in the suburbs, with excommunication from the safety of his cathedral within the walls of the *bourg*.

The *bourg* was of a substantial size, with a perimeter wall over a mile in length enclosing about forty acres. The walls had stood since at least 1204, and over the years had fallen into disrepair. In 1352 and 1353, however, work to restore the defences had been given priority over all other expenditure. By 1356 the *bourg*, or the Ville de St Front as it was more correctly known, had shrunk to some 800 households compared to a peak of 2,450 in 1320, but it would have been a challenging prize to take, with its newly repaired perimeter walls. Certainly it does not seem that the prince made any attempt to take the *bourg*, presumably, as with the *chevauchée* of the previous autumn, judging that the time and resources required to do so were not merited, particularly with the goal of battle with the French in mind.[20] The *cité* was still occupied by the English, and the *bourg* by the French, in October 1356 after the Battle of Poitiers, and the dauphin granted a subsidy of 500 *livres tournois* per month 'to make engines and other repairs necessary for the guarding and defence of the said town against our enemies who hold the *cité* of Périgueux'.[21]

The prince moved off north on Monday 8 August in the direction of Brantôme, probably taking the route of the old Roman road through Château-l'Evêque, five miles north of Périgueux. This small village is dominated by the imposing château of the bishops of Périgueux, built by Bishop Adhémar between 1347 and 1349, and thus relatively new at the time of the passage of the prince. Some historians believe that it was here that the prince lodged rather than at Périgueux.[22]

On Monday 8 August the prince stayed near a strong castle called 'Ramesforde' in the *Eulogium*, the château of Ramefort, which still stands on a rocky outcrop 100 feet above the valley on the north of the Dronne, three miles south-

west of Brantôme. The origins of the castle go back to the ninth or tenth century
when a cave was burrowed out of the rock with an embrasure opening out over
the river to allow surveillance of the river. This was succeeded by a wooden
fortress, and in due course a stone castle. The existing keep is thought to date
from the end of the thirteenth century. The castle is currently owned by Gérard
Durand de Ramefort, having passed into the hands of his family in 1697, but in
1356 Ramefort owed dual allegiance to the Lord of Bourdeilles, a further three
miles to the south-west on the Dronne, and to the abbot at Brantôme. There
is a tradition, related to the present owner by his great-aunt who lived in the
castle throughout her life, that at one time during the Hundred Years War a
detachment of English soldiers hid in a chamber under the courtyard of the
castle. There is evidence of the existence of such a chamber, but to uncover it
would require destroying a fine parquet floor. As the present owner says 'perhaps
my successors will have the courage to demolish the floor!' If there is truth in
this tradition the event belongs to a later period in the war, possibly during the
capture of Brantôme by the French in 1376. There was certainly no reason for
English troops to seek refuge in the castle in 1356.[23]

The next day, the prince moved three miles to Brantôme, but from here until
he reached Rochechouart three days later, there is uncertainty over the route, and
intermediate points at 'Quisser' and 'Merdan' have proved difficult to identify.

The night of 10 August was passed at Quisser, where the army crossed a ford
near a mill, above which stood a strong castle. Bussière-Badil has been proposed
as Quisser, but this is implausible since it does not stand on a river and is well to
the west of the general line of march. However, Quinsac, six miles north-east of
Brantôme along the Dronne, fits Baker's description well. It has an ancient mill,
now in ruins, on the banks of the Dronne which, although the earliest existing
archive reference is dated 1520, is thought to be medieval in origin.[24] The château
of Vaugoubert stands on the hillside 100 feet above the river valley and about
400 yards from the mill. Although the current château dates from around 1860,
and records only survive back to the sixteenth century, there are traces of a moat
and two towers believed to date back to a medieval castle. In the Middle Ages
there were three fords and an improvised wooden bridge across the river over a
distance of about a mile, making a crossing here straightforward.

If Quinsac is Quisser, however, we have a conundrum, since if the prince
passed through Brantôme, as would seem logical, he would have crossed the
Dronne and would have no need to do so again, as this would take him away
from his line of march and across to the wrong side of the river to the east. The
solution may lie in the two days spent moving the ten miles from the vicinity of
Ramefort to Quisser.

Brantôme is a natural choke-point on the route north. It stands on an island
in an ox-bow bend of the Dronne. It was fortified with ramparts, traces of which
remain, overlooking the wide, natural moat formed by the river. To the west,
immediately across the river, stands a Benedictine abbey, founded by Charle-
magne, which was protected by fortifications on the river side, with natural

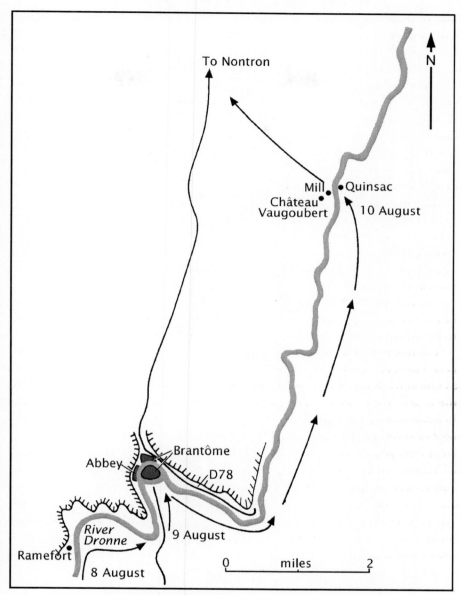

Map 19 The passage of Brantôme, 8–10 August 1356.

protection behind from cliffs 200 feet high. To the east high ground again rises steeply more than 200 feet above the town. The road north passes through the town over bridges spanning the river to the south and north. There is a narrow strip of land between the town and the high ground to the east, which currently carries the minor D78 road, which could afford a passage past the town. However, it would be well within bow-shot of the ramparts.

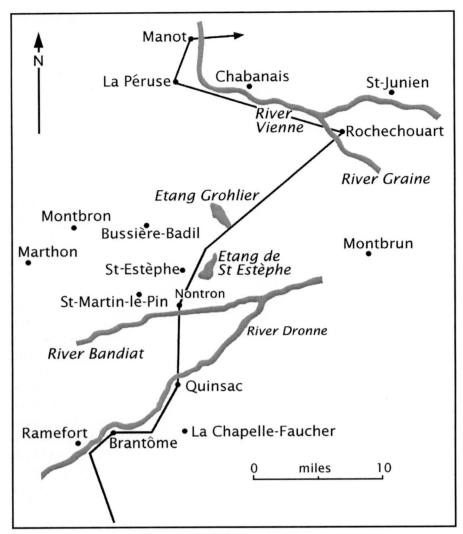

Map 20 Brantôme to the Vienne.

The castle and village of La Chapelle-Faucher, five miles east of Brantôme, are said to have been destroyed on the prince's orders.[25] This could indicate that the area, including Brantôme, was in the hands of forces loyal to King Jean, and it is possible that the time spent in the vicinity of Brantôme might be due to consideration of the possibility of an assault of the town to force a passage, reconnaissance for an alternative crossing, or negotiations to attempt to persuade a garrison undecided about where its best interests lay to come over to the English cause and allow the prince's army to pass. In the absence of an unmolested passage through the town, the option of taking the town by assault would probably have been feasible. However, banners had not yet been unfurled and the decision not to assault the town may have reflected a desire to avoid unnecessary combat and casualties. Action at this stage, with the nearest substantial French force almost 200 miles away with the count of Poitiers at Bourges, would deplete resources without the prospect of provoking the French into battle. If a passage of the Dronne could not be made at Brantôme, the best option would be to move east for two miles, follow the river north to Quinsac, and then to cross the river and move across country for another two miles to rejoin the main route north from Brantôme, probably along the tracks of an ancient road close to or along the route of the current D675.[26] This would explain a crossing of the Dronne, from east to west, at Quinsac and not at Brantôme.

What then of 'Merdan', which has been variously interpreted as Marthon, Nontron and St-Martin-le-Pin?[27] Marthon is the closest approximation in sound to the name recorded in the *Eulogium*. However, it is well to the west of the line of march, and the march to Rochechouart would mean a large detour in the route from Brantôme. It would also mean two days of marches each of almost twenty-five miles, which would have been very much out of keeping with the almost leisurely progress to date on this *chevauchée*. In addition, an exhaustive study of the archives of Marthon conducted towards the end of the nineteenth century reveals evidence of an attack on the town in 1347, but not in 1356.[28] This absence cannot, of course, be conclusive proof that the prince did not pass through Marthon, but it seems an unlikely candidate for Merdan. Two other places with similar sounding names are the small town of Montbron, twenty-four miles north-west of Quinsac, and the castle of Montbrun near the small village of Dournazac a similar distance to the north-east. Other than the toponymy there is nothing else to support Montbron being Merdan, and as with Marthon it would have entailed long marches and an unnecessary deviation from the generally northerly route. The castle of Montbrun is more likely, in that the onward march to Rochechouart is shorter at twenty miles, but there is no other evidence to support this proposition.

However, we are told that the prince and his men were able to buy large quantities of fish at Merdan and this is perhaps a clue to the location of the town.[29] Five miles north of Nontron is an artificial lake, over half a mile in length and 250 yards wide in places, belonging to the Grandmontain abbey of Badeix in St-Estèphe. There is another lake of similar size, Grolhier, a further five miles to the north. Such lakes were originally constructed for the production of fish, possibly in the case of the Grandmontains as a result of a dispensation by Pope John XXII in 1317 relaxing their earlier vegetarian regime and authorising them to follow the conventional Benedictine code.[30] The account of the supply of fish is unusual, and would be consistent with either Nontron or St-Martin-le-Pin, both close to the lakes, being Merdan.

Merdan could feasibly be a corruption of St-Martin-le-Pin, three miles north-west of Nontron, but in the fourteenth century, the village had only 102 inhabitants in seventeen households.[31] Nontron, on the other hand, is not an obvious candidate on the basis of toponymy, but, it is, and was, a good-sized town on a more or less direct line of march north from Périgueux, through Brantôme, to Rochechouart. The approach to Nontron from the south would have confronted the prince's army with a formidable obstacle if it were in enemy hands, with a steep descent into the valley of the Bandiat running across the line of approach. Behind the river is an escarpment rising 200 feet above the valley floor. The town is on a steep rocky spur jutting out from the escarpment like an upturned boat before broadening out to the north. Nontron had come into hands sympathetic to the Anglo-Gascon cause in 1345, but it had been retaken for the French by Arnoul d'Audrehem in the autumn of 1352 and it would have been in French hands in August 1356.[32] Thus, with the road north running through the town, Nontron would have presented a significant obstacle. However, in a letter dated 29 May 1357 one Ietier de Maignac forfeits 'all his goods, either in the manor of Nontron or elsewhere, since the said de Maignac is accused of having delivered the castle of Nontron into the hands of the enemies of the Viscount of Limoges'.[33] It is possible that this refers to some later action after the Battle of Poitiers, but most military action before a truce agreed in Bordeaux on 23 March 1357 was in Brittany and Normandy and not in the Dordogne. It may be that this letter relates to the surrender of the castle to a company of routiers active after the truce, but in that case the timescale of two months between the truce, surrender, and forfeiture is short, particularly as the letter was signed in distant Avignon. If this surrender was related to the passage of the prince, then the army could have passed through the town unmolested. Casualties which would have resulted from an assault to the detriment of fighting strength could have been avoided. Nontron therefore seems the most plausible location for Merdan.

Having spent a peaceful night at Merdan, the prince moved on to Rochechouart on Friday 12 August across gently rolling hills. Rochechouart is on high ground to the north of the river Graine, atop an escarpment, with the castle on a steep spur that thrusts out into a bend in the river. The castle has been much modified over the years since construction began in the twelfth century, but approached out of the river valley it is still an impressive sight. The town, which retains some of the towers of the twelfth-century walls, stretches away to the north and east of the castle. It appears not to have been molested, and the next day the prince was on the move again, this time turning west for the twelve-mile march to the Benedictine priory at La Péruse, said in the *Eulogium* to stand above the bank of the river Vienne but in fact two miles west of the river. Only the solid, squat, eleventh-century church remains of the priory where the nobles and magnates in the army were entertained.[34]

On Sunday 14 August the army left La Péruse and crossed the Vienne. The logical route would have been along an ancient road running a little west of north, known variously as La Route des Métaux and Le Chemin de Meules because of its use for the transport of tin and mill-stones, between the Charente and Vienne rivers. This intersected another road, probably Roman in origin, which ran north-east through Manot, possibly along the lines of the modern GR48 long-distance footpath, to a ford across the Vienne, approximately 500 yards north of the modern road bridge, which had been in use at least since Roman times and would have been a well-known crossing point.[35] But why cross here? The prince had been progressing in a more or less direct route from Périgueux towards Bourges. In view of the known points on his itinerary for the next few days, it would have been more logical to have crossed the Vienne at either Chabanais or St-Junien, respectively six miles north-west and north-east of Rochechouart. Both towns had had bridges over the river since at least the thirteenth century, and routing via St-Junien would have saved more than thirty miles, well over a day's marching, compared with the route via La Péruse. The drawback with these routes was that both bridges were in the vicinity of fortified towns. Chabanais was on both banks of the river, with the stone bridge linking the two parts leading directly into the gates of the eleventh-century castle on the north bank, which was surrounded by a ditch on the other sides. A crossing at Chabanais would have required the reduction of the castle to secure the crossing. This would probably have entailed an assault through the town and across the bridge, since fording the river, although quite shallow here in dry weather, would have been likely to be impractical in the wet summer of 1356.[36] At St-Junien the medieval town stood a few hundred yards back from the river and the Pont Notre Dame, but those crossing the bridge would inevitably move within bow-shot range of the town's ramparts.[37]

In comparison to towns assaulted on the *chevauchée* of the previous autumn, the reduction of either Chabanais or St-Junien should have been within the capacity of the prince's army, but in both cases casualties would have been incurred and the losses to fighting strength would have been irreplaceable. If the priority was to maintain maximum fighting strength for the anticipated battle either with the count of Poitiers at Bourges or with greater French forces subsequently, then an uncontested crossing would be preferred. The use of the ford at Manot met this tactical preference.

Accounts of the *chevauchée* of the summer of 1356 generally treat the conduct of operations, at least until the latter stages immediately before the Battle of Poitiers, as being consistent throughout. However, circumstantial evidence points to three distinct phases to the campaign: a deployment phase with the advance to and the crossing of the Vienne, a classic phase of *chevauchée* operations during the advance to the Cher, and a manoeuvre phase leading to battle at Poitiers.

There are some general comments on widespread destruction during the *chevauchée*, the burning and devastating of the county of Périgord, and to Bartholomew Burghersh capturing two unnamed walled towns on entering Périgord.[38] One historian also assumes that because mention is sometimes made when a town was spared, then by inference any town not noted as having been spared must have been burned. However, there are no reports of destruction of named towns on the itinerary in the *Eulogium* before the crossing of the river Vienne, apart from the bishop fulminating against looters at Périgueux and the possible destruction of La Chapelle-Faucher near Brantôme.[39] In addition, the author of the *Eulogium* is quite specific in stating that banners were not unfurled until the Vienne had been crossed.[40] Rogers has suggested that the invaders were 'travelling at a moderate pace so as to leave plenty of time for a thorough devastation of the French countryside'.[41] However, an examination of the crossing of the Dronne, the route through Quisser and Merdan, the route chosen for the crossing of the Vienne, and the lack of other than generalised statements of widespread destruction indicate limited combat operations during this phase. The rate of progress may have been due either to a planned meeting with the duke of Lancaster, as Rogers points out the prince's arrival at the Loire was in the event well-timed, or indeed to take account of the longer, more easterly route being followed by other elements of the Black Prince's army.[42]

11

Romorantin

Manot to Romorantin
Sunday 14 August to Monday 5 September 1356

> When the summer came, he reassembled his forces and made a march
> upon Saintonge, Périgord, and Quercy, and came, I assure you, as far
> as Romorantin. Then he took the tower by assault, and made prisoner
> messire Boucicault and the great Lord of Craon, and very many others.
>
> Chandos Herald[1]

Once across the Vienne banners were unfurled and the character of the campaign
changed. Bourges, where the declared objective of the prince was to join the
count of Poitiers in battle, was about 125 miles away in a direct line. The countryside in between was generally easy going and the prince could be there in a week
if he so chose. A campaign of destruction might draw out the count of Poitiers
or perhaps King Jean could be drawn south. The previously cautious approach
was now set aside, and the itinerary becomes a catalogue of towns and castles
taken and destroyed.

The route to Lesterps, ten miles beyond the river Vienne, would certainly have
taken the army through St-Maurice-des-Lyons.[2] From the thirteenth century
Lesterps had been defended with walls and ditches. There was a fortified Augustinian abbey, also walled with an internal gate to the town, forming an integral
part of Lesterps.[3] After the soft, honey-coloured sandstone prevalent during the
march north to the Vienne, the hard, grey granite of the Massif Central now
begins to predominate and is evident in the vestiges of the town walls and the
remaining thirteenth-century houses.

At Lesterps we have the first specific reference to hostile action since Burghersh's capture of two towns at the outset of the expedition, with the abbey
surrendering after resisting the assault of the prince's troops for a great part of
14 August. Unusually, both by the general standards of the time and the conduct
of the previous *chevauchée*, those who had resisted were spared. The church was
also spared and still stands. The prince took a day's rest at Lesterps on Monday

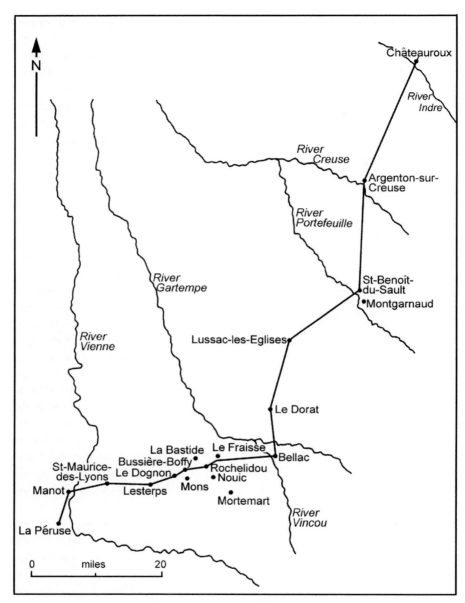

Map 21 Manot to Châteauroux.

15 August, the feast of the Assumption of the Blessed Virgin Mary. This was the first day of rest since leaving Bergerac eleven days before.[4] Even during the march to cross the Garonne in November, there had not been a longer period without rest. However, only 113 miles had been covered, compared to the 146 in nine days in November. Nevertheless, no doubt a pause was required to rest men and horses and to repair equipment. For the prince there were also admin-

istrative matters to deal with and there is a surviving letter originating during the pause at Lesterps to the constable of Bordeaux concerning a land transfer.[5]

On Tuesday 16 August the prince moved on to Bellac. The likely route between La Péruse and Le Dorat, reached on Wednesday, has been thoroughly researched.[6] From Lesterps to Bellac the route was marked by a number of castles close to or on the road. Among these were Le Dognon, Mons, Rochelidou, and Le Fraisse. The modern roads and tracks pass close to the castles. However, the medieval route was more direct and, in one case at least, at Rochelidou passed through the gates of the castle. Part of this castle, although now abandoned, survives about 200 yards to one side of the modern road. The gate through which the ancient road passed can still be seen, although at some time the associated buildings have been adapted for farm use. There are also substantial remains of the castle's keep, standing about 100 yards from the entrance gate, indicating a castle of significant size. Two miles further on, and a little to the left of the route, is the Château du Fraisse. At the time of the Black Prince's passage a thirteenth-century castle stood here. Now there is a substantial Renaissance château with some elements of a fifteenth-century castle. The property has been in the hands of the same family since 1220, and the current marquis attributes this remarkable achievement to 'a considerable fortune'. The marquis recounts that the thirteenth-century castle was destroyed by the Black Prince's troops on or about 20 August, four days after the prince is said by the *Eulogium* to have been in the vicinity, and that the older part of the present castle was built by his ancestor, Jacques des Monstiers, in the 1450s, at the end of the Hundred Years War, to replace the ruined buildings.[7] The delay in rebuilding is far from unusual in the Limousin area, in contrast to the Languedoc where damage inflicted by the 1355 *chevauchée* was frequently repaired rapidly. Such delays were probably due to the area being subject during the war to more frequent and prolonged fighting than the Languedoc. There is evidence of both the ebb and flow of fortunes and the enduring nature of the conflict in the region where fortifications were constructed by the French some 800 yards from the castle at Rochelidou to help retake the castle from the English. The fortifications themselves have long since gone, but are recalled in the name of the village La Bastide.[8]

The old road from Lesterps to Bellac bypassed Bussière-Boffy by a mile. This small town was protected by walls and ditches in the fourteenth century but, although there is no documentary evidence to suggest that it was attacked, it is difficult to imagine that, lying so close to the line of march, it did not receive the attention of the prince's army. Indeed, there is an oral tradition that the prince did pass by the village, and the door to the thirteenth-century Church of the Assumption of the Virgin is known as the Portail des Anglais. The door is also said to bear a mark of the prince. However, as local historian Nicole Raynaud has remarked,

> The oral sources in the Limousin, are unreliable. The Black Prince has become a person of legend: not a castle, not a village would have been spared! One of these traditions for example relates that the Black Prince left his mark on the door of the

church of Bussière-Boffy. This enigmatic statement cannot with certainty establish
that he passed through the village in 1356.[9]

However, we need be less wary of the report, since this time it is recorded,
that the castle in the village of Mortemart, four miles south-east of Bussière-
Boffy, was devastated by the prince's army. Mortemart is now a small village,
but between 1325 and 1329 Cardinal Gauvain, a native of the village, founded
Augustinian, Carthusian and Carmelite institutions. The Augustinian church,
the chapel of the convent, remains as do the Augustinian and Carmelite convents
and part of the twelfth-century castle, which was then protected by ditches and a
drawbridge. We can also be certain of the mark the Hundred Years War left on
the lords of Mortemart. Aimery I, the king's captain-general for Poitou, had been
taken prisoner at Crécy and was to lose his life at Poitiers. Jean I of Mortemart
was left for dead at Agincourt in 1415, and captured by the English. Having been
released after payment of a ransom he then brought disgrace upon his family in
1417 by surrendering the castle at Tours to the duke of Burgundy, then an ally
of the English.[10]

On approaching Bellac the prince would have found two bridges across the
river Vincou on the edge of the town. The more westerly of these is the Pont du
Vincou, on the more direct route from Lesterps to Bellac, and the other is the
thirteenth-century Pont de la Pierre on the road from Mortemart, built to facilitate trade along this route in salt, fish and wine. The town had a castle standing
on a steep escarpment overlooking the river crossings 200 feet below, with the
old town being on a V-shaped promontory within a right-angled bend of the
river and protected by ramparts with three gates. Inside the town ramparts was
the church of Notre Dame de Bellac, once the chapel of the castle, which remains
standing, as do some of the walls.

Fortunately for the soldiery on that Tuesday in August 1356 there was no need
to launch an assault on the town. Although it had once been in the possession of
the count de la Marche, the town had passed into the hands of the countess of
Pembroke, Marie de Châtillon, as part of her dowry on her marriage to Aymer
de Valence.[11] On his death in 1324 the countess had sought refuge in England,
but the town remained her property and was, as a consequence, spared from the
flames.[12] It is indicative of the nature of the campaign at this stage that the fact
that the town was spared was worthy of comment.

On Wednesday 17 August the prince moved north, probably crossing the
river Gartempe on the thirteenth-century Pont de Beissat, three miles north
of Bellac.[13] The difficulties over names in source documents is illustrated on
the approach to the bridge, where even today there are differences in spelling
between the names on maps and the locally used names, with the Château de la
Chaisse on the map signposted as Le Chèze.

The stop on Wednesday for the prince's division is not named in the *Eulogium*, but it is clear that Le Dorat was the unnamed town since we are told that
it and its strong castle belonged to Jacques de Bourbon and that his wife was

residing there. In fact this is not strictly accurate, since Le Dorat was a possession of Pierre I de Bourbon in 1356. However, it was held on his behalf by his
brother, Jacques de Bourbon, as count de la Marche et Ponthieu. He was absent
with the army of King Jean, but his wife, Jeanne de Châtillon, was present in
the town.[14] The Bourbons were unfortunate at Poitiers to lose Pierre I, killed in
the battle, and Jacques as a captive, later purchased from his captors by Edward
III for £4,709.[15] It seems that there was both a castle and a fortified church in
Le Dorat. The twelfth-century church remains, but the residual fortifications
belong to defences constructed between 1420 and 1431. However, we know that
there were earlier defences from instructions given by King Philippe IV in 1298
to the seneschal of Poitiers 'to rebuild forthwith barriers and fences'. It seems that
these, however, were of wooden construction with the fifteenth-century walls
being the first to be built in stone.[16] Nothing remains of the castle, built in 1173,
which stood on a hill outside the town to the north-east. The occupants of the
fortified church resisted for the greater part of the day and then surrendered,
much as had been the case at Lesterps. In this instance, however, we are not told
of the fate of those who surrendered. Another source, albeit not contemporary
and with some confusion over the date of events, recounts that the castle was
assaulted and held out, but that the town was destroyed.[17]

On the same day the vanguard took two strong castles by assault. The prince
stayed in one of them on the night of Thursday 18 August. Since we know that
he arrived at Lussac-les-Eglises the following day, twelve miles north-east of Le
Dorat, we can infer that these castles were either in the vicinity of Le Dorat or
between that town and Lussac, but we can get no closer to identifying them.

On the Friday the prince was on the move again, this time to Lussac-les-
Eglises. Little is said of the town or events at Lussac, beyond the fact that large
quantities of fish were found here and that the town was burnt before the departure of the prince the following day. About one mile north of Lussac, on the track
of a Roman road, is a monument consisting of a rough stone block with a cross
carved in it, said locally to mark the tomb of a knight of the prince.

Having left Lussac in ruins, the prince's next port of call was St-Benoît-du-
Sault sixteen miles to the north-east. The chronicle tells us that St-Benoît was
a beautiful town with an abbey where two kinsmen of the lord de la Brette had
a huge quantity of gold and 14,000 écus. Even without the gold this was a good
prize to take, with the écus worth around £2,000 sterling. It is possible that de
la Brette was in fact Bernard d'Albret, now in joint command of the army left at
Bergerac to defend Gascony. We do not know if he had a claim on the money.[18]

The approach to St-Benoît from the south reveals the Benedictine priory, not
an abbey as stated in the Eulogium, standing on a promontory 100 feet above
the road from the south. The river Portefeuille was dammed to provide a lake
for fish for the priory, which could account for the fish found at Lussac. There is
now a bridge across this small lake for access to the town, but in the fourteenth
century the only access across at this point was by way of the dyke damming the
river. Road access was further round to the east across a bridge and through one

of the town gates. The walls and ditches of the town had initially surrounded
the priory, but they had been extended in the twelfth century to embrace the
administrative quarter that had grown up around the priory. They were further
extended to include the town in the fourteenth century. Traces of these walls
remain, together with the twelfth-century gate between the administrative area
and the town proper. However, the weakness in the defences was that the side of
the town next to the escarpment to the south had not been fortified, presumably
on the assumption that the slope itself provided sufficient defence. However, it
is not particularly steep and little more than a scramble would be required to
gain the top. It is not surprising that local tradition has it that the prince's men
gained access by this slope rather than by assault across the walls and ditches.

On Sunday 21 August the prince advanced a further fourteen miles to
Argenton-sur-Creuse, where there was a strong fortress.[19] Almost all the
sprawling modern town is to the north on the right bank of the river Creuse, as
indeed was the Gallo-Roman town of Argentomagus. In the fourteenth century,
however, the town was on the left bank with its castle on a spur of high ground
standing prominently above the river. Argenton does not seem to have been
fortified before the fifteenth century, when it started to expand across the river
to the north and this new part was fortified around 1420. However, although
lacking town walls in 1356, Argenton was protected by a formidable fortress,
with ten stone towers and 600 metres of ramparts. The entrance to the south
was defended by two massive towers 12 metres in diameter with walls 3.5 metres
thick. Both of these towers had water tanks to provide a reserve for the garrison.
Much of one of the towers, La Tour du Midi, and vestiges of the walls remain.
Also still remaining are vestiges of a Gallo-Roman bridge, originally 110 metres
in length and 5 metres wide, which afforded a crossing of the Creuse and access
to Argentomagus.[20] We do not know if the town was destroyed, although since
it was undefended this seems likely. A further unidentified strong castle was
captured.

Meanwhile events elsewhere would have a significant impact over the coming
month. On 10 August the Aragonese galleys allied to the French had moved
from the river Seine and were sighted off the Kent coast. This posed a serious
threat to English shipping and to the planned expedition by King Edward. As
an immediate measure shipping was ordered to take refuge in harbour, and by
26 August men were being arrayed for coastguard duty. Edward would not be
coming to meet his son. However, Lancaster could still do so. From 13 July he
had been at his headquarters at the abbey of Montebourg, twenty miles south-
east of Cherbourg, and he was, therefore, 220 miles north-west of Tours.[21] He
would need at least fifteen days to effect a rendezvous with the prince, even in
ideal conditions, but a date of departure in the third week of August could still
bring him to a rendezvous in good time. Meanwhile, on the French side, the
count of Poitiers had withdrawn from Bourges on 18 August while the prince
was in the vicinity of Le Dorat and Lussac-les-Eglises. The count had been
instructed to hold the line of the Loire to the east of Bourges until reinforced

by the king and the Dauphin Charles. By 20 August he was at Decize, more than fifty miles south-east of Bourges.[22] King Jean, having concluded that the progress of the Black Prince presented the greater threat, lifted the siege of the castle at Bretueil where his Navarrese enemies were keeping him effectively at bay, and, having paid the garrison to surrender the castle and allowed them a free passage to retire to the Cotentin, moved to Chartres around 20 August. The marshal, Jean de Clermont, was sent to organise the defence of Touraine, and two detachments, one under the leadership of Philippe de Chambly, otherwise known as Grismouton, and the other led by Jean de Boucicaut and Amaury de Craon, were sent south as advanced reconnaissance parties as the king set about gathering his army.[23]

How aware the prince was of these events we do not know, but the army rested at Argenton on Monday 22 August before moving on Tuesday twenty miles across gently undulating countryside with widely scattered villages to Châteauroux. The defence of Châteauroux was in the hands of André de Chauvigny, son of Louis de Chauvigny, the viscount of Brosse. The town's defences were in a poor state of repair and the prince's troops were able to enter the town without difficulty.

However, the castle, in the north-west corner of the town, with one wall close up to the river Indre, proved to be another matter. The prince's men, in an attempt to force an entry, filled an ox-cart with oil and dry wood with the aim of burning the drawbridge and gate. The defenders showered the attackers with missiles, and the cart escaped from those man-handling it towards the gates and fell into the ditch. The attackers suffered some casualties including, it is said, one knight whose arms were described by one source as 'a band with a silver shield and a green lion rampant', while a second describes the knight as wearing a tabard with 'seven silver shields and seven green lions rampant'. Unfortunately neither description is sufficient to allow the knight to be identified. The prince now took charge of the assault. In an attempt to achieve the surrender of the castle the prince sent four Gascon knights, including Lords d'Albret, Lesparre, and Pommiers, forward under a sign of truce. Albret told André de Chauvigny:

> My lord, the prince sends greetings to you as his close relation, in whom he has great confidence, and asks you to open the fortress, for as you are his relation, you should respect his rights more than those of others.

The reply was courteous but uncompromising:

> Gentlemen, I thank my lord the prince for his recognition of our relationship, but as for opening this place, in truth, I cannot do so, for my father holds it for the King of France to whom he has sworn an oath and my father has ordered that I neither open nor surrender this place.

Albret told him that, if he failed to surrender, then 'certainly tomorrow you have an assault'. With this assertion in mind, the strength of the castle was now assessed. Two knights protected by shield-bearers went forward to make a recon-

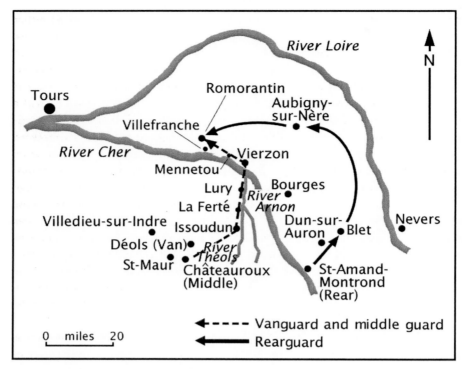

Map 22 Châteauroux to Romorantin.

naissance. They identified the weakest part of the defences, and marked it with oats for the benefit of the assailants. The prince now held a council to consider the options. The consensus was that the defenders were determined and valiant, that an attack would cost many men, and that success was not certain. In view of the overall aim to do battle with the French king, an attack was not deemed necessary, the assault was abandoned, and orders were given for a departure the next day.

Contrary to his usual practice of sleeping outside towns, the prince is said to have lodged at an inn called the Pilier, held by one Penin Thomas, close to the Porte St Denis, near to the corner of the current place de Lafayette and the rue des Etats-Unis.[24] The Wednesday was a rest day for the feast of St Bartholomew, but before leaving on Thursday 25 August the town was burned, leaving the viscount to survey the ruins from his castle. No doubt the message would not have been lost on the townspeople that, once again, in the face of the Anglo-Gascon army, the king and the local lord had been unable to fulfil their duty to protect the population. As for André de Chauvigny, he was to die at Poitiers only three weeks later along with his father.[25]

Unusually we are told where all three divisions lodged on 23 and 24 August. The prince was at Châteauroux, while the vanguard was at 'Burgo Dei' and the rearguard at 'Seynt Yman'. Burgo Dei has been variously identified as either Villedieu-sur-Indre, about eight miles to the west of Châteauroux, or Déols, now contiguous with Châteauroux but just across the river Indre. At first sight Villedieu seems an obvious translation of Burgo Dei, but in earlier times Déols was known as 'Bourg Dieu'. We can add further weight to the case for Déols as Burgo Dei by going back to the *Eulogium* which tells us that Burgo Dei had a fortified abbey.[26] Villedieu did not have such an abbey, while Déols had the forti-fied Benedictine abbey of Notre Dame protected by walls and five large towers. It seems most likely that the vanguard was at Déols, a little over a mile from the prince's middle guard.[27] Seynt Yman is generally taken to be St-Amand-Montrond, twenty miles to the east of Châteauroux, although one historian believes this to be St-Maur, three miles to the west of the middle guard.[28] These differences of interpretation are important because the locations of the three divisions on 23 August give an indication of the conduct of operations. At one extreme we have the three divisions concentrated within three miles of each other at St-Maur, Déols and Châteauroux. At the other extreme, the army is spread out across forty-eight miles between Villedieu-sur-Indre and St-Amand-Montrond. An examination of the activity on the right flank helps to resolve the location of the rearguard.

As we have already seen, it is probable that one of the other divisions was following a more easterly route than that of the prince for the initial part of the *chevauchée*. We also have accounts of some of the army, but not the prince, in action at Bourges. Bourges was a large city, on a par with Toulouse, and it was well protected with walls, towers, and seven fortified gates. The archbishop, Roger le Fort, seems to have taken charge of the defence of the town. He was assisted by Guy II de Damas and Hutin de Vermeilles with their troops, together with Louis de Maleval with 100 men-at-arms. There was skirmishing around the southern Porte Bourbonnoux and an attempt to gain entry in the vicinity of the Porte d'Auron with the help of a citizen of Bourges, Perrot Monein, who had leased land close to the wall by this gate and started to build a house. He offered to show the English a way into the town for an undisclosed sum of money. This came to nought, and the rearguard left without entering the town but having burnt the suburbs. The unfortunate Monein, however, was discovered. His house was confiscated and sold for the profit of the king, and he was decapitated for treason.[29] The skirmishing and destruction of the suburbs of Bourges is further evidence that the army was widely dispersed at this stage.[30]

By Sunday 28 August the rearguard, under the command of John Chandos and James Audley, was at Aubigny-sur-Nère, thirty miles north of Bourges. It is likely, therefore, that it was this division in action at Bourges. According to Bartholomew Burghersh's letter, the army also visited Nevers, forty miles east of Bourges. This can only have been the rearguard, and yet four days later they were at Aubigny-sur-Nère. There are also accounts of visitations on Dun-sur-Auron and Blet, where one Jean de Grivel is said to have defended the castle successfully, close to the route from St-Amand-Montrond to Bourges.[31] We do not have dates for the army at Nevers, but a logical course of events would have been for the main body of the rearguard to have gone to Bourges with a detachment going further out to the right to Nevers. The troops of this detachment would have covered 110 miles from St-Amand-Montrond before reaching Aubigny-sur-Nère four days later, 24 August having been a day of rest. All this would have been demanding enough, but to have made the same journey from St-Maur would have added forty miles to the itinerary making the overall march 150 miles. Even if the rearguard had foregone the rest day, this would have been a very demanding and exceptional march. St-Maur is not a plausible location for the rearguard.

In sum, it is probable that the vanguard and middle guard were in close proximity at Déols and Châteauroux, with the rearguard to the east at St-Amand-Montrond. The rearguard, having taken a more easterly route than the other divisions, had very likely been converging to concentrate the army's strength in anticipation of an encounter with the count of Poitiers in the vicinity of Bourges. With news of the count having withdrawn some days previously, this convergence would no longer have had the same urgency, but it would have been prudent to verify that he had indeed withdrawn and to know what was happening on the Loire. At St-Amand-Montrond, the rearguard would have been best placed of all the divisions for this mission, and it is probable that they moved out north-east to Nevers and Bourges, then north towards Aubigny-sur-Nère and the Loire, fifteen miles beyond the town, before turning south-west to rejoin the prince at Romorantin at the end of the month.

Déols was undefended in the fourteenth century, with fortifications authorised late in the Hundred Years War in 1443. Only the abbey was fortified, but this did not save it from devastation on the departure of the vanguard on Thursday 25 August.

On Thursday the prince moved twenty miles north-east across open flat plains from Châteauroux to Issoudun, where according to local legend Richard the Lionheart, King Philippe Auguste of France and the Emperor Frederick Barbarossa met and feasted in 1189 before leaving for the Third Crusade. Unfortunately the legend is no more than that, since Richard and Philippe met at Nonancourt on 30 December 1189, and not at Issoudun, and by then Frederick had long since gone on crusade, having left Regensburg along the course of the Danube in May 1189.[32] In the twelfth century Issoudun was on the ill-defined border between the Plantagenet empire and the kingdom of France. In the struggle between Richard and Philippe Auguste it changed hands several times, and it had been well fortified as a consequence.[33] Issoudun consisted of two distinct parts. To the west was the château, which the *Eulogium* describes as a large castle belonging to the king of France, mainly the seat of government, and home to the Benedictine abbey of Notre-Dame. To the east was the larger town given over largely to commercial and residential use. The château had one exterior gate, the Porte St Jacques, through which the road from Châteauroux passed over the bridge across the river Théols. The ramparts to the south, west and north had numerous towers, seven of which still exist in varying states of

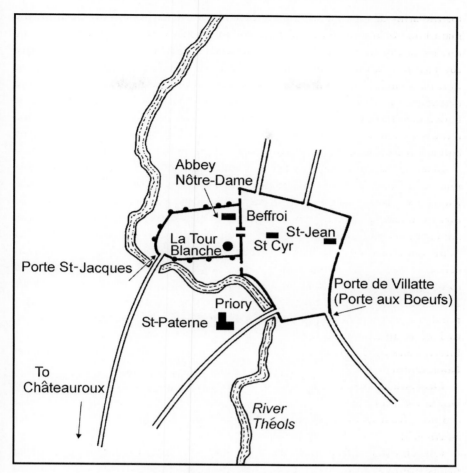

Map 23 Issoudun.

completeness, with five other probable locations identified. To the east a second gate, still existing and allowing passage through the Beffroi, gave access to the town. There was a large keep, La Tour Blanche, built by either Richard the Lionheart or King Philippe Auguste towards the end of the twelfth century, and still dominating the skyline. In sum, the château, with its strong keep, ramparts and towers around the perimeter of about three quarters of a mile, was a formidable fortress. The defended part of the town itself covered an area about four times the size of the château. It was protected by ramparts and ditches and seven gates but few towers. Outside the town walls there were further suburbs, including that of St-Paterne with its Benedictine priory to the south across the river. The town and its suburbs were much more vulnerable than the château.[34]

The river is not a significant obstacle, and a crossing by the bridge and through the gate of the château was certainly not necessary. Nevertheless, an

assault on the castle was attempted. This was repulsed, but the town itself could
not resist the prince's division. The entry to the town was forced at the Porte de
Villatte at the south-east corner of the ramparts. Some accounts have described
the entrance as having been made at the Porte aux Boeufs, and there is still a
street with this name, but there was no gate where the modern street joins the
line of the rampart. It is probable that this was a popular name for the Porte de
Villatte. The entrance was forced by setting fire to adjacent houses, with the fire
quickly consuming the gate and then spreading throughout the town. Among
the buildings destroyed inside the town was the church of St Cyr, of which only
the bell-tower and part of its façade remain standing. Outside the town walls,
the suburb of St-Paterne, including its priory and church, was also put to the
torch. The damage to the priory and the church was so extensive that they did
not merit repair, and the ruins were still evident for all to see three centuries
later. Indeed, to this day much of this suburb remains open ground despite its
proximity to the main town. We have a clear picture of the impact of the devastation of 1356 on Issoudun, which was still being felt almost seventy years later.
Jacquemin Coran, the owner of the tavern Porte aux Boeufs outside the town
and close to the gates, possibly close to the current hotel-restaurant Ste Catherine, was aggrieved that the abbey of Notre-Dame was pursuing him for rent
in 1357. As he said in his appeal:

> all the town was set afire, destroyed, and consumed by the flames, especially the
> gate and house, in such a manner that nothing remained and the said town and
> gate rendered uninhabitable in such a way that no one had lived there since.

We do not know whether or not his case received a sympathetic hearing, but
we do know that repairs to the town stretched over many years. In 1358 nobles,
ecclesiastics and townspeople assembled at the abbey of Notre-Dame to consider
'repairs and defence of the castle and the good people of the town and the
surrounding area'. A tax of six *deniers* in the pound was agreed on the sale of
goods in the castle, town and suburbs of St-Denis and St-Paterne. However, in
1376 the remaining citizens of the town were still living within the castle, and
around 1390 the repairs had still not been made. A further tax, this time on salt,
was authorised in 1412, but in 1423 some work still remained outstanding.

Having wrought such extensive destruction, and demonstrated yet again the
impotence of the king of France, the army set out north for Vierzon on Sunday,
having spent all of Friday and Saturday at the unfortunate Issoudun.[35] The countryside from Issoudun north towards Vierzon remains open with gently undulating ground. The main axis of advance for the prince's division would have been
along the river Théols and then along the Arnon after the two rivers converge
ten miles north of Issoudun. A mile to the west of the confluence of the rivers,
on the left bank of the Théols, is the small village of La Ferté, then with a strong
castle, possibly on the site of the present seventeenth-century château close to
the bridge, belonging to the viscount of Thouars.[36] Here the lords Berkeley and
de la Ware stayed for the night, apparently having sent their baggage carts on

ahead, implying some confidence in their security. Whether the stay at the castle implies that the viscount was friendly to the English cause or that the castle was not garrisoned is not known.

While Berkeley and de la Ware settled in for the night the prince pressed on, coming after a further five miles to the small town of Lury on the right bank of the Arnon. The author of the *Eulogium* makes a point of recording that in earlier days the town was close to the ancient border of the duchy of Aquitaine which ran only a few miles further north along the banks of the river Cher. Lury was walled, with a small castle to the south-west. It is likely that the town, if defended at all, only had a small garrison, and the local governor decided that the best course of action was to destroy the defences to deny them to the prince. When the Anglo-Gascon troops arrived much of the wall had already been destroyed but the castle keep remained standing.[37] At the time the castle at Lury, along with that of Vierzon, was the property of Guillaume IV, the margrave of Juliers. However, since he was an ally of Edward III, both castles had been taken into the custody of King Jean. The castle at Lury had been destroyed in 1196 by Richard the Lionheart and then rebuilt. We do not know in detail what occurred in 1356. The castle was still standing in 1361 when it was returned to Guillaume, but judging by the records of an inquiry held in 1412 to establish the state of the town on the transfer of its ownership to the chapter of St Etienne of Bourges, the town had suffered substantially.[38] Lancelot Buisoon, a groom aged forty-six, testified that 'the town has been deserted since the *chevauchée* of the Prince of Wales through the realm of France, it must have been 56 years ago', and Martin Piot, aged fifty, sergeant of the town living in Vierzon, stated that 'Lury is a small ancient town which is now deserted other than for about ten to twelve households'.[39] At some point the prince would have had to cross the Arnon for the approach to Vierzon and Lury is as likely a spot as any.

Vierzon was also close to the frontier between Plantagenet and French territory, and in 1196 or 1197 the castle was captured by Richard the Lionheart. Its strong defences in the fourteenth century had resulted from this event, when Philippe Auguste replaced wooden ramparts with stone walls for the town. The prince would have been presented with a view of a rectangular town, standing back 200 yards from the river Yèvre, surrounded by its stone walls, with four principal gates and numerous towers. Outside the town walls, on the banks of the Yèvre, was the abbey of St Pierre, and to the east, forming part of the defensive walls, was the castle with its keep, known as the Tour des Fiefs, standing on a motte. Although the itinerary of the prince indicates that he arrived on 28 August, there is an account which indicates that the attack may have begun two days earlier with the capture and sacking of the town, but that the castle held out until Monday 29 August when it was overrun and the defenders killed.[40] This same account relates that the attack on the town was made from the hamlet of Puits Berteau about one mile to the north-east. With the town walls to the south, close to the river Yèvre, a frontal attack, even if the town were lightly defended, would entail unnecessary risks and there would be obvious advantages in crossing the river away from the town and choosing an easier place for the assault. Another historian speculates that redoubts, still visible in the nineteenth century, one of these a mile to the east of the town and the other close to Puits Berteau, were built by the prince's forces. This seems unlikely given the nature of operations on the *chevauchée*. Whatever the truth about the attack, we do know that the result was the destruction of the castle and the town. The slow pace of reconstruction in the area is illustrated here once again with work on the castle starting in 1358 but dragging on for more than a hundred years until 1460.[41]

During the three preceding days, the captal de Buch had been wreaking havoc throughout the local area. The destruction included the burning of one 'fine and noble' abbey, probably the Benedictine abbey of St Pierre at Vierzon.[42] The pace of events was now picking up. On Sunday 28 August, while Chandos and Audley were conducting a reconnaissance to the north with the rearguard and pillaging and burning the fortified town of Aubigny-sur-Nère, King Jean had arrived at Chartres, 100 miles to the north, and was gathering his army.[43] There was also contact with the reconnaissance parties sent out by King Jean. The first of these, under Philippe de Chambly, known as Grismouton, variously described as having 200 men-at-arms or eighty lances, came up against some of the rearguard of Chandos and Audley. Although the Anglo-Gascon detachment, with only ten lances, was considerably less numerous than the French force they had much the better of the encounter. Grismouton's men were routed, with many killed and eighteen knights and men-at-arms captured.[44]

On the following day, Monday 29 August, the prince moved fifteen miles west from Vierzon along the river Cher to Villefranche-sur-Cher on the ancient border between the kingdom of France and the duchy of Aquitaine. The obvious route would have been along the old road from Vierzon to Romorantin, the Chemin de la Fringale, which ran about two miles north of the town of Mennetou-sur-Cher. Mennetou was fortified with thirteenth-century stone ramparts, five towers, and gates to the north, south and east, with a castle embedded in the wall adjoining the southern gate on ground rising gently to the north of the river. There was a local regulation dating from 1269 which required inhabitants to mount guard on the ramparts. Whether or not they did so on this day we cannot say. Nor can we say if there is any truth in the local legend that the prince flew his banner from the ramparts.[45]

In the vicinity of Villefranche-sur-Cher, five miles beyond Mennetou, there was further contact with the French. There was an ebb and flow in fortunes as the day progressed, but the day in the end went to the prince. The start of the events was a clash between the lord of Caumont for the prince and some of the French force, resulting in the capture of eight French knights and men-at-arms. From these prisoners the prince learnt that a French army was assembling and moving towards Orléans with the intention of doing battle with the prince. He was also able to confirm that Grismouton's party encountered the day before had been sent to gather intelligence. Similarly, it became apparent that the prisoners were part of a second scouting party in the vicinity under the command of the lords Craon and Boucicaut, with sixty lances and many other troops, possibly amounting to 300 men-at-arms. Later in the day Craon and Boucicaut ambushed and captured a small Anglo-Gascon foraging party of ten men-at-arms under Sir John Willoughby and Ralph Basset, together with their booty. However, reinforcements quickly came to their relief, and some 150 of the French were captured and the English prisoners released. The remaining French fled with Craon and Boucicault and, finding the drawbridge down and the gates open, took refuge in the castle at Romorantin, five miles north of Villefranche.[46]

On the next day, Tuesday 30 August, the prince's army converged on Romorantin. The modern town sprawls out across the river Sauldre, with suburban housing and light industry, but in 1356, as the army approached from Villefranche, it would have come first to the unprotected suburb of Le Bourgeau on the south of the river. Beyond that was an island in the river with a twelfth-century church, and beyond again on the other bank was the walled town with the castle and its substantial keep.[47] The town fell with little if any resistance. The following day the army attacked the castle where Craon and Boucicault had taken refuge. The outer walls were scaled and the gates forced with little difficulty, and the French withdrew further to the keep. The prince and his council decided that they would remain until they had taken the castle.

At first sight this departure from the policy to date seems strange. Why would the prince now take the risks of losing valuable resources and remaining static that a siege would entail? After all, only a week earlier at Châteauroux he had rejected a siege precisely because he wished to conserve his resources for battle with the French main army. The answer seems to be that the situation had changed to the extent that he now knew that King Jean was approaching with a view to do battle. From Baker's account it seems that the prince thought that the enemy were about ten leagues away, much closer than was in fact the case. Since the prince also wished to do battle, if he remained at Romorantin and laid siege to the castle the French might be provoked into an ill-timed attack.

The keep proved to be difficult to take. On 31 August there were two notable casualties amongst the prince's forces, with Bernadet d'Albret and a knight in the company of the captal de Buch both killed. The next day three successive assaults were made by the earl of Suffolk, Bartholomew de Burghersh and an unnamed Gascon knight. The keep still held. A change of tactics was required, and the emphasis was placed on undermining and setting fire to the keep. This was achieved over the next two days: by Saturday 3 September the keep was burning so badly that the garrison had no hope of extinguishing the fire with their remaining stocks of water and wine. Their choice was between losing their lives to the fire and surrender. They opted for surrender.[48] Of those who surrendered, Amaury de Craon was subsequently held in Bristol until liberated without ransom on the orders of Edward III after the Treaty of Brétigny in 1360.[49] As for Boucicaut, he had only been released from imprisonment by the English in February 1355 on parole to return himself to custody in April of that year, subsequently extended to Christmas. We do not know why he was still at large in August 1356, but he was once again a prisoner. He was fortunate to pass a relatively short period in custody; by May 1358 there are records of his appointment to office in France.[50] Of the other defenders we know that one Robert de Gien, a soldier-cleric from the Maison-Dieu in Romorantin, received 40 *écus* as compensation for the armour that he had lost in the service of his master, the count of Blois, in defence of the keep.[51]

Fresh intelligence came that King Jean was moving towards Tours. Clearly the French were not as close has had been thought, and there was now little point in remaining at Romorantin. The prince and his council now had a new target to make for, and having rested the troops on the Sunday, they set out towards Tours on Monday 5 September.[52]

12

Manoeuvre

Romorantin to Poitiers
Monday 5 to Saturday 17 September 1356

But the English, to amuse themselves, gave the whole country to fire and flame. There made they many a widowed dame and many a poor child an orphan.

Chandos Herald[1]

The epigraph above relates to the campaign leading to the Battle of Crécy, but could equally well apply to the prince's *chevauchées* of 1355 and 1356. The continuing provocation could no longer be tolerated by King Jean and his forces were gathering to pursue and confront the prince. Thus, after the prince's departure from Romorantin, until the Battle of Poitiers fought in the vicinity of Nouaillé-Maupertuis two weeks later to the day, both armies entered a new phase of manoeuvre. For King Jean, it has been generally accepted that, during the coming days, he had to continue to marshal his forces and maintain contact with the Anglo-Gascon army in order either to bring it to battle in a favourable position for the numerically superior French forces, or to trap it and cut it off from its route back to Gascony and force its surrender. For the prince, however, there have been two distinctly different views concerning his objective. The predominant view has been that the Black Prince was seeking to avoid battle and that he was attempting to disengage and return to Bordeaux with his booty. The other view is that his objective was to join battle provided that this could be done in a favourable position, and that he manoeuvred his army accordingly, ensuring that he avoided becoming trapped in the process.[2] An understanding of this phase of the *chevauchée*, after the departure from Romorantin until arrival in the vicinity of the battlefield twelve days later, is instructive, both for gaining an insight into the prince's conduct of operations and within the context of the wider debate among historians in recent years as to whether the predominant strategy in medieval warfare was to avoid or to seek battle.[3]

We shall return to an assessment of the prince's intentions later, but first of all let us look at the sequence of events, and the relative positions and movements of the two armies as events unfolded.

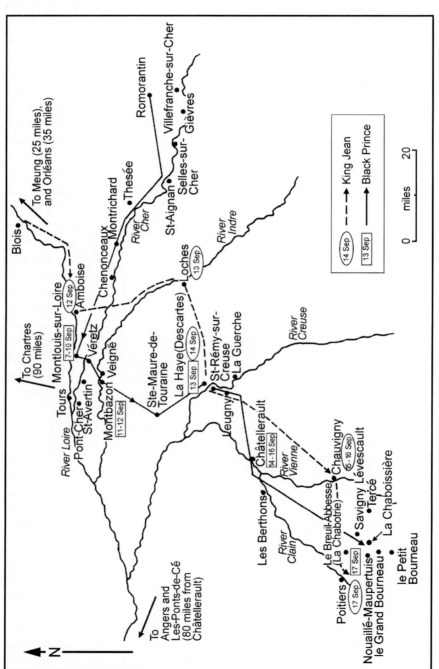

Map 24 Romorantin to Nouaillé-Maupertuis.

Before departing from Romorantin the intelligence available to the prince from prisoners was that King Jean was gathering his army and 'had made up his mind for certain to fight with us, at whatever time we should be on the road towards Tours, he meeting us in the direction of Orléans'. He also believed that the bridges across the Loire had been destroyed, although it is probable, in view of the need for the French to cross the river, that some of them at least were simply well guarded. This much we know from the prince's letter written to the City of London in October.[4] We do not know what news he had at this stage either of the progress of Lancaster or of the nature of the French forces at Tours, but it seems that a detachment from the prince's army may have made a reconnaissance towards the Loire at Amboise.[5]

In any event, it was towards Tours that the prince advanced from Romorantin. We do not have his precise itinerary between leaving Romorantin on Monday and arriving at Montlouis on Wednesday 7 September. The *Eulogium* simply tells us that on the Monday he came into lands belonging to the counts of 'Bisser' and 'Bourgillon'. It is likely that he first of these was the count of Auxerre, and the second the count of Bourgogne.[6] It has been suggested that the first stop was at St-Aignan, twenty miles to the west of Romorantin along the valley of the Cher, which could be reached in a good day's march.[7] This is plausible since the seigneur at the time was Jean II, count of Auxerre.[8] Similarly, the *Eulogium* does not name the prince's lodging place on the Tuesday, although we are told that he came to a castle in the county of Blois which was situated above the river Cher. Montrichard, twelve miles along the river Cher from St-Aignan, fits this description well. It is a reasonable day's march to the next destination on the itinerary, and it has a strong fortress standing on the ridge to the north of the river. The keep of the castle, dating from 1109 and rising high above the town, is imposing. However, following a siege by Philippe-Auguste in 1188, the castle had been strengthened with additional walls and the town defences had also been improved with solid, crenellated ramparts 8 metres high standing on embankments. There were four gates, and those to the east and west were considered to be the most vulnerable points in the defences. However, to the east, the logical direction from which the prince would come, the approach was narrow and dominated by high ground, with an escarpment rising steeply 150 feet above the river. Furthermore, only five months before, Marshal Clermont had visited the town on a tour of inspection to ensure that the defences were in good order. It would have appeared a formidable town as the army approached along the river and, if well garrisoned, it could only have been taken at some cost.[9] In view of the prince's need to conserve resources it is probable that Montrichard was not assaulted, and very likely that the army moved through the forest to the north of the town to avoid the narrow passage between the high ground and the river.

The countryside between Romorantin and Montlouis-sur-Loire on the banks of the Loire near Tours is sparsely populated and heavily forested with ancient oaks. It is relatively flat, but the network of roads and tracks does not provide an obvious route, other than along the ancient Roman road from Bourges to

Tours which followed the north bank of the Cher from Villefranche-sur-Cher through Gièvres, Selles-sur-Cher, Thesée, Montrichard, and Chenonceaux.[10] This route is consistent with the army passing in the vicinity of both St-Aignan and Montrichard.

On Wednesday the *Eulogium* reports that the prince came to 'Aumounk sur Leire'. The identification of this town led to a protracted debate amongst French historians in the late nineteenth century before this was resolved in favour of Montlouis-sur-Loire.[11] It is possible that the army continued to follow the Roman road along the Cher until close to Montlouis although, since there was a reconnaissance towards Amboise, it may be that from Montrichard at least some of the army moved north-west to cut through the forest of Amboise. The army had covered fifty miles in three days, and the prince arrived at Montlouis on Wednesday 7 September.[12]

The prince was now six miles to the east of Tours. The medieval city stood on the left bank of the Loire, which served to protect its northern side, and it was, therefore, vulnerable to attack from the south without the need to cross the river. This vulnerability had been recognised by King Jean who, in March 1354, had issued a charter to the town to galvanise the townspeople in their work of improving the town walls and ditches. As well as providing encouragement, including the grant of wood from royal forests, it provided for substantial fines of 60 *sols*, 3 *livres*, for those who did not co-operate. The importance attached to this work can be seen in the demolition of buildings, including churches and abbeys, with the church and walls of the abbey of St Marc, the abbey of St Vincent, and the ruined basilica of St Lidoire all contributing stone. Provision was also made to improve the arrangements for local defence, with the raising of seven companies of town militia.[13] In addition, by the time the prince arrived there was a large French force in the city with the count of Poitiers, the count of Angers and Marshal Clermont.[14] It is unlikely that the prince planned to assault the city, but it is possible that he hoped to entice the French out for battle before King Jean brought further troops to the scene. This may have been the motive for the attacks which took place on the suburbs. Baker explains that orders were given for the town to be burned, but that due to the intervention of St Martin, the patron saint of Tours, it rained and thundered for three days and it was impossible to burn the town. A fuller account attributes the escape of the town to the intervention of not only St Martin but also St Gatien:

> The Prince of Wales, eldest son of the king of England, after having ravaged a part of France, came to Touraine, to take the town of Tours ... The prince, who was at Montlouis, where he stayed for three days, detached from his army one thousand men-at-arms and five hundred archers to take the town of Tours, and if it could not be held to burn it and take the men of the town into captivity. And this would have happened if it had not been for the intervention of the blessed Sts Gatien and Martin. There came, in effect, a great tempest, thunder, and rain, so that the English men-at-arms could neither see nor mount their horses. Many times they tried to execute the orders of the prince. But each time the tempest was renewed,

and they had to abandon their expedition. The prince, recognizing the intervention of God, ordered the cessation of the attack on the town, and several times he was heard to recount this story, adding that the town was saved by the merits of the Saints Gatien and Martin.[15]

Meanwhile contingents had been joining the growing army of King Jean at Chartres from 28 August until the first days of September. As his army continued to grow, Jean moved towards the Loire, reaching Meung-sur-Loire on Thursday 8 September. He continued south-west along the north bank of the Loire, reaching Blois and crossing the river there on Friday. He was now only thirty miles northeast of the prince's position at Montlouis and on the same side of the river. With the Loire in front of him and the Cher behind, the prince would have been mindful of the potential dangers of his position if he remained at Montlouis. Here the two rivers are only four miles apart and they gradually converge to meet seven miles to the west of Tours. A further consideration was that the bridges across the Cher in the vicinity of Tours, at Pont-Cher and St-Avertin, had been cut, and small villages burnt down, on the orders of Marshal de Nesle, who had been sent to command the troop in Tours, to avoid them being of use to the Anglo-Gascon army.[16] This may have been because he appreciated that it might be possible to keep the prince penned between the rivers, but, in view of the proximity of these bridges to Tours, it is more likely that this was a defensive measure to protect the city. Nevertheless, now that King Jean had crossed the Loire, the destruction of the bridges would have increased the risk of the prince being bottled up in the funnel between the Loire and the Cher.

No doubt other crossings to the east of Tours had been held by the prince's army to secure his rear, but in a day, or two at the most, the French could close the trap. As it was, on 11 September Jean moved twenty miles to Amboise, only eight miles east along the Loire from Montlouis. He paused briefly to await other contingents crossing at Meung, Orléans, Blois, Tours and Saumur, but it was time for the prince to move if the trap were to be avoided.[17] Of necessity this move must be to the south. Although this would take him closer to Bordeaux this did not indicate a desire to disengage from the French. If he had wished to do that he would surely have moved at a greater speed than he did. Indeed, it seems that he was moving at a pace which might still allow for a rendezvous with Henry of Lancaster. Baker claimed that the prince's men could see the camp fires of the duke of Lancaster's men while at Montlouis. This is implausible, and it must now have been clear that there was no longer any prospect of bringing the two armies together near Tours. However, the prince clearly still had hopes of effecting a union of the two armies, for in his letter to the City of London he wrote:

and on departing from thence [Montlouis], we took the road so as to pass certain dangers by water, and with the intention of meeting with our most dear cousin, the Duke of Lancaster, of whom we had certain news that he would make haste to draw towards us.[18]

The Indre flows east to west only a few miles south of the Cher before joining the Loire. A short move beyond the Cher would simply replicate the risk of entrapment a little further south. Thus, the prince needed to move further than the Indre. This he did on Sunday 11 September. It is probable that his crossing of the Cher was somewhere near Véretz, about three miles south of Montlouis, and from there the army may have followed the route of the ancient Chemin des Boeufs which led to Montbazon.[19] Montbazon had possessed a bridge over the river since the eleventh century, but there were two drawbacks for the prince's men. The bridge, which comprised seventeen arches and ran across water meadows as well as two arms of the river, was wooden and it could easily be destroyed, and the town was split into two parts, one each end of the bridge, both of which were fortified with walls. Thus, crossing the bridge was likely to be problematic, and would require the reduction of the town and, if there were one, its garrison. The town also had a strong castle, thought to be the earliest constructed of stone in France, built around 996, which still stands on a promontory in a dominant posi- tion over the river, and was integrated into a corner of the town's fortifications.[20] A local history relates that the gates were opened and the army slept in the town. This implies that the town and castle were not garrisoned and that the seigneur, Barthélémy de Savary, was absent, possibly with the gathering French army. If this were the case then it would suggest that the bridge would be undefended and available, but the *Eulogium* emphasises that the crossing of the river was dangerous, which implies a crossing at a ford rather than over a bridge. If so the crossing was probably made at fords near the hamlets of the Village des Gués and Gués de Veigné, a mile north of Montbazon, close to a bend in the Indre with low land on both sides.[21]

The prince now had room to manoeuvre since the next serious obstacle, the river Creuse, was twenty miles to the south, and he remained at Montbazon on the Monday. While here he received a visit from the cardinal of Périgord, together with many of his household and several bishops, who came to try to persuade the prince to negotiate either a truce or peace. The cardinal told him that the dauphin was at Tours with 1,000 men-at-arms and that the king was drawing near and intended to join battle on Wednesday 14 September. Presum- ably this news was intended to persuade the Black Prince of the advantages of suing for peace. He politely rebuffed the cardinal's approach, as he explained in his letter to the City of London:

> Upon which parley we made answer to him, that peace we had no power to make, and that we would not intermeddle therewith, without the command and the wishes of the King, our most dear lord and father; nor yet as to a truce were we at that time of opinion that it would be the best thing for us to assent thereto, for there we were more fully certified that the King had prepared in every way to fight with us.[22]

The final clause is a further indication that the prince did not wish to avoid the

chance for battle, but in addition his approach reflected the terms of his indenture with his father which gave him some restricted powers to agree a truce:

> And if it shall happen that the prince is besieged or so beset with enemies that
> his person is in peril, and no rescue can come in time, then, to save himself and
> his men, he may help himself by making a truce or armistice, or in any other way
> that seems best to him.[23]

Even if the prince had been inclined to negotiate a truce, at this stage he was
neither 'so beset with enemies that his person was in peril' nor without hope of
rescue in the shape of Henry of Lancaster. A truce, which would have allowed
the French to tighten the net further to the disadvantage of the Anglo-Gascons,
would certainly have been premature.

The discussions with the cardinal having proved fruitless, the prince moved on
again on Tuesday. He covered twenty-five miles, moving through Ste-Maure-de-
Touraine, a small town similar to Montbazon in size and with a castle standing
on a promontory at one end of the town. The prince kept moving, reaching the
river Creuse that day and spending the night at La Haye, now called Descartes,
on the east bank of the river.

Meanwhile, Jean had also been on the move and on the Tuesday night rested
at Loches, a massive Plantagenet fortress built by Henry II, twenty miles north-
east of the prince. At this point the French were not in a position to block the
Anglo-Gascon army's route south, but it was while the prince was at La Haye
that he received information of the position of the French and the news that
King Jean was trying to get ahead of him to cut him off. It would seem that
King Jean was afraid that the Anglo-Gascons would escape to the south, and the
attempt to overtake them made eminent good sense for the French. However, for
the prince, the prospect that he might be trapped and held at bay as his victuals
dwindled was not a happy one.

On Wednesday 14 September, the prince moved fifteen miles to Châtellerault
a 'beautiful and large town' on the eastern bank of the river Vienne, having crossed
the river Creuse either at La Haye, or possibly a mile to the south at St-Rémi-
sur-la-Haie, now St-Rémy-sur-Creuse, a small town founded by Richard the
Lionheart in 1184 which had a bridge over the Creuse in the medieval period.[24]

Between the Creuse and the Vienne the land rises to a spur about 300 feet
above the rivers. The most probable route for the prince would have been along
the valley of the Creuse until a mile or so to the south of Leugny. From here he
could take the Roman road from La Guerche to Châtellerault, much of which
can still be traced through the forest, to climb over the hills and descend to
Châtellerault. On reaching the town, it must have seemed that they had moved
on sufficiently to keep ahead of the French. However, the prince still needed
to be alive to the risks of becoming trapped while keeping in touch with the
enemy so as to be able to bring them to battle. Also, if he still held out hopes of
meeting the duke of Lancaster, he needed to avoid moving too far too quickly.
Thus, he remained here for two days. Meanwhile, the French had moved rapidly,

passing through La Haye on Wednesday, and moving on to secure the bridge at Chauvigny on the river Vienne. Jean had overtaken the prince and was twenty miles to the south-east of him. Seventy-five miles away to the north-west, as the French were approaching Chauvigny, Lancaster had tried unsuccessfully to force a crossing of the Loire at Les-Ponts-de-Cé. The prince could not have been aware of the news at this point, but all hope of joining up with Lancaster had now gone. However, although the duke could not come to join the Anglo-Gascon army, he continued to engage the French, seeing off an attack by Guillaume de Plessis during his withdrawal.[25]

The prince then executed a bold stroke. Hearing on Friday evening that the French would be moving from Chauvigny to Poitiers the next day, he determined to attempt to intercept the French column. The Anglo-Gascon army had more than twenty miles to cover if they were to catch the French. They could not move quickly enough if they tried to stay with the baggage train, and so instructions were given for it to cross the bridge to the west of the river Vienne that night to avoid impeding the combat elements the next morning as they hastened to find the French. Once across the Vienne, however, the river Clain also needed to be crossed almost immediately. This crossing was probably made three miles south-west of Châtellerault where there is evidence of a ford dating from Roman times serving the road from Poitiers through the site of the old Roman town, now known as Vieux Poitiers, adjacent to the modern hamlet of Les Berthons.

On the Saturday morning the prince set off quickly, hearing fresh news that the main French army was on the move towards Poitiers where there were other French troops, probably both garrison troops and men who, having responded to the king's summons and crossed the river Loire at Saumur, were converging on the main French army. The prince moved quickly across country, through the forest of Moulières which extended across much of the land between the rivers Vienne and Clain, and crossed the main road from Chauvigny to Poitiers. Meanwhile, the baggage train, left to look after itself in the prince's haste to catch the French, is likely to have used the Roman road, which runs south-west from Vieux Poitiers to Poitiers alongside the river Clain, rather than also try to move across country. This would have allowed for faster progress initially, although at some point they would need to turn towards the south-east to avoid Poitiers itself and to rejoin the remainder of the army.

Having crossed the road from Chauvigny to Poitiers, the prince emerged from the woods to find that the main body of the French army had passed already. However, 200 Anglo-Gascon men-at-arms fell on the rearguard. The French were clearly unprepared for combat, since some at least were wearing ostrich-feathered caps rather than their bascinets, and were taken by surprise.[26] In the ensuing engagement with 700 French knights and men-at-arms, the French were put to flight, with 240 killed or captured, including the counts of Joigny and Auxerre and the lord of Châtillon.[27] As well as taking the two counts out of the French order of battle, this proved a profitable encounter, with Auxerre eventually being ransomed for £563 paid to the earl of Suffolk, and £2,734 shared between the three Gascons, Bertrand lord of Montferrand, Bonet de Grayns 'dit Saint-Sever' and Gaillard de Saint Germain. The viscount of Orthez received £2,828 in ransom for Joigny.[28] In Froissart's account there is the suggestion that the prince sprung a trap: that the French, upon seeing his scouts, donned their helmets, unfurled banners and pursued the Anglo-Gascons only to find themselves drawn into contact with the main force. The prince admits to losses, but we do not know how many. Some of the prince's men pursued the routed French towards Chauvigny, but the majority of the army was held back in case of a French counter-attack. This did not materialise, but the prince camped for the night near the scene of the engagement so that, in his own words, 'we might collect our men', which presumably included the baggage train and those who had pursued the French. An unfortunate consequence of this choice for an overnight bivouac was a shortage of water for the men and horses.[29]

The location of the engagement on Saturday is generally taken to be the *lieu-dit* of La Chabotrie, probably a fortified farm in that period, in the hamlet of Le Breuil-Abbesse, three miles to the east of Poitiers, mainly on the evidence of the letter of Bartholomew de Burghersh written after the battle to Jean de Beauchamp in which he refers to a castle called 'Chabutorie'. Since Burghersh was with the prince, the case for La Chabotrie seems strong. However, this is the only source which records anything close to 'Chabutorie'. There is one further source which gives a precise place-name. This is a letter from Sir Henry Peverel to the prior of Winchester Cathedral. Apart from differences in spelling in several places, much of this letter is identical to that of Burghersh, and Peverel, who was a warden of the coast and is not known to have been with the prince, was probably passing on the news with a copy of Burghersh's letter. Peverel gives the location as 'Tanne', which does not tally with any local place-names and must have been an error in transcription. Other sources give approximate locations rather than a precise place-name.[30] Clifford Rogers has argued that, despite Burgersh's 'Chabutorie', it is more likely that the fighting was in the vicinity of Savigny-Lévescault, three miles south-east of La Chabotrie.[31] This makes sense in that Savigny is the right distance from Chauvigny, quoted as three leagues by the prince, and is south of the road, the modern N151, from Chauvigny to Poitiers. This is consistent with the description in the *Eulogium* of the prince having crossed the road from Chauvigny to Poitiers before emerging from the woods to fall on the French whereas La Chabotrie is on the road. The sources leave some room for interpretation, but the prince's intention seems to have been to intercept the French at the river crossing at Chauvigny and in this case Savigny would also fit better than La Chabotrie.[32] Furthermore, with both armies camped for the night south-east of Poitiers, but not apparently in close proximity or aware of each other's precise locations, it seems likely that, with the French between them and Poitiers, the Anglo-Gascon army would be further out from the city than La Chabotrie's three miles. Clifford Rogers suggests that 'He [the prince] therefore took up position in the woods by a small stream (which did not provide enough water for the army), probably between Savigny-

Lévescault and Tercé.'³³ There is a further source which tends to support this general location:

> on 20 September [*sic*], the two armies took up positions somewhat close to Poitiers, about one league, that is to say between a manor of the Bishop of Poitiers, called Savigny-Lévescault, and a wood belonging to the Abbey of Nouaillé called Borneau, in which wood was the greatest part of the Anglo-Gascon army.³⁴

The distance quoted of one league from Poitiers is wrong, as is the date, and the context of the statement is that this was the site of the battle which does not make sense. However, there are woods adjoining two *lieux-dit* called Le Petit Bourneau and Le Grand Bourneau, just over a mile to the south of Nouaillé, five miles south-west of Savigny. There is also a *lieu-dit*, almost equidistant between the woods at Bourneau and Savigny-Lévescault, La Chaboissière, which is on the edge of woods with a minor watercourse in the vicinity. In 1334 this was recorded as 'la Chaboucère', which could possibly have been corrupted into Burghersh's 'Chabutorie'.³⁵ There is also some rather tenuous evidence that there may have been a castle here, which would also fit with Burghersh's account that King Jean had lodged there the night before.³⁶ However, it has to be said that this, three miles south of the road from Chauvigny to Poitiers, seems an unlikely halt for the king and is probably also a little distant from the road for Saturday's engagement. Nevertheless, as with Rogers' suggested location, the vicinity of La Chaboissière and the woods at Bourneau would be consistent with the prince turning from there to advance towards the French on Sunday 18 September and coming to the battlefield. La Chabotrie does not fit this picture. The best that can be said is that the skirmish and overnight bivouac on the Saturday were more probably in the vicinity of Savigny-Lévescault than La Chabotrie.

Let us now look at what contemporaries, or near contemporaries, had to say of events in this phase of the *chevauchée*. There are some general comments in the chronicles to the effect that when the prince heard that Jean was approaching he turned for home.³⁷ Froissart also states that the 'English took the road to go to Poitiers'.³⁸ However, Baker is quite specific: 'the prince eager for battle ... led his army towards the camp of the usurper'.³⁹ Chandos Herald, relating the movement of the French and the prince's response states that 'they [the French] departed from Chartres and rode without any hesitation straight towards Tours. Very noble was their array. The news then reached the prince, and good tidings did they seem to him; towards Poitiers he took his way'.⁴⁰ This short passage is ambiguous. Was the prince's delight due to the approach of the French or because they were heading towards Tours and this gave him time to move away from them towards Poitiers? It would be interesting to know what Jean thought the prince was trying to achieve. Le Bel gives a tantalising taste of what might have been the king's view: 'when he [King Jean] knew for certain that they were so close to him, he thought that they would wait for him, and that the next day or the one after it would be necessary to fight them.'⁴¹ What are we to make of the last clause? Was Jean himself that keen to fight, or did he simply see battle as inevitable? As we shall see later, on the eve of battle he and his advisors were in two minds as to whether the best course was to starve the prince into submission or take the risks of battle.

Other contemporary evidence includes the report from Sir Henry Peverel, and the letter written by Bartholomew de Burghersh, both discussed above, and three letters by the prince: to the prior of Winchester Cathedral, to the bishop of Worcester and to the mayor, aldermen and commonality of the City of London. The letter to the prior of Winchester Cathedral deals with fact and not intentions, and Burghersh's letter is also very matter of fact, only briefly alluding to intentions when he talks of crossing the Loire to 'pass into France'. The prince's letter to the bishop of Worcester is, however, explicit: 'and we had news that the King of France with great strength very close to those marches [Bourges, Orléans, and Tours] came to fight with us, and we approached so that battle was joined between us'.[42] In his letter to the City of London the prince is also explicit over his intentions. As a general intent he states that 'it was our purpose to ride forth against the enemies in the parts of France', and he also links the intelligence that Jean was seeking battle with his decision to move towards him at Tours. Similarly, he explains the halt at Châtellerault because he was 'waiting to know for greater certainty of him'.[43]

Next let us look at the prince's options on the eve of his departure from Romorantin on Sunday 4 September and subsequent events within the context of the documentary evidence. His options at this stage were: to await the arrival of the French, to advance to the Loire and attempt to either find or force a crossing, to turn for home, or to move towards Tours in the hope of confronting the French army.

The first option would not have been attractive. They had already been in the vicinity of Romorantin for six days, and the longer that they remained in place the harder it would be to provision men and horses. Also, if a rendezvous with Lancaster were still possible, then the prince should be moving towards him in order to effect the meeting as quickly as possible. Finally, and most importantly, by remaining static he would cede the initiative to King Jean.

As we know from his own account, the second option, attempting to cross the Loire, was discounted by the prince on the basis of intelligence: 'And there [Romorantin] we were certified that all the bridges upon Leyre [the Loire] were broken down, and that we could nowhere find a passage'.[44]

We know that he decided to move towards Tours, but rather than being seen as an attempt to close with the French, this has been portrayed as the prince having decided to turn for home. As Hewitt put it: 'The best way from Romorantin to Bordeaux lay in going west along the Cher and, at some suitable point, turning south'.[45] Even a cursory glance at the map shows that this is nonsense. A quicker escape could have been achieved by either retracing the route taken in the previous month or cutting south-west to join the route from Poitiers to Bordeaux. In either case he could have kept well ahead of King Jean. Indeed, even if he had marched at only twelve miles a day, the average distance covered on march-days since leaving Bergerac, he would have reached Poitiers on 13 September, well ahead of King Jean who arrived at what was to be the battle-field on Sunday 18 September. If escape had been his aim he could have moved much faster. As Appendix 2 shows, marches of twenty miles a day were by no means unusual during this *chevauchée*, and on the days after leaving Montlouis he covered twenty-three and twenty-five miles. There can be no doubt that if his primary objective were to disengage from the French and return home with his booty he could have done so with ease. The route taken and the pattern of movements and halts are simply not compatible with the thesis that he was running for safety.

What the prince's movements show us is his tactical appreciation of the situa-tion and his skilful execution of the necessary manoeuvres, to strike what Rogers rightly describes as 'the delicate balance between avoiding a trap and not avoiding a battle'.[46] His itinerary from Romorantin was no more, nor less, than sound tactical movement to maximise the opportunities to join forces with the duke of Lancaster, to keep the initiative, to stay close enough in touch with the French that King Jean would not be tempted to give up the chase, and yet avoid being trapped. The risk of entrapment was entirely linked to the position of the two armies in relation to major rivers. The prince's movement out of potential traps is exemplified by his departure from Montlouis and the passages of the Cher and the Indre before halting at Montbazon, and his crossing of the Creuse and the move to Châtellerault, followed by another halt. In each case he paused long enough to stay in touch and then moved on again before the next trap could be sprung, all the while keeping the opportunity for battle alive. His bold move on Saturday 17 September not only gave him a successful morale-boosting skirmish, but also brought the two armies into close proximity. There was now the oppor-tunity for battle without the prince facing the risk of entrapment with a major obstacle at his back. The question now was whether battle would come the next day on Sunday 18 September.

13

Battle Joined

Nouaillé-Maupertuis
Sunday 18 and Monday 19 September 1356

'Sirs', said he, 'advance for God's sake, let us win this field, if we regard
our honour.'   The Black Prince in the thick of battle[1]

The manoeuvre phase which had characterised operations since the prince and
his army left Romorantin was now over and the armies were at last in close
proximity.

However, the most pressing need for the Anglo-Gascon army as the sun rose
on Sunday 18 September 1356 was to find water, and, if possible, other provisions
for men and horses. The nearest water source was the river Miosson, only about
two miles from the overnight bivouac. Furthermore, the Benedictine abbey of St
Junien on the banks of the river in the village of Nouaillé and the commanderie
of the Knights Hospitaller at Beauvoir were close at hand and could be expected
to provide at least some provisions for the army. Once the men and horses had
been fed and watered as best they could, attention could then turn to the best
course of action. If, as some believe, the prince was intent on avoiding battle, the
obvious move, with the French somewhere to the north between the prince and
Poitiers, would have been to continue south towards Bordeaux and safety at all
speed. Instead he chose to advance towards the French and select a position for
battle:

> And on the morrow we took our road straight towards the King, and sent out our
> scouts who found him with his army; and he set himself in battle array at one
> league from Poitiers, in the fields; and we went as near to him as we could take
> up our post, we ourselves on foot and in battle array, and ready to fight with him.[2]

So where and how was the prince's army arrayed on Sunday, and were these
the positions in which they started the battle on Monday morning? There are
numerous primary sources which deal with the battle. However, they vary in
detail, are often obscure, and are imprecise concerning the location. As a conse-

quence it has proved impossible to resolve the many differing accounts with certainty, and there have been significantly different interpretations. My conclusions, in common with those of others, inevitably involve a large measure of conjecture.[3] In this context I should also add a caveat to the sketch maps which I have used later in the chapter to illustrate the progress of the battle. I recognise that such maps could be taken to imply that it is possible to reduce a medieval battle to accurate plans of well-ordered blocks of men moving in disciplined parade-ground fashion to some master-plan. This is of course not the case, and such maps cannot accurately represent the chaos of battle. I hope that the sketch maps are helpful, but they are nothing more than visual aids provided to guide the reader through the main events of the combat based on my interpretation of the battlefield. To avoid too much detail only main contour lines have been included. However, without the contour lines the steep gradients on some parts of the battlefield, notably around the Champ d'Alexandre and to the north of the Gué de Russon, are not apparent and the hatching around the 115-metre contour line has been added to show these slopes.[4]

Froissart tells us that the battle took place 'somewhat close to Poitiers in the fields of Biauvoir and Maupertuis', and 'in the fields of Maupetruis [*sic*] two leagues from Poitiers'.[5] Biauvoir is unambiguous, it is the small settlement of Beauvoir, five miles south-east of Poitiers, close to Froissart's two leagues. Maupertuis has been the subject of debate over the years, hinging on whether this was a place or a description. It has been suggested that Maupertuis was the current farm of La Cardinerie, a mile to the west of Beauvoir, based on a concession which passed land named Maupertuis to a Richard Delyé, known as Cardin, in 1495.[6] However, it has been argued that this is not conclusive and that Maupertuis is more likely to be a description of a place than a proper noun.[7] It has been asserted that Maupertuis means 'bad road', and that this description was applied to the minor road running from north to south to the west of the woods at Nouaillé. Unfortunately it is not quite as clear cut as that, as *pertuis* has a variety of meanings in Old and Middle French, including a hole, hollow, den or hiding-place or passage.[8] Thus, although the description Maupertuis can conveniently be applied to the road, it could equally well be applied elsewhere.

In the nineteenth century there were reported to be a number of local names, *le champ de la bataille*, *la masse* (mound) *aux Anglais*, and *l'abreuvoir* (watering-place) *aux Anglais* in the vicinity of La Cardinerie and the settlement of Les Bordes to the south. Unfortunately these names are on neither modern maps nor cadastral plans going back to Napoleonic times and do not help to locate the battlefield. Mention is also made of the *lieu-dit* Carthage, two miles east of Nouaillé and the Champ d'Alexandre, on the spur of ground in the bow of the Miosson to the west of Nouaillé. It has also been claimed that archaeological finds were made in the area in the eighteenth and nineteenth centuries, including jewellery said to belong to King Jean found near La Cardinerie. There were also said to be signs of defence works still visible in the nineteenth century.[9] Even if all this information were correct it would give us little useful help, since the places mentioned are dispersed across a wide area.

The *Eulogium* gives us a brief description of the English position as being near a dense wood with pasture lands and glades with a ditch, surmounted by a high thorn hedge. This hedge had one gap, wide enough for only five men-at-arms to pass at a time.[10] This is too general to be of any great help, other than the proximity to the dense wood. So what of Froissart? According to his account, on the Sunday King Jean sent forward four knights to reconnoitre the prince's position, with Eustace de Ribemont, credited with making the report to the king. On his return he was asked by the king: 'And how do they lie?' This is said to have been Ribemont's description of the English position:

> Sire, they are in a very strong position, and we can see and imagine that they are prepared for battle, very well and very cleverly arrayed. They have taken the length of a road well fortified with hedges and bushes, and have lined this hedge, from one end to the other, with their archers such that one cannot enter, nor ride in the road, save being among them if one wants to take this road or fight them. This hedge has only one way in and out, where only four men-at-arms could ride abreast, and the same goes for the road. At the end of this hedge, where one can neither go nor ride, are their men-at-arms, all on foot, and they have put in front of them archers in the manner of a harrow. It is very well organized it seems to us, for whoever wants or is able to come up to them by feat of arms, will not be able to do so save among the archers who will not be easy to defeat.[11]

Although this places emphasis on a road and hedges, it does not give us enough information on its own to determine the location of the Anglo-Gascon deployment. Baker gives the most detailed description:

> he [the prince] perceived that there was near-by on one side a hill, encircled with hedges and ditches on the outside, but with different land inside, on one side a pasture thick with thorn bushes, but, on the other side sown with vines, and the rest of it arable land. And in the arable part of it he thought a French column lay. Between us and the hill was a broad deep valley, and a marsh which was fed by a certain stream. At a fairly narrow ford the prince's column crossed the stream, with its wagons, and coming out of the valley across ditches and hedges occupied the hill, where amid the thickets they were easily hidden by the natural fortification of the place, which lay higher than the enemy. The field in which our first and second columns lay was separated from the open ground which the French occupied by a long hedge with a ditch on the far side, one end of which fell away into the marsh aforementioned. The earl of Warwick, commander of the first column, held the slope going down to the marsh. In the upper part of the hedge, a good way from the slope, was a certain large gap or hiatus, which carters made in the autumn, distant a stone's throw from which lay our third company, which the earl of Salisbury commanded. The enemy, seeing the standard of the prince, previously visible, but now starting to move and to be hidden from their eyes by the slope of the hill, thought that he was trickling away.[12]

The last sentence clearly relates, as we shall see later, to the opening moves of the battle, and this raises the issue of whether or not this description refers

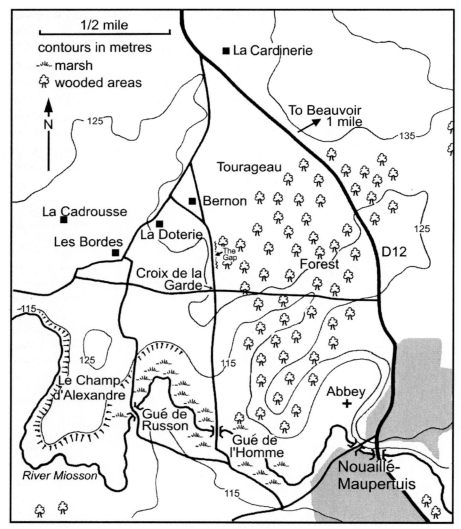

Map 25 The battlefield.

to an appraisal made by the prince on the Sunday morning as they advanced towards the French in the direction of Poitiers or the morning of battle, Monday 19 September. We shall return to this later, but for the moment let us see what we can determine about the position of the Anglo-Gascon army from Baker's account, keeping in mind the descriptions in the *Eulogium* and by Froissart, since it is the only one which gives specific features which might be identifiable, albeit not without ambiguity. Before doing so, however, it is important to appreciate that although Baker talks of 'a broad deep valley' and a 'hill' these terms can give a distorted impression of the terrain. There are valleys and hills, but this is not

Plate 5 View south from the ridge above the marsh. This view, taken in the spring after a period of moderately wet weather, shows the nature of the marsh. The river Miosson follows the tree-line in the background with the Gué de Russon on the right beyond the embankment on the edge of the water.

hilly terrain and they are of a modest nature. The maximum change of elevation across the whole battlefield area is no more than 35 metres or 115 feet.

The features which are the most distinctive in the description given by Baker are the 'fairly narrow ford' and the 'marsh'. The 'fairly narrow ford' could be either the Gué de l'Homme, on the road north to the west of the forest, or the Gué de Russon crossed by the track towards Les Bordes. From the Gué de Russon to the east, following the bend in the river, is an area of very marshy land, with a steep bank rising to the north. It is tempting to assume that this was the extent of the marsh at the time of the battle, but even after a prolonged spell of dry weather the ground further round towards the Gué de l'Homme is wet under-foot. Indeed, the Miosson today, particularly after a period of dry weather, gives a very misleading picture. It is only about 5 metres wide, slow running, and gently meandering. However, heavy rain can dramatically change the character of the river, and as recently as 1982 the modern road bridge was carried away by flood water. It is likely that in the wet conditions experienced in the summer of 1356 the marsh extended out as much as 150 yards from the river in places, mainly on the northern side, and from west of the Gué de Russon to well to the east of the Gué de l'Homme.[13]

Plate 6 Facing south at the Gué de l'Homme. This photograph was taken after the driest summer for fifty years. The Miosson was little more then a minor stream but in wet weather it can be a much more significant river. The bridge replaced an earlier structure washed away by the river in flood in 1982. The land in the foreground would be susceptible to flooding in such conditions. Beyond the road on the right, where grass has not been planted, marsh plants are evident even in dry weather.

It is interesting that, although the *Eulogium* mentions dense woods, Baker does not refer to the woods at Nouaillé. This may have been because their extent and nature have changed since the fourteenth century and that at the time this was an area of thickets of bushes and young trees and not the mature woodland we see more than 600 years later. The absence of comment on the woods might tend to support the case for the view being from the Gué de Russon, but equally there are substantial woodlands to the west and south of the Champ d'Alexandre which we might have expected Baker to mention if this were the location and we cannot draw conclusions from this absence of evidence. It is possible to visualise the description given by Baker from both fords. From the vicinity of the Gué de Russon he would have seen the hill with Champ d'Alexandre about a half mile distant, and if this is the view that the prince saw, then we could envisage the army deployed near the Champ d'Alexandre, facing north-east across the throat of the large loop in the Miosson. The weakness of this position is that there are steep banks around the spur, which would make it a dangerous position if the army were pushed back by the French attack. Although today the slopes are

Plate 7 The Gué de Russon. This photograph, also taken after the driest summer for fifty years, shows the low banks of the Miosson but how easily the low ground on both sides can flood.

obscured by trees, the line of the road south from Les Bordes which traverses the contours is evidence of the difficult nature of the slope. A better position can be found looking back to the north from south of the river somewhere near the Gué de l'Homme. From here the prince would have looked across the valley of the Miosson and seen rising ground, stretching away for about a mile to the north and a hill, more properly a spur coming out from the higher ground to the north-east, near Croix de la Garde. If this were his view then the deployment could have been along the axis of the road to the west of the woods at Nouaillé, possibly Froissart's 'length of a road well fortified with hedges and bushes'. It would be easier to disengage from such a deployment than from the Champ d'Alexandre, and there would not be the same risk of being driven back to steep slopes. There is also more space for manoeuvre, and on balance I believe this to be the more probable location for the prince's army.

On the assumption that this was the general location, how might the army have been deployed? Clifford Rogers calculates the frontage of the English army at the Battle of Agincourt on the basis of four ranks of men, each man with a frontage of 3 feet.[14] He also argues that depths of three or four men-at-arms were typical in the period.[15] As we shall see below, the Anglo-Gascon army

Plate 8 The rim of the bowl north of the Gué de Russon. The slopes around the Champ d'Alexandre are obscured by trees. Their gradients vary, but in some places they are as steep as the 45-degree gradient illustrated here on the slope above the marsh to the north of the Gué de Russon.

probably consisted of 3,000 men-at-arms, 1,000 sergeants and 2,000 archers. We do not know with confidence the number of men in each division: Froissart's figures give a more or less equal distribution of forces between the three divisions, although his total is well in excess of the number believed to have been present.[16] In addition, we are told that there were 400 men-at-arms in reserve around the prince's banner. Notwithstanding Froissart's account of Ribemont's reconnaissance report of archers along the length of the road, it seems that the archers were deployed on the flanks and, again as we shall see later, the fighting implies that the archers were in two contingents.[17] If, for the sake of argument, we divide the men-at-arms and sergeants equally with the reserve as additional troops for the prince then we have 1,200 men fighting on foot in each division with an additional 400 men in reserve with the prince. We also have 1,000 archers with each of the vanguard and rearguard. Thus, if the men-at-arms were arrayed in four ranks, each division would have a frontage of 300 yards. In his discussion on Agincourt, Rogers proposes that at that battle archers were probably deployed in seven ranks with a frontage of 3 feet per man.[18] If, again solely for the sake of argument, we assume a similar formation at Poitiers, we would have a block of archers on the flanks, each with a frontage of about 140 yards.

Plate 9 View north across the Gué de l'Homme. Baker's 'broad deep valley', with the river Miosson in the middle ground and the road running up the hill towards the prince's position near the Croix de la Garde.

From the description in Baker above it seems that the vanguard, under Warwick, on the left, and the prince's division were close together, but that they were separated initially from the rearguard under Salisbury on the right. Based on these assumptions, the army could have deployed over an overall frontage of around 1,200 yards, with archers on the flanks, centred on the prince on the spur near to the Croix de la Garde.

A serious flaw with the army deployed in this manner, however, is that the archers would not be able to bring effective fire to bear on the centre of the frontage, so this seems an implausible deployment. This problem would be resolved if the archers were distributed between the three divisions and deployed on the flanks of each, but this would have broken them up into small units of not many more than 300 men. In addition, we know that the French deployed two squadrons of mounted men-at-arms with the express purpose of riding down and eliminating the archers, implying again that the archers were deployed in two blocks. It may be that descriptions of the initial deployment, the formation taken up when the army started to move off on the Monday morning, and the positions when battle was joined have become conflated. A possible initial deployment, with a narrower frontage, could be along the axis of the road with the prince's division stepped back from the other two, and with Warwick and

Plate 10 The hedge near Bernon. This hedge has been allowed to grow to more than 3 metres, or 10 feet, in width. Such hedges would be formidable obstacles.

Salisbury on the left and right respectively. It is impossible to know how much store to place on the words used by Baker, but his statement that Warwick 'held the slope going down to the marsh', may have meant just that and not that the archers were in the marsh initially. This deployment, although more compact than that described earlier, does not entirely resolve the problem that fire from the archers could not cover the entire front of the army. It may be that the formation was based on the expectation that there would be a need to disengage and then move off with the divisions in column; in the event of battle, the three divisions could then either form up one behind the other or close up as a single unit with, in both cases, the archers on the flanks. This would avoid a dead spot for the archers along the front of the men-at-arms. As we shall see, although the closing-up happened in the chaos of battle, this was effectively what happened with the three divisions in the end fighting as one mass.

A road runs north from the ford at the Gué de l'Homme, as it did then.[19] A little to the north, near Bernon, the modern road turns left but a length of farm track continues north on what was probably the route of the original track. This section of road is bordered on both sides by thick hedge typical of the region, which gives a useful insight into the nature of the hedges mentioned in the sources and why they received so much comment. The hedges in this region of France are planted with two rows of saplings a metre or more apart and undergrowth develops between the two rows. They frequently grow several metres in height and as they grow the saplings become trees embedded within

Plate 11 View from the possible French position. This view is taken from Les Bordes looking east up gently rising ground towards the prince's position near Croix de la Garde.

the hedge. They are formidable obstacles which would slow the attackers and give the defenders an initial advantage until the hedges had been breached and cut through.

With hedges along the sides of the road and, assuming that the prince's division as indicated by Baker's account had occupied the higher ground initially, then the gap in the hedge for the carters would be somewhere to the north of the Croix de la Garde with Salisbury's rearguard stepped back somewhat to put them a 'stone's throw' from the gap. Some interpretations of the battlefield imply that the gap was to allow a road to pass. Since we are told that the gap was opened in the autumn by carters this does not make sense. They must have been opening a gap to allow access either to fields or woodland.[20]

We have no detailed information on the French position. One analysis suggests that on the night of Saturday 17 September the French army was positioned with its right flank near to the right bank of the Miosson, a mile northwest of Les Bordes, and its left towards La Cardinerie and Beauvoir.[21] If this is correct then the prince's deployment would have brought him within sight of the French about three-quarters of a mile away, but one source records that there was only a bowshot between the two armies and the French may have moved forward close to a line south-east of Les Bordes.[22] From that position the French would have a clear view of the location of Anglo-Gascon rearguard and middle guard, but with the road falling away towards the Gué de l'Homme the position of the vanguard would be masked by the terrain. Chandos Herald tells us that 'as I have heard, the one camped before the other, and pitched their tents so near that, by Saint Peter, they watered their horses at the same river'.[23] It is not clear whether this is supposed to refer to Saturday night after the engagement between the prince and the rearguard of the French or the positions taken up on Sunday. However, on the assumption that the prince's army was short of water on the Saturday, it seems more likely that he means when the armies were deployed. That both should use the water of the Miosson is very likely, given the meandering course of the river.

Accounts of the battle give varying numbers for the strengths of the armies deployed. The figures cited above for the Anglo-Gascon army of 6,000 men with 3,000 men-at-arms, 1,000 sergeants, and 2,000 archers, are widely accepted as the probable strength of the Black Prince's army. The figures for the French vary widely from 11,000 cited in letters by Bartholomew de Burghersh and Henry Peverel to Froissart's 60,000. There are numerous other figures in between, but an assumption that at the start of the battle the French outnumbered the prince's men by around two and a half to one is probably not far off the mark.[24]

Having moved his army into position along the road north from the Gué de l'Homme the prince and his advisors would no doubt have considered the possible turn of events. Sunday was likely to be free of fighting under the provisions of the doctrine of the Truce of God which tried to prevent combat on holy days, although the prince could not count on this and would need to be on his guard. Meanwhile the French army continued to grow as fresh contingents arrived, adding perhaps an additional thousand men-at-arms during the day.[25] If the French attacked on the Monday morning the prince would adopt the preferred English tactic of the period of fighting a defensive action with his archers and dismounted men-at-arms. Although the size of the French host led some in the prince's army to mutter about the number of troops left behind to defend Gascony, many of his captains had been at Crécy and they would be confident that, given the right circumstances and God's blessing, they could prevail against the numerically superior French army. Recent successes during encounters with the French reconnaissance parties, the siege at Romorantin and Saturday's skirmish would have added to their confidence.

However, if the French did not engage early on the Monday the situation could rapidly deteriorate. The prince's men were short of supplies, and the longer that they stayed the greater the risk of them being starved into submission. As things stood they had an escape route over the fords of the Miosson, but the distance from the northernmost French positions round the east of the woods to the Gué de l'Homme was no more than three miles. A substantial French force could easily be in a blocking position within a couple of hours of first light. Indeed, it is something of a mystery that the French did not cut the way south on the Sunday. So if the French were not to show signs of engaging soon after first light on Monday then the prince would have to consider withdrawal. This should not be seen as a sign of wishing to avoid battle. Once again it would be a prudent measure to avoid being trapped. A move south and the chance to feed and water men and horses would possibly present another opportunity for battle.

In any event, on Sunday morning the prince's army had watered and fed as well as circumstances allowed and had moved into position facing the French. Meanwhile Talleyrand, the cardinal of Périgord, still had hopes for peace. He approached the king, and suggested that in view of the might of his army in comparison with the handful in the prince's army it would bring him more honour to secure a peaceful outcome than to risk the lives of many when it was not necessary. With the agreement of King Jean, Talleyrand rode out towards the English army with two fellow cardinals, the bishop of Urgel, a fellow papal dele-gate, and the archbishop of Rouen, an ambassador for the French. The English did not trust Talleyrand to be impartial, since both he and the pope were French. Thus, initially the prince rebuffed his approach, suspecting that the cardinal was buying time for the French to supplement their forces, and told Talleyrand this was a time for fighting and not sermons. However, having heard the cardinal out and held discussions with his council, he agreed to negotiations. These were conducted on the ground between the two armies by representatives of the king and the prince, under the chairmanship of the cardinal. For the prince the nego-tiators included the earls of Warwick and Suffolk, Bartholomew de Burghersh, John Chandos and James Audley. The result of the negotiations was the offer of terms by the prince. The details of the terms vary from one source to another but included some at least of the following provisions: the surrender to Jean of all the properties that had been captured from the French in the last three years, an indemnity reported variously between 100,000 écus (about £14,000) and 200,000 nobles (about £67,000), the release of all prisoners, the hand in marriage of one of the king's daughters and the promise not to take up arms against Jean for seven years. The sting in the tail was that the terms would be subject to the agreement of King Edward. The prince promised to secure this quickly but, given the speed of communications and the imminence of battle, his sincerity in entering these negotiations must be questionable. As we saw in Chapter 12, the prince's indenture with King Edward empowered the prince to make a truce or armistice in extremis, and it seems very likely that he was simply buying time while he prepared for events on the Monday. During the negotia-tions King Jean asked for the surrender of the prince and 100 knights as a sign of good faith. Also, according to Chandos Herald, there was a proposal from Geof-froi de Charny for the battle to be settled by combat between 100 knights from each side. Warwick's reported reply is interesting, in that it implies that perhaps the French were seeking to select a field for the battle which would offer them better circumstances. If so this would clearly not be in the interest of the English and the Gascons, outnumbered as they were, and Warwick replied:

> Sire, what will you gain by this encounter? You know well that you have more men-at-arms and steel clad, by four times than we are, and we are on your terri-tory; here is the field and the place, let each side do its best. Nowhere else will I

be, nor agree to any other conditions. May God defend the right, as it shall seem best to him.[26]

It seems that Jean may have been inclined to accept the terms on offer, and some of his advisors were of the opinion that he should do so. However, many of his entourage were opposed, and in the argument d'Audrehem implied that Clermont was lacking in courage to which he retorted: 'You will not be brave enough today to put the muzzle of your horse to the backside of mine!'[27] The bishop of Châlons reminded the king of the damage done by King Edward, the duke of Lancaster and the prince throughout his realm. He also reminded the king of his inaction to date to exact revenge on the English, and expressed some incredulity that Jean, bearing in mind his strong position, should be negotiating with the prince when he could have little confidence in his good faith. He was strongly supported by Marshal d'Audrehem, Geoffroi de Charny and Earl Douglas, a Scot in the service of Jean with 200 men-at-arms, who argued that given the relative strength of the armies, the fact that the French were on their home soil, and the difficulty the Anglo-Gascon army was in with provisions, 'by common reason it could not come to passe that the Englishmen should at that time prevaile.'[28] The position of the prince's army with regard to provisions, and the possibility of holding the Anglo-Gascons in position and forcing their surrender, would no doubt have figured in the king's deliberations with his advisors and, having taken counsel, Jean refused all terms and demanded the surrender of the prince and his army, trusting in his mercy.

When the prince heard that terms had been rejected by the king, he is said to have announced that he would willingly put himself in God's hands; that he only had one life and he would prefer to risk death than live in shame. There was an offer from the king of a formal truce until the Monday morning provided that the prince undertook not to depart under cover of night. The prince was not going to be caught like this and replied to the effect that he had not come to these parts with the assent of King Jean, and would stay or go at his own pleasure. Although Talleyrand was mistrusted by the prince and his advisors he was not held in much greater regard in some quarters in the French camp. As Chandos Herald put it: 'and on both sides it was said "This cardinal has betrayed us".'[29]

It could be argued that these negotiations revealed the reluctance of the prince to fight, and Chandos Herald adds some weight to this with his comment that 'and willingly, as I think, [the prince] would have been spared the action, could he have avoided it'. However, none of the other principal sources make similar reference, and we should see the negotiations within the religious context of the times. Strange as it may seem to us today, God's support for his cause would have been very much in the prince's thoughts. To reject the cardinal's overtures without negotiation, particularly on a Sunday and a day of the Truce of God, would have been tempting providence.

It is likely that both the king and the prince saw the prospects of a peaceful issue as remote, and both would be considering the coming battle. For the prince, whose army had been together for six weeks on this campaign, the allocation of captains and their companies to divisions was in accord with the organisation to date. Warwick would command the van with Oxford and numerous Gascon lords including the captal de Buch; the prince commanded the centre with John Chandos and James Audley, and Salisbury the rearguard with Suffolk and Berkeley. On the French side, King Jean assigned the vanguard, comprising according to Chandos Herald, men-at-arms, infantry, and crossbowmen to the two marshals, Audrehem and Clermont, and the duke of Athens, constable of France. The vanguard also included a number of men-at-arms from Lorraine, modern Switzerland and Savoy, under the leadership of the counts of Saarbruck, Nassau and Nidau. The dauphin, the duke of Normandy, commanded the second division with the duke of Bourbon. The king's brother, Philippe duke of Orléans, took command of the third division. A fourth division was constituted under the command of the king with his three sons Louis, Jean and Philippe.

King Jean also had to decide on his tactics. He knew, of course, of the standard tactic for the English to fight on foot. He would also have known how effective the archers could be, and the experience of Crécy would have been much in his mind and those of his advisors. When he had heard the reports from the reconnaissance party he had asked for advice on how best to fight. Eustace de Ribemont advised that he should select 300 men-at-arms (500 according to Baker) to make a mounted attack 'to split and open and disrupt the English archers, and then our divisions, which are large, powerful, and well equipped with good men-at-arms, to follow quickly on foot, for there are too many vines for the horses'.[30] This advice was supported by William Douglas, since this was the practice of the Scots. The king readily agreed, and orders were given to shorten lances to 5 feet in length, and to remove spurs.

While all this had been going on a dispute had arisen between Marshal Clermont and Sir John Chandos over the fact that they were wearing identical arms. Clermont challenged Chandos: 'Chandos, since when have you borne my arms?' 'And you mine', replied Chandos, 'because they are as much mine as yours.' 'I will show you', replied Clermont in turn, 'that you have no right to wear them.' Chandos had the final word: 'Ha! Tomorrow morning you will find me prepared to defend and prove by feat of arms that you have no right to wear them!'[31]

With the prospect of peace gone, the prince addressed his army, and no doubt held a council to finalise plans for the Monday morning.[32] Sunrise on 19 September would have been at 5.40 a.m., with the two armies facing each other and arrayed for battle. Shortly thereafter the cardinal arrived in the English camp to try once again to secure a peaceful outcome. It was clear to all that his efforts were in vain, and even the cardinal in the end had to concur that there was now no option but battle.

Let us now return to the final sentence in Baker's description of the location of the prince's army: 'The enemy, seeing the standard of the prince, previously visible, but now starting to move and to be hidden from their eyes by the slope of the hill, thought that he was trickling away.' This passage follows immediately after Baker's account of events on the Sunday, including the conclusion reached by the prince that the French were resolved on battle and a report of the speeches made by the prince to his army as a consequence. The implication is that on Monday morning the prince's army moved to the position in Baker's description in anticipation of battle. The prince, however, recounted that:

> the battalions on the one side and the other remained all night, each one in its place, and until the morrow [Monday], about half prime [7.30 a.m.]; and as to some troops that were between the said main armies, neither would give any advantage in commencing the attack upon the other. And for default of victuals, as well as for other reasons, it was agreed that we should take our way, flanking them, in such a manner that if they wished for battle or to draw towards us, in a place that was not very much to our disadvantage, we should be the first; and so forthwith it was done.[33]

This implies that the armies stood in position overnight and that, a little less than two hours after sunrise, the prince's army started to disengage. If we return to the description in Baker that 'at a fairly narrow ford the prince's column crossed the stream, with its wagons, and coming out of the valley across ditches and hedges occupied the hill', it is difficult to see how this fits with the prince's army starting to disengage and move away from the French on Monday. It is more probable that the prince adopted the position described by Baker after moving towards the French on Sunday, and that he then started to disengage from these positions on Monday morning.

At some point the prince sent Sir Eustace Daubriggecourt and another knight, probably the Gascon Petiton de Curton, to reconnoitre the French position. This may have been a diversionary tactic, but equally it may have been to gain intelligence before the prince started to move. In any event, the unfortunate Sir Eustace, having become involved in combat with Louis de Recombes, in the service of the count of Nassau, was overwhelmed by Louis' companions and made prisoner.

Chandos Herald describes the prince as outlining the plan for disengagement thus:

> At first you [Warwick] will cross the pass and protect our carriages; I shall ride after you with all my knights, so that if you meet with any mischance, you may be reinforced by us; and the Earl of Salisbury shall also ride after me, bringing up our rearguard; and let each be on his guard, in case they fall upon us. Each may dismount and engage as quickly as he possibly can.[34]

The instruction to 'protect our carriages' can be interpreted to mean that the baggage train was moving across the Miosson that morning, but it could mean that some at least of the baggage train was already positioned south of the river. Certainly it would have been prudent, in view of the possibility of needing to disengage, to leave non-essential vehicles south of the Miosson on the Sunday to minimise the risk of congestion at the crossing, retaining north of the river only those carts carrying necessary provisions and stocks of arrows.

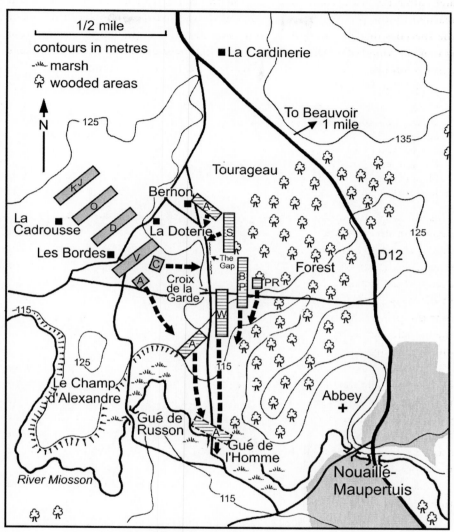

Map 26 The battle – initial deployment and first moves.

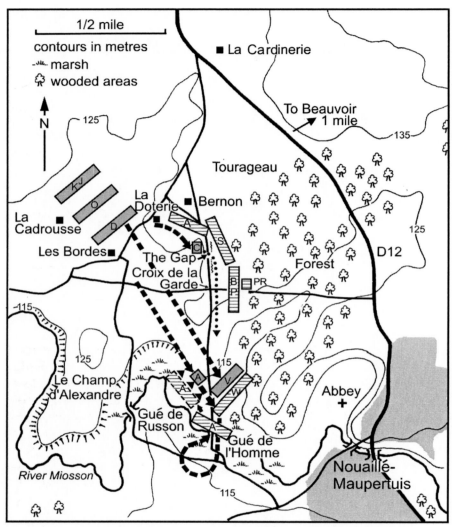

Map 27 The battle – the attack of the French vanguard.

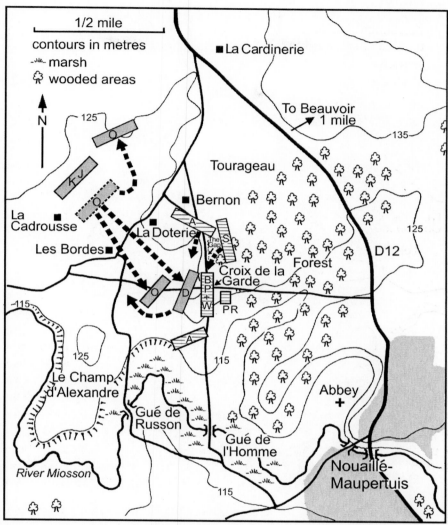

Map 28 The battle – the attacks of the dauphin's and Duke of Orléans' divisions.

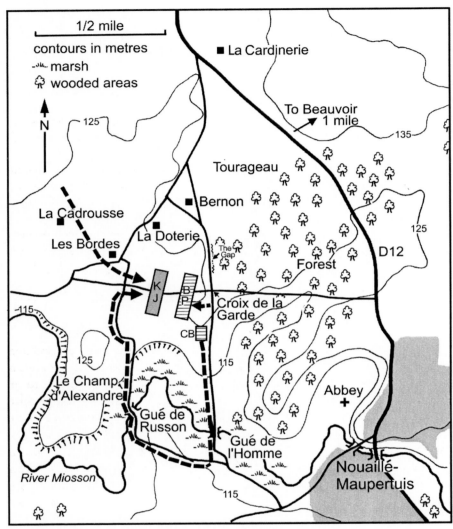

Map 29 The battle – the final phase.

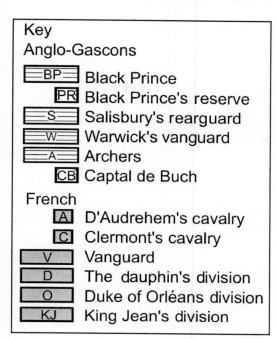

Key
Anglo-Gascons

BP Black Prince
PR Black Prince's reserve
S   Salisbury's rearguard
W   Warwick's vanguard
A   Archers
CB Captal de Buch

French

A   D'Audrehem's cavalry
C   Clermont's cavalry
V   Vanguard
D   The dauphin's division
O   Duke of Orléans division
KJ King Jean's division

Key to the battlefield maps. Note: Although the sizes of the Anglo-Gascon units are approximately to scale, they are based on the assumptions in the text on disposition between divisions and spacing when dismounted. When mounted, as they were initially for the withdrawal, they would occupy a larger space. In any case, sizes should be taken as indicative only, for the purposes of illustration.

French awareness of the movement of the Anglo-Gascon army precipitated the start of the battle, with Baker telling us, as we have seen, that the French saw 'the standard of the prince, previously visible, starting to move and to be hidden from their eyes by the slope of the hill'. This is consistent with the prince moving off to the south between the road and the wood, where he would become partially hidden from French view by the reverse slope of the spur, with Warwick already having moved off out of sight of the French because he was further down the slope. It is likely that by the time the French realised what was afoot both the vanguard and middle guard of the Anglo-Gascon army had started to move from their positions. On a modern parade-ground well-drilled troops can move off simultaneously in large numbers. This would not have been possible with troops in the fourteenth century. They would, no matter how well disciplined they were, have tended to move off much as a queue of cars when traffic lights change to green, with movement extending progressively down the line. Thus, it would be probable that the vanguard would be well under way before the prince's middle division moved off, and that Salisbury would still be stationary by the time Warwick was crossing the Miosson.

Marshal d'Audrehem concluded that the English were seeking to disengage, and considered that there was no time to lose if they were to be prevented from escaping. Marshal Clermont and William Douglas took a different view, and cautioned against haste. However, d'Audrehem set off and Clermont, apparently goaded into action by a mixture of insults and pride, followed. It may be that the speed of the response was the undoing of the attack. Clearly there would have been some confusion, and the constable would have taken a few minutes at least to get the dismounted troops of the French vanguard moving. In addition, the distances from the French vanguard to each of the two wings of the Anglo-Gascon army would be significantly different. If the cavalry was somewhere in the vicinity of Les Bordes, they would have had about 500 yards to cover to reach Salisbury's rearguard and possibly as much as 1,000 yards to the left flank of Warwick's vanguard. Thus, d'Audrehem's cavalry on the right of the French would quickly outstrip the infantry, who of necessity would be some way behind the mounted troops when contact was made, and would probably be in contact with Warwick after about seven minutes. On the left, Clermont's cavalry would probably take about three minutes to come into contact with Salisbury and could expect the infantry to be closer on their heels, assuming that the constable took the initiative to advance promptly when he saw the cavalry move.[35]

A co-ordinated attack at a more measured pace might well have caught the prince's army at its most vulnerable, with infantry coming into contact quickly after the cavalry on both wings. However, the die was cast and the mounted troops of Marshal d'Audrehem and Marshal Clermont fell upon the vanguard and the rearguard respectively. It seems that Warwick had at this point already crossed the Miosson with a part of his force, but that there was an initial clash between some of Warwick's mounted men-at-arms and d'Audrehem's cavalry. This initial encounter led to some hesitation on d'Audrehem's part, but he renewed the attack heading south-east down the spur of land converging with the road and the Gué de l'Homme. It appears that by now elements of the French vanguard on foot were coming into contact since d'Audrehem's men turned their armoured horses face-on to protect them from the English archers, who had been positioned in the marshy ground close to the river, most probably as a prudent measure to cover the initial stages of the withdrawal. Oxford, recognising what was happening and that the fire was proving less effective than it might be, took the archers forward to allow them to strike the horses in their unprotected flanks. It is probable that the archers were not deployed where the current marsh is most visible. If they had been it is difficult to see how their fire could have been effective with the very steep ground to their north. Furthermore, the slope would have been difficult for cavalry to descend and a head-on confrontation between archers and cavalry would have been most improbable. It is more likely that the archers were close to the Gué de l'Homme and were then moved to the left along the edge of the marshy ground to engage the cavalry in the flank. The result of this movement and the flanking fire was chaos as some horses fell, taking their riders with them, and others turned and ran into those coming behind. The men on foot were now exposed to flanking fire from the archers. Those of Warwick's men-at-arms who had already crossed the Miosson, realising what was happening, had now recrossed the river and joined the fray.

Meanwhile, on the English right flank, Clermont led a determined attack with the aim of exploiting the gap in the hedge to fall on the vanguard. This implies that the prince's division was separate from the van, as would be expected if they were now both moving, and Clermont, with the aim of cutting off the withdrawal, intended to move across the front of the prince, which he could do safely if the archers were on the flanks with Warwick's and Salisbury's divisions. Salisbury anticipated the problem and countered Clermont by moving forward with his men-at-arms. He positioned his archers so that they were protected by the hedge and brought fire to bear on the French mounted men-at-arms. Since Clermont, goaded into action, had set off promptly and had a shorter distance to cover than d'Audrehem, the first action was between his men and those of Salisbury, as reflected in the words of Salisbury reported by Chandos Herald: 'Advance, Sirs, in God's name! Since it hath pleased Saint George that we who were the rear, should now be the front, let us take care to do honourably.'[36]

We know little of the part played by the dismounted men-at-arms, infantry and crossbowmen in this initial phase of the battle, other than that the constable, the duke of Athens, lost his life. Amongst the mounted elements of the vanguard, Clermont was killed and d'Audrehem captured. William Douglas fled the field, possibly in fear of his treatment if, as a Scot in theory subject to a truce between England and Scotland, he should fall into English hands. In a disastrous start to the battle the king had lost three of his key commanders. Among the dead was Robert de Duras, the nephew of Cardinal Talleyrand, and a further member of the cardinal's family, the châtelain d'Emposte, had been captured. According to Froissart the prince was enraged that members of the cardinal's entourage had joined the fight. He gave orders for Duras to be carried to the cardinal with the prince's compliments. He also ordered that d'Emposte should be decapitated, but was dissuaded by Sir John Chandos from carrying through this act. With the defeat of the French vanguard fortunes changed for Eustace Daubriggecourt who was now released from captivity.

There had been no general pursuit of the remnants of the French vanguard. As successful as this opening encounter had been, the battle was far from over. The Anglo-Gascon vanguard closed up with the prince's division, probably on the spur near the Croix de la Garde, and waited for the next phase. The dauphin's division now advanced to join battle. Baker tells us that this was a harder and longer fight than that with the vanguard, lasting two hours, and at some time early in this phase the Anglo-Gascon rearguard must also have closed up. At some stage the French penetrated the gap in the hedge, but the fire of the archers was so intense that the French were driven back beyond it again. The dauphin's banner-bearer, Tristan de Maignelières, was captured, and the division fell back, albeit in good order.[37] Suffolk seems to have played a key part in this phase, moving among the men to encourage them and to restrain the less experienced from foolhardy pursuit of the retiring French. The duke of Bourbon was among the French dead, and among the English casualties was Sir Maurice Berkeley who, wounded and isolated, was taken prisoner.

The prince's men were exhausted and many were wounded, but once more they kept their composure and did not pursue the French. They now awaited the next onslaught, and in the meantime moved the wounded away from the immediate area of combat, laying them under hedges and bushes. Men with broken or damaged weapons replaced them with those of the fallen, and archers went forward to recover arrows, including pulling them from the dead and wounded. Much would depend now on the 400 chosen men who had been kept in reserve with the prince's standard. No doubt Sir John Chandos, Sir James Audley and Sir Bartholomew de Burghersh, as his close advisor were with the prince. Of these, it is noteworthy that Chandos remained close by the prince throughout, and that Audley single-mindedly pursued the combat without thought of personal gain. Neither of them joined in the pursuit of prisoners to secure ransoms.[38] Also among the men close to the prince were Sir Walter Woodland, carrying the standard, William Shank and William de Harpenden in attendance on the standard, Sir Nigel Loring, John de la Haye, Sir William Trussell, Sir Alan Cheyne and Sir Baldwin Botetourt who attended on the prince, all of whom received annuities from him in recognition of their service at the battle.[39]

The next division into action should have been that of the duke of Orléans, but instead it, or at least a great part of it, left the field of battle and withdrew towards Chauvigny. With the duke went the king's sons, other than the youngest, Philippe, who remained with his father to the last. What remained of the duke of Orléans division seems, however, to have made a somewhat half-hearted attack which was driven off. To many in the English camp it must have seemed that, after three phases of combat, the day was theirs, since the common practice was for a medieval army to comprise three divisions. However, the remaining French troops, including the survivors of the crossbowmen, now rallied to the king. The final act was about to begin.

King Jean had held his division to the rear, which gave the English some breathing space as he advanced, but now the exhausted English and Gascon troops, having successfully withstood three successive attacks, watched with fear and consternation as a fourth division, described as arrayed in a broad and dense body, approached. They had every reason to be concerned since this fourth battle brought fresh men-at-arms as well as those who had been rallied from the earlier fighting. In addition, with the Oriflamme banner flying above the French, the traditional signal that no prisoners would be taken, they would have clearly understood the fate that awaited them if they lost the day. According to Baker, one of the prince's men close to the prince cried out, 'Ah, we are beaten!' The prince, however, rebuked him: 'You're a liar and a fool! How can you say we're beaten while I'm still alive?'[40] No doubt there is some licence in this account, but it is indicative of the challenge facing the prince. His army had fought courageously but was suddenly faced with having victory snatched away. The prince's response was to seize the initiative, and he took two decisive steps. First, he despatched the captal de Buch with sixty men-at-arms and 100 archers to move round behind the French. Second, possibly in part to stiffen the resolve of his men as they saw the captal apparently leaving the field, he called

'Advance, advance banners!', and moved down the slope of the spur towards King Jean's advancing men. Froissart states that, for this advance, the prince and his men remounted. This is not reported by other writers and is improbable, given that the fighting that followed was clearly intense and hand-to-hand. The battle was now renewed. This phase started with an exchange of fire between French crossbowmen and English archers. The archers were proving less effective than hitherto as the French advanced with their shields across their chests and their heads turned away from the fire, but in any case the archers had soon exhausted their already depleted supplies of arrows and joined the hand-to-hand fighting with any weapon that came to hand. It is possible that Warwick had earlier left the field in pursuit of fleeing French troops, but if so he returned just in time to add his forces to those of the prince. However, it seems that the decisive stroke was delivered by the captal de Buch who:

> made a wide sweep, retreating down the slope of the hill [the spur near Croix de la Garde] which he and the prince had recently left and circling the battlefield, reached a point just below the original position of the usurper. From there he rode up to the battlefield by the path just taken by the French and suddenly bursting out of hiding, signalling his presence to our men with the noble banner of St George.[41]

His appearance behind the French, with his archers firing into the less well-protected sides and rear of the men-at-arms, caused many now to flee the field. Tradition has it that the final combat took place inside a loop of the Miosson on the Champ d'Alexandre.[42] If so, it may be that the flanking attack by the captal crossed the river to the south over the Gué de l'Homme, recrossed at the ford further to the west at the Gué de Russon, followed the track north, and then turned to come onto the hill. Alternatively, if the final combat, as seems more probable, took place further north on the flat ground to the west of Croix de la Garde, the captal may have taken his men across the Gué de Russon, along the track north and then along the re-entrant to between Les Bordes and La Cadrousse to shield himself from the view of the French.

King Jean remained fighting to the last with his youngest son Philippe at his side shouting warnings: 'Father, look out to your right! Look out to your left!' Among those to fall were Geoffroi de Charny, seen by many as the epitome of chivalry, bearing the Oriflamme. There was an unseemly scramble to receive the surrender of the king as many claimed to have taken him, with cries of 'Surrender, surrender, or you are dead!' The king, recognising his position as hopeless, wished to surrender to the prince: 'To whom should I surrender, to whom? Where is my cousin the Prince of Wales? It is to him that I wish to speak.' Froissart records that Denis de Morbek, a knight from Artois who had been exiled from France following a murder committed in his youth and was now in the service of Edward III, intervened: 'Sire, he is not here, but surrender to me and I will lead you to him.' Subsequently Bernard de Troyes claimed that it was he who had taken the king prisoner, but in due course King Jean gave testimony that he had surrendered to de Morbek.[43]

To all intents and purposes the battle was now won, but fighting continued as the English pursued the fleeing French, many of whom lost their lives outside the gates of Poitiers which remained closed to them.[44] However, not all those fleeing were either killed or captured, and one at least, Oudart de Renti, managed to turn the tables on an unnamed English knight, capturing and releasing him in due course in return for a ransom. It is possible that Maurice Berkeley was wounded and captured by Jean de Hellenes during the final pursuit, rather than after the defeat of the dauphin's division, but in any case he was taken to Châtellerault where his wounds were tended. He was subsequently taken to Picardy pending his release for a ransom of 6,000 nobles (£2,000).[45]

The difficulties that could arise with the taking of prisoners in the confusion of battle are well illustrated by the case of the count of Dammartin, a member of the king's division. There was a dispute, principally it would seem between the prince and Salisbury, over ownership of the count which was still not resolved by 1360. On 31 January of that year the prince gave written testimony that he had made an ordinance before the battle, which was publically proclaimed to all the army, that 'no man should linger over his prisoner on pain of forfeiting him, but that each man without hindrance or dispute should have the prisoner to whom he should first be pledged'. There then follows testimony from Warwick and Cobham that the ordinance had indeed been proclaimed. The unfortunate Dammartin then gave a lengthy account of events in the presence of the prince, Warwick and Cobham which was authenticated by a notary public. The following extract gives a flavour of events:

> First of all an esquire came up to me on the battlefield. I do not know his name, but I was told that he was one of the prince's household and was called John Trailly. He called on me to surrender, and I immediately did so and gave him my fealty in such wise that he should save me. He said I should be quite safe and should have no fear. Then he went to take off my bascinet, and when I prayed him to leave it to me he answered that he could not properly save me unless he took it off. So he took it off, as well as my gauntlets; and as he did so another man came up and cut the strap and frog of my sword, so that it fell from me altogether. Then I told the esquire to take the sword, for I preferred that he should have it rather than anyone else. After that, the esquire once more demanded my fealty that I would be his faithful prisoner whatever the result of the day might be, and I gave it to him in such wise that he should save me. He said I should be quite safe and need have no fear. Then he made me mount his horse and handed me over to the safe keeping of a yeoman of his, and left me thus. Immediately afterwards the yeoman left me all alone and went off. Then a Gascon came up and demanded my fealty. I answered that I was already a prisoner; but all the same I gave him my fealty, simply so that he should save me. He took an escutcheon of my coat armour and left me. As he went, I told him that since he was leaving me in this way I should give my fealty to any other person who might come up and be willing to save me. He answered: 'Save yourself, if you can.' Then another man, who belonged to Sir John de Blankmouster [Blaunkminster], came up and demanded my fealty. I answered that I had already been taken by two persons; but I gave him my fealty, simply so that he should save me. This man stayed with me,

guarded me and brought me to the Earl of Salisbury, and I gave my fealty to the earl at the wish and with the consent of my last captor.

The count then goes on to promise not to put himself to ransom 'with the Earl of Salisbury or any other person until it is definitely decided whose prisoner I ought to be'. Matters were finally resolved, and the count was released, in February 1361 when the prince acknowledged receipt of £1,000 from Salisbury 'in full payment of what belongs to him of the ransom of the count of Danmartyn [Dammartin]'.[46]

It had been a hard-fought battle, and the result had been uncertain throughout much of the day. The *Eulogium* tells us that in the past one could almost always judge the outcome of a battle from the release of the sixth arrow while at Poitiers, when each archer had fired 100 arrows, the result remained uncertain. As calm settled over the battlefield the scale of the French losses became apparent. The prince's account named twenty nobles killed and reported another 2,426 men-at-arms killed, with forty-two senior nobles and a further 1,933 men-at-arms taken prisoner. Attention was rarely given to the losses of those of lower social status, but the letter, entitled 'News of the Prince Overseas' from Sir Henry Peverel to the prior of Winchester refers to 500 common folk captured and 3,300 slain. Many of the senior personages killed and captured are listed in the sources. French sources tend to give lower figures, with one account stating that 800 were killed and 700 captured. Indicative of the ambivalent role of the Church in the medieval period are the capture of the archbishop of Sens and the death of the bishop of Châlons in the fighting. Many of the prisoners were released on parole with conditions for payment of ransoms, but others were taken with the king, initially to Bordeaux and then on to England. Reports of English casualties, forty to sixty killed including four men-at-arms, seem improbably low, but we have no other means to judge them.[47]

After the battle the prince's army rallied, and set about gathering in and tending the wounded. It has been suggested that the prince took the king to the bishop of Poitier's château at Savigny- Lévescault.[48] This seems improbable, and Chandos Herald and Froissart are quite clear that the prince lodged on the battlefield that night and this is implicit in Baker's account. Among the wounded was the close associate of the prince, Sir James Audley, who was brought in seemingly near to death. The prince is said to have been entertaining the king to dinner when Audley was brought in and left his guest to tend personally to Audley, raising his morale with the news of the capture of the king. It is said also that the prince waited on the king, and during dinner asked him: 'Fair cousin, if you had taken me today, as by the grace of God I have taken you, what would you have done with me?' The king did not answer, and out of courtesy the prince did not press the point.[49]

Geoffrey Hamelym, a groom in the prince's chamber, was despatched with the tunic and bascinet of King Jean as evidence of his capture, and a messenger was sent with letters. The news was known in England by 10 October, when King Edward gave orders for the proclamation of the victory.[50]

Once again a smaller English army had prevailed over a much larger French force. No doubt the skilful combined arms approach of the English with the mix of archers and dismounted men-at-arms had much to do with it. Andrew Ayton has argued that, in assessing the success of English armies under Edward III, we should in addition 'devote more attention to the continuities provided by traditions of service, at personal, familial and institutional levels, and to the symbiotic relationship that could form between the work of men and the functioning of impermanent institutions'.[51] This seems particularly apt at Poitiers where so many were old comrades-in-arms, and had also, most unusually, notwithstanding the interlude between the 1355 and 1356 chevauchées, been together for a year. These continuities no doubt contributed to the discipline that the Anglo-Gascons displayed in the battle. Crécy had started with an ill-disciplined French charge against a disciplined English army, and much the same had happened here with a precipitate charge by the marshals. Perhaps a better co-ordinated initial attack with the dismounted elements of the vanguard following close behind the marshals would have resulted in a better start, and if the other divisions had moved more swiftly to the attack, denying the prince's army any respite, the French could well have won the day through force of numbers. Certainly a cardinal principle of war, 'concentration of force', had been ignored. Perhaps the reported sighting by the French army of an armed and mounted knight flying to and fro in the sky and fighting against them would be seen by some as a reason for the defeat, but many more in France would see it as a result of cowardice and treachery on the part of much of the nobility of France.[52]

14

The Return to Bordeaux

Nouaillé-Maupertuis to Bordeaux
Tuesday 20 September to Sunday 2 October 1356

> We take not pleasure in the slaughter of men, but we rejoice in God's bounty and we look forward to a just and early peace.
>
> Edward III after receiving news of the victory at Poitiers[1]

Although a famous victory had been achieved and, in modern parlance, the French command structure had been decapitated, the prince and his advisors would have been only too aware that a substantial part of the enemy army had escaped unscathed. In the event any concerns that they may have had were misplaced, with the French apparently more worried about a possible follow-up assault on the town of Poitiers. Indeed, Froissart tells us that they watched from the gates and towers of the city all night, and the next morning armed all manner of men to help the defence. He attributes the prince's lack of interest in Poitiers, and indeed places on the route to Bordeaux, to the fact that the Anglo-Gascons were so charged with gold, silver, jewels and valuable prisoners that they had neither the time nor the need to attack towns and fortresses.[2] Nevertheless, despite the French preoccupations with Poitiers, an attempt to liberate the king could not be ruled out. This was not a time to dally, and a return to Bordeaux without delay was advisable.

However, before they could leave time was required to identify and bury the dead, at least those of higher social status, to tend to the wounded, and to arrange for the release on parole of those prisoners who were not to be taken to Bordeaux. It was also important to get news to both the duke of Lancaster and King Edward and letters had to be written and despatched.

With so much to be done, the prince and his army moved only the short distance of three miles from the battlefield, south-west to Roches-Prémarie-Andillé, on the day after the battle. It is appealing to think that perhaps the small château of Prémarie was a likely lodging for the prince and the king, but that could not have been so since it dates from the fifteenth century and there

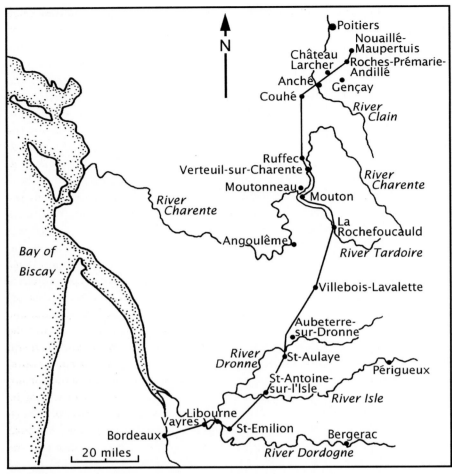

Map 30 Nouaillé-Maupertuis to Bordeaux.

does not seem to have been an earlier castle on the site.[3] Two further days were required before the army moved on from Roches-Prémarie-Andillé on Thursday 23 September. Once they had started their march back to Bordeaux, however, no further rest days were taken, other than pauses following river crossings when the journey had almost been completed, until the 168-mile journey was completed eleven days later. The priority now was to ensure a safe passage rather than to spread destruction along the line of march, and they moved in one body, save for an advance party of 500 men-at-arms under Warwick and Suffolk which went out ahead to reconnoitre and secure the way. According to Froissart they need not have been concerned since, on account of the disaster at the battle and the loss of so many nobles and the king, any men-at-arms along the route shut themselves up in castles.[4]

Once the prince and his army had left Roches-Prémarie-Andillé they seem to have felt the need to get some distance behind them and Poitiers, since they marched twenty miles south-west to Couhé on the Thursday and a further twenty miles the next day. They would certainly have passed near Château-Larcher, with substantial fortifications, including a castle and a fortified church which was integrated into the castle curtain wall. Six miles to their south-east of Château-Larcher is Gençay which had a formidable fortress. There is a claim that King Jean was held prisoner here en route to Bordeaux. This is not substantiated, although it does seem that the seigneur of Gençay had been captured at the battle. As a consequence it may be that the castle was both undefended and potentially available to the prince.[5]

The going once they were on the move was easy, with gently undulating terrain, but the march included a crossing of the river Clain. This was not a major obstacle by the standards of many of the rivers crossed, but nonetheless it has steep banks with difficult access in many places. The most direct route would have taken the army close to the small village of Anché. There is a ford three miles north of here which could have been used to cross the river, and from here south to Anché the river has wide flat banks which might have allowed crossings in a number of places. A mile north of the village is a spring called La Fontaine des Anglais. According to local tradition this is so named because during the Hundred Years War an English soldier tied his horse to an oak, which can still be seen, and his horse, being thirsty, scratched with his hoof until a spring burst forth which runs to this day. We can do no more than speculate whether or not this story is associated with the events of 1356. Couhé has little to show of its medieval past, but there are some vestiges of the château, forming part of a much later building, which was initially built by Hugues de Lusignan in about 1025.[6] However, unless the town and château had been abandoned, it is likely that the prince and the king lodged outside the walls on the night of 22 September.

On the Friday they moved on to Ruffec, a little to the west of the river Charente. Ruffec was fortified at the time and had a castle with its origins in the tenth century. Although it was to be ceded to Edward III by the Treaty of Brétigny, in 1356 it was still in French hands.[7] The pace slackened a little on the Saturday with a march of fourteen miles to 'Mortoun', with a crossing of the Charente on the way at Verteuil-sur-Charente. Verteuil was well protected with a strong fortress dating from the eleventh century. The châtelain, Aimery de Rochefoucauld, had been killed at the battle, and it is possible that the castle was not garrisoned. Five years later, however, it was held by Peyran du Sault who initially refused to surrender the castle to Sir John Chandos, as he was required to do by the Treaty of Brétigny. Chandos went on to Ruffec and seized Peyran's brother, Bertrand. He imprisoned him for two days and then, having given Peyran time to reflect, returned to Verteuil. Bertrand was forced to kneel in front of the entrance to the castle with an executioner at his side. The message was clear to Peyran: surrender the castle or watch your brother die. He opted for surrender.[8]

Saturday's destination, 'Mourton', has been interpreted as one of two villages about one mile apart, Moutonneau and Mouton.[9] At first sight Moutonneau is more likely in that it appears to have had a castle while Mouton does not.[10] However, to reach Moutonneau the army would have needed to recross the Charente. This is most improbable, and Mourton is more likely to have been Mouton.

On Sunday the prince moved on, once more at a slower pace, covering fourteen miles to La Rochefoucauld. The countryside now was much more open than on previous days, with numerous villages, castles and abbey churches in view. The castle of La Rochefoucauld can be seen from some miles away, dominating the two parts of the town which are separated by the river Tardoire. The prince would have approached the newer part of the town, fortified with walls, six gates and five towers. Beyond was the smaller Basse-Ville, also fortified with walls and joined to the main part by a bridge, above which towered the twelfth-century fortress. It is said that Charles VII was staying at the castle when he received news that on 17 July 1453 his army had defeated an Anglo-Gascon army at Castillon, now known as Castillon-la-Bataille, and, as it was to transpire, bringing the Hundred Years War to a successful conclusion for France.[11] It is possible that the prince entered the town to cross the river Tardoire but it is more likely that the army crossed this minor river elsewhere in the vicinity.

The next day, Monday 26 September, brought the army to Villebois-Lavalette after a long march of twenty-two miles across increasingly undulating terrain. On approaching the town from the north the castle, dating from the eleventh century and on a spur of ground above and a little apart from the town, suddenly comes into view little more than a mile away. We cannot know whether or not King Jean had been here before, but certainly the name would be familiar to him since the castle, which had been in the hands of the Lusignan family since the thirteenth century, had passed to him on the extinction of the family line. Only the year before this visit, on his way to Bordeaux, Jean had exchanged the castle for some property held by the seigneur of Mareuil.[12]

Another long march followed on Tuesday 27 September, twenty-three miles to St-Aulaye across a succession of ridges separated by wide valleys. The *Eulogium* then tells us that on Wednesday they crossed the river Dronne and stayed the night at St-Antoine-sur-l'Isle, a further fifteen miles south and on the north bank of the river Isle. This only makes sense if they stopped for the Tuesday night to the north of St-Aulaye rather than in the town itself, which sits on the southern bank of the river.[13] Thus, before moving on to St-Antoine on Wednesday, since the first bridge at St-Aulaye was not built here until 1836, the Dronne would have been forded in the vicinity of the town.

On the Thursday they crossed the Isle and then stayed close by for the night. This may indicate a difficult crossing since, although this is a relatively minor river, there does not seem to have been a bridge across the Isle in the vicinity of St-Antoine even as late as the eighteenth century.[14] Indeed, even today the bridge is a modest single-track affair. However, an alternative explanation may be that since they were now only thirty miles from Bergerac, where the remainder of the prince's initial army had been left in August for the defence of Aquitaine, the prince and his advisors felt that the danger of pursuit was behind them and that they could now move at a slower pace. The following day, Friday 30 September, they passed through St-Emilion which during Edward III's reign was, at the request of the municipal officers, granted the privilege of remaining attached to the English crown in perpetuity. They stayed overnight near the Dordogne river.[15] Since Libourne is on the east bank of the Dordogne and only five miles beyond St-Emilion this implies that they stopped outside Libourne for the night, having marched nineteen miles since the previous night's bivouac to the south of St-Antoine-sur-l'Isle.

The great adventure was now almost over, and the army crossed the Dordogne on Saturday 1 October. Presumably they did so somewhere in the vicinity of Libourne. As at St-Antoine, the river did not have a bridge and the crossing may have been made at the ford at Vayres to the west of Libourne on the route of the Roman road from Bordeaux to Périgueux.[16] If so, the army would have crossed the Isle once again to the north of Libourne and then forded the Dordogne. Having crossed the river the army made its way towards Bordeaux the following day. The Garonne, which is navigable and more than 500 yards wide near Bordeaux, could not have been forded and those of the army that needed to cross would have had to be ferried over. It is possible that much of the army remained to the east of the river initially and either dispersed from here or made their way further up river to cross at the first available ford.

Meanwhile the prince waited in Libourne for preparations to be made for his and King Jean's reception in the city. Libourne was a relatively new town, founded by Edward I and built by his seneschal Roger de Leyburne around 1270.[17] It was only in 1314 that it had been felt necessary to fortify Libourne, and the work may not have been completed until 1358. Indeed, in May 1356 before his departure on the Poitiers *chevauchee*, to encourage completion of the work and provide financial support for the costs of fortification, the prince had confirmed the privileges of the town and given the magistrates the right for the next thirty years to measure and weigh, and presumably exact taxes upon, merchandise sold retail in the town.[18] Of the dressed stone ramparts, double ditches and nine gates which constituted the defences only the gate once known as Le Grand Portail de la Mer remains, close to the confluence of the Dordogne and the Isle rivers. It is flanked by two towers, one of which, La Tour Richard, commemorates the prince's son and future King Richard II, Richard of Bordeaux. About a fortnight later the prince crossed over the Dordogne and made his way to Bordeaux with King Jean. They were received with great celebrations and the prince and the king were lodged in the abbey of St André.[19] It was now time to turn to thoughts of peace.

PART V

EPILOGUE

15

Aftermath

We, the aforesaid ambassadors, demanded 1,600,000 crowns, of which two shall be worth an English Noble, which ought to have been paid to the aforesaid former King Edward, for the ransom of John, lately his brother of France of excellent memory, which yet remain unpaid.

The final demands of the ambassadors of Henry V before the Agincourt campaign, March 1415.[1]

With the prince back in Bordeaux with his prisoners, and the news having reached London of his momentous victory, attention turned on the diplomatic level to capitalising on the advantageous situation in which King Edward found himself. The French were in disarray, with a crisis of leadership and governance. Both sides had an interest in securing peace: the English to press home their advantage, and the French to restore government, stop the continuing military action of English troops under the duke of Lancaster in Brittany and Normandy, and nullify the threat posed by the English forces in Calais.

The English negotiating team was led by the dean of Chichester, William Lynne, and the constable of Bordeaux, John Stretelee. They acted on behalf of King Edward. Although members of his entourage were involved, the prince took no part in the peace negotiations. The negotiators were in contact with London throughout the winter, but serious negotiations started in early 1357 when the Dauphin Charles had re-established a modicum of control in France.

On 22 March 1357 a truce was signed which would extend until 9 April 1359. The truce made provision for a cessation of hostilities and for the prisoners held by the English to go to England. King Edward had already put arrangements in hand for the return of the prince with his prisoners, and on the Tuesday after Easter, 11 April 1357, the prince set sail from Bordeaux for Plymouth. According to Froissart and Jean le Bel the departure caused some consternation on the part of the Gascon magnates who are said to have felt uneasy that, since they had played such a large part in the capture of the king, they should see him leave for England. Froissart says that the prince had to pay 100,000 florins (£14,160) to put the Gascons' minds at ease, but there is no other evidence to support this contention.[2] The prince and King Jean landed at Plymouth on 5 May, which brings us full circle to the start of Chapter 1. However, it is by no means the end of the story.

On the diplomatic front, negotiations now turned to securing a permanent peace. In June the cardinal of Périgord, who had been involved in the negotiations in Bordeaux, and the cardinal of San Vitale arrived in England to join the renewed discussions. These dragged on until eventually, in May 1358 at Windsor, King Jean ratified the peace treaty known as the First Treaty of London. The terms of the treaty set the ransom for King Jean at the enormous sum of four million gold *écus* (£568,000), of which the first instalment of 600,000 was to be paid before his release. Edward agreed to drop his claim to the French crown in return for the transfer to the English crown of great swathes of France in full sovereignty. The territories to be ceded, which by one estimate amounted to as much of one third of France, comprised: Aquitaine, Saintonge, Poitou, Angoumois, Périgord, Agenais, Limousin, Rouergue, Quercy, Bigorre and Gaure in the south and west and Calais, Guînes and the county of Ponthieu in the north. The first payment of the ransom was due by November 1358, but despite strenuous efforts on the part of King Jean the money could not be raised.

With the expiry of the truce of Bordeaux fast approaching, Edward increased the pressure. In December arrangements were made for Jean to be moved from the comfort of the Savoy Palace to the more austere Somerton castle in Lincolnshire. This transfer was put in abeyance until July 1359, but nevertheless Jean was now held in the Savoy without the freedom of movement that he had enjoyed hitherto. On 18 March 1359 it was agreed to extend the truce of Bordeaux until 24 June 1359. Jean was presented with a revised treaty, the terms of which were much more severe than those of the preceding year, known as the Second Treaty of London. He signed the draft on 24 March, a treaty which the French historian R. Delachenal understandably termed 'disastrous'. In addition to the territories in the earlier treaty, Jean now agreed to cede Touraine, Maine, Anjou and Normandy. In effect, the Angevin empire of Henry II would be restored and the west of France would pass to the English crown. In addition the English king would have sovereignty over Brittany. As for the ransom, the sum was reduced to three million *écus*, but with a bond of a further million which would be forfeit if payment was not made by 24 June 1360. A first payment of 600,000 *écus* was due on 1 August 1359.[3] The Estates General were summoned to consider the treaty. They met on 25 May 1359. They judged that the terms were displeasing to all the people of France, and that they were neither feasible nor acceptable. They advised the regent, the Dauphin Charles, to make war on England.

The renewal of the war was now inevitable, and in 1359 King Edward mustered the largest army that ever went to France during his reign.[4] It was 12,000 strong and organised in three divisions led by the king, the prince and the duke of Lancaster. By early November the army had crossed the Channel to Calais. The objective was clear. The king would go to Reims and be crowned and anointed as king of France.

When the army approached Reims it became apparent that the English were not going to be welcomed with open arms, and that the fortifications and defence of the city had been well prepared and the storehouses well stocked. In mid-

December the English army started a blockade. Early in the siege an attempt was made to take the city by storm, but the attack was repulsed and not repeated. By early January a shortage of supplies for Edward's army was causing concern, and on 11 January the king had no alternative but to lift the siege. He departed towards Burgundy, and then swept round to the north-west to approach Paris. During this period he hoped to entice the French to face him in battle, but the dauphin was too smart to fall into this trap again. On 7 April the army drew near to Paris, and until 12 April ravaged the suburbs in the hope of drawing the French out. This was to no avail and, since there was no prospect of Edward sustaining an effective siege of Paris and supplies were running short, the army set out for Chartres on Monday 13 April. Disaster then struck. After weeks of warm weather a great thunderstorm storm broke, bringing high winds and driving rain which turned to sleet and hail with the temperature dropping below freezing. On this day, which became known as Black Monday, men and horses died of exposure, others were killed by the effects of the storm, and much of the baggage sank into mud and was abandoned. Rogers argues that, although his military position was by no means desperate, Edward interpreted these events as a sign from God that it was time to settle, and he decided to resume negotiations for peace.[5]

These talks started in the village of Brétigny on 1 May 1360. With so much groundwork done before, terms were rapidly agreed and sealed on 8 May. The terms of the Treaty of Brétigny were essentially those of the First Treaty of London agreed between Edward and Jean almost exactly two years before. Edward was to hold in full sovereignty all the provinces in the south-west which his ancestors had held. He was also to hold the county of Ponthieu, Montreuil and Calais. The ransom for King Jean was reduced to three million écus, £426,000, and was to be paid in six annual instalments. Jean was to renounce the territories by 29 September and in exchange Edward would renounce his claim to the throne of France. Since the additional claims of the Second Treaty of London had been abandoned, the reversion to the previous terms has been portrayed by some historians as a defeat for Edward. However, Clifford Rogers argues that it was only the renewal of war which finally brought the French to the point of signing the treaty, the terms of which still remained a triumph for King Edward. He also suggests that the willingness of Edward to accept these terms reflects his belief that it was God's will that it was time to settle, and not a result of a weak military position. Indeed, despite the English setbacks of the 1359–60 campaign, France was in a parlous state and needed a settlement.[6] The English returned to England, and Jean started to raise the first instalment of his ransom. This proved far from easy, and by the time Edward arrived in Calais in October for what should have been the formal ratification of the treaty, only two thirds of the first instalment had been raised. In addition, the detailed negotiations for the mutual renunciations were proving difficult. It was decided to make these renunciations the subject of a side-agreement and they were removed from the main treaty, which was signed in the Church of St Nicolas in Calais on the 24 October 1360.[7]

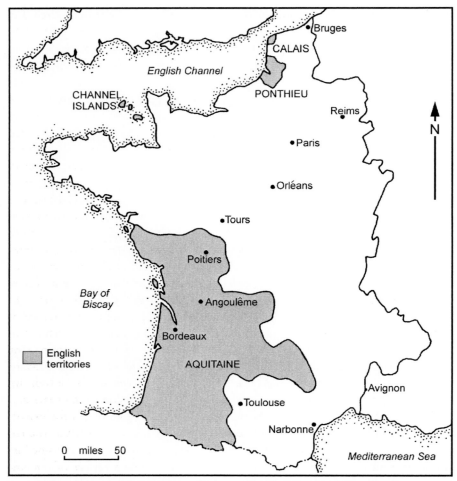

Map 31 English territories in France after the Treaty of Brétigny, 1360.

The separation of the renunciations from the main treaty would in due course prove fatal to both peace and English hopes in France. However, in the meantime Jean was now a free man once again and work started on the implementation of the treaty. Neither the transfer of territories nor the raising of the ransom proved straightforward. After the conclusion of the treaty Warwick had been left to see to its observance on behalf of the king, and not the least of his problems was prising English troops out of strongholds that they had seized. In August 1361 Sir John Chandos began the process of transferring ceded French territories into allegiance to Edward. This was largely completed by February 1362, although some disputes lingered on. In January 1364 Jean travelled to England and was reinstalled in the Savoy Palace. He seems to have hoped to be able to resolve the outstanding territorial matters and the arrears on his ransom. Agreement may have been reached but fate intervened and Jean was taken ill in early March. He died in London on 8 April 1364. The dauphin took the crown as King Charles V.

Charles had sworn to abide by the treaties but he had room for manoeuvre in that the renunciations had not been made. In 1368 a dispute over taxation between the count of Armagnac and the prince, who since 1363 had been prince of Aquitaine, over taxation was referred by Armagnac to King Charles. If Charles were to accept the appeal he would be in clear breach of the Treaty of Brétigny in that sovereignty had been ceded to Edward. Charles would have been well aware of the consequences, but in November or December he issued a summons for the prince to appear before Parlement in Paris on 2 May 1369. In early 1369 Charles sent ambassadors to London purportedly to resolve outstanding disputes associated with the treaty. However, this was purely window dressing. When the prince failed to appear before Parlement the result was a *de facto* return to war.

By June both sides were again actively pursuing the war. By now the prince was bedridden as a result of an illness contracted in the Nájera campaign of 1367, and he left Aquitaine for England around the end of 1370, never to return. All chances of implementation of the Treaty of Brétigny were now gone, and over the coming years the gains that the English had made were steadily eroded.[8] Scenes of the prince's earlier *chevauchées* were now exemplars of the change of fortune: English troops were cornered and virtually wiped out in Lesterps in the spring of 1370, and Bazas was captured by the French in February of that year. In October 1372, when the prince formally relinquished the principality, it had shrunk to less than one fifth of the area it had been when he took up the reins as prince of Aquitaine. The prince was now in his declining years and he died on Trinity Sunday, 8 June 1376, just one week short of his forty-sixth birthday. Whether or not he knew at this stage of further losses such as the fall of Brantôme in April we do not know. His death was commemorated not just in England but also in France, where King Charles V held a service of remembrance in the Sainte Chapelle in Paris in the presence of many prelates, barons and knights. King Edward followed the prince the next year leaving the prince's son, the ten-year-old Richard of Bordeaux, to become king as Richard II.[9] Now all of the prince's close associates except Salisbury were dead, and all the gains had been lost.

It would be two generations later before the English once again made significant inroads into France, and the epigraph at the head of this chapter illustrates how the unfulfilled Treaty of Brétigny still remained at the heart of matters when Henry V came to the throne. Following his victory at Agincourt in 1415 Henry made huge gains for England once again, and indeed his claim to the crown of France was accepted. He was to die before he could accede to the throne, and as the fifteenth century progressed English gains were eroded once again until in 1453 the English were expelled from France, save for Calais which they held for another century. Crécy, Poitiers and Agincourt trip off the tongue as famous English victories, but how many know of the Battle of Castillon, fought in 1453? At Castillon the English were soundly trounced. In the end it is the final battle of a war that counts; after Castillon the Hundred Years War was over and, although the English royal arms would be quartered with those of France until George III renounced the claim to the crown of France in 1801, English monarchs would never again hold wide swathes of territory in France. With the benefit of hindsight we can see that England could never have sustained its position in France, but in 1356 the prince had presented Edward III with the best opportunity he was to have to achieve his aims, only for the king to see it all turn to dust by his death in 1377.

Appendix 1

Summary Itinerary for Prince's Division, 1355

The distances below are approximations of the minimum distances covered along the likely axis of advance of the prince's division. The distances travelled by some elements would often have been greater.

Monday 5 October	Bordeaux to Villenave-d'Ornon	4 miles
Tuesday 6 October	Villenave-d'Ornon to Castets-en-Dorthe	28 miles
Wednesday 7 October	Halt	
Thursday 8 October	Castets-en-Dorthe to Bazas	11 miles
Friday 9 October	Halt	
Saturday 10 October	Bazas to Castelnau	13 miles
Sunday 11 October	Castelnau to Arouille	25 miles
Monday 12 October	Halt	
Tuesday 13 October	Arouille to Monclar	8 miles
Wednesday 14 October	Halt	
Thursday 15 October	Halt	
Friday 16 October	Monclar to Nogaro	14 miles
Saturday 17 October	Nogaro to Plaisance	13 miles
Sunday 18 October	Halt	
Monday 19 October	Plaisance to Bassoues	12 miles
Tuesday 20 October	Halt	
Wednesday 21 October	Bassoues to Mirande	11 miles
Thursday 22 October	Halt	
Friday 23 October	Mirande to Seissan	11 miles
Saturday 24 October	Seissan to Simorre	10 miles
Sunday 25 October	Simorre to Samatan	12 miles
Monday 26 October	Samatan to St-Lys	14 miles
Tuesday 27 October	Halt	
Wednesday 28 October	St-Lys to Lacroix-Falgarde	14 miles
Thursday 29 October	Lacroix-Falgarde to Montgiscard	12 miles
Friday 30 October	Montgiscard to Avignonet	14 miles
Saturday 31 October	Avignonet to Castelnaudary	9 miles
Sunday 1 November	Halt	
Monday 2 November	Castelnaudary to Alzau	15 miles
Tuesday 3 November	Alzau to Carcassonne	9 miles

Wednesday 4 November	Halt	
Thursday 5 November	Halt	
Friday 6 November	Carcassonne to Rustiques	10 miles
Saturday 7 November	Rustiques to Canet	21 miles
Sunday 8 November	Canet to Narbonne	10 miles
Monday 9 November	Halt	
Tuesday 10 November	Narbonne to Aubian	9 miles
Wednesday 11 November	Aubian to vicinity of Homps	12 miles
Thursday 12 November	Vicinity of Homps to Azille	10 miles
Friday 13 November	Azille to Villemagne	20 miles
Saturday 14 November	Villemagne to Pennautier	23 miles
Sunday 15 November	Pennautier to Prouille	16 miles
Monday 16 November	Prouille to Belpech	17 miles
Tuesday 17 November	Belpech to Miremont	25 miles
Wednesday 18 November	Miremont to Carbonne	14 miles
Thursday 19 November	Halt	
Friday 20 November	Carbonne to Mauvezin	19 miles
Saturday 21 November	Mauvezin to Auradé	19 miles
Sunday 22 November	Auradé to Aurimont	20 miles[1]
Monday 23 November	Halt	
Tuesday 24 November	Aurimont to Montaut-les-Crénaux[2]	14 miles
Wednesday 25 November	Montaut-les-Crénaux to Réjaumont	12 miles
Thursday 26 November	Halt	
Friday 27 November	Réjaumont to Lagardère	15 miles
Saturday 28 November	Lagardère to Mézin	18 miles
Sunday 29 November	Halt	
Monday 30 November	Mézin to Casteljaloux	22 miles
Tuesday 1 December	Casteljaloux to Meilhan-sur-Garonne	15 miles
Wednesday 2 December	Meilhan-sur-Garonne to La Réole	6 miles

The *chevauchée* covered 606 miles in fifty-nine days, averaging a little over ten miles per day. On those days on which the army was on the move the average rate of movement was about fourteen and a half miles per day.

Appendix 2

Summary Itinerary for Prince's Division, 1356

The distances below are approximations of the minimum distances covered along the likely axis of advance of the prince's division. The distances travelled by some elements would often have been greater.

Thursday 4 August	Depart Bergerac	⎫
Saturday 6 August	Enter Perigord	⎬ 30 miles
Sunday 7 August	Arrive Périgueux	⎭
Monday 8 August	Périgueux to Ramefort	13 miles
Tuesday 9 August	Ramefort to Brantôme	3 miles
Wednesday 10 August	Brantôme to Quinsac	7 miles
Thursday 11 August	Quinsac to Nontron	9 miles
Friday 12 August	Nontron to Rochechouart	25 miles
Saturday 13 August	Rochechouart to La Péruse	12 miles
Sunday 14 August	La Péruse to Lesterps	14 miles
Monday 15 August	Halt	
Tuesday 16 August	Lesterps to Bellac	18 miles
Wednesday 17 August	Bellac to Le Dorat	7 miles
Thursday 18 August	Halt	
Friday 19 August	Le Dorat to Lussac-les-Eglises	12 miles
Saturday 20 August	Lussac-les-Eglises to St-Benoît-du-Sault	16 miles
Sunday 21 August	St-Benoît-du-Sault to Argenton-sur-Creuse	14 miles
Monday 22 August	Halt	
Tuesday 23 August	Argenton-sur-Creuse to Châteauroux	20 miles
Wednesday 24 August	Halt	
Thursday 25 August	Châteauroux to Issoudun	20 miles
Friday 26 August	Halt	
Saturday 27 August	Halt	
Sunday 28 August	Issoudun to Vierzon	20 miles
Monday 29 August	Vierzon to Villefranche-sur-Cher	15 miles
Tuesday 30 August	Villefranche-sur-Cher to Romorantin	5 miles
Wednesday 31 August	Halt	
Thursday 1 September	Halt	
Friday 2 September	Halt	
Saturday 3 September	Halt	

Sunday 4 September	Halt	
Monday 5 September	Romorantin to St-Aignan[1]	20 miles
Tuesday 6 September	St-Aignan to Montrichard[2]	12 miles
Wednesday 7 September	Montrichard to Montlouis-sur-Loire	18 miles
Thursday 8 September	Halt	
Friday 9 September	Halt	
Saturday 10 September	Halt	
Sunday 11 September	Montlouis-sur-Loire to Montbazon	12 miles
Monday 12 September	Halt	
Tuesday 13 September	Montbazon to La Haye (Descartes)	25 miles
Wednesday 14 September	La Haye to Châtellerault	15 miles
Thursday 15 September	Halt	
Friday 16 September	Halt	
Saturday 17 September	Châtellerault to the vicinity of Savigny-Lévescault	23 miles
Sunday 18 September	Deploy to battlefield, Nouaillé-Maupertuis	5 miles
Monday 19 September	Halt – Battle of Poitiers	
Tuesday 20 September	Battlefield to Roches-Prémarie- Andillé	3 miles
Wednesday 21 September	Halt	
Thursday 22 September	Roches-Prémarie-Andillé to Couhé	20 miles
Friday 23 September	Couhé to Ruffec	20 miles
Saturday 24 September	Ruffec to Mouton	14 miles
Sunday 25 September	Mouton to La Rochefoucauld	14 miles
Monday 26 September	La Rochefoucauld to Villebois-Lavalettte	22 miles
Tuesday 27 September	Villebois-Lavalette to St-Aulaye	23 miles
Wednesday 28 September	St-Aulaye to St-Antoine-sur-l'Isle	14 miles
Thursday 29 September	Crossing of river Isle	1 mile
Friday 30 September	Near Libourne and river Dordogne	19 miles
Saturday 1 October	Crossing of river Dordogne	1 mile
Sunday 2 October	To Bordeaux	20 miles

The *chevauchée* covered 561 miles in sixty days, averaging a little over nine miles per day. On those days on which the army was on the move the average rate of movement was just less than fourteen miles per day.

Notes

Introduction

1. *WCS*, p. 314.
2. See Clifford J. Rogers, 'By Fire and Sword: *Bellum Hostile* and "Civilians" in the Hundred Years War', pp. 36–9, in *Civilians in the Path of War*, ed. Mark Grimsley and Clifford J. Rogers, for a detailed description of the scope and method of the *chevauchée*. The quotation by Professor Rogers describing the progress of the army was given to me in response to a question posed to him during my research.
3. *WCS*, p. 310.
4. Baker, pp. 127–39, 292–7. See also *Life and Campaigns*, pp. 61–70, for a translation from the Latin of the passage on the 1355 *chevauchée*. *Eulogium*, pp. 215–26.
5. Baker, pp. v–vi, 293.
6. *Eulogium Historiarum*, ed. F. S. Haydon, vol. 1, pp. iii–v; vol. 3, pp. xxx–xxxvi.
7. There is a more detailed but concise explanation of currency in the period in Jonathan Sumption's *Trial by Fire, The Hundred Years War*, vol. 2, pp. 592–3, and tabular values can be found in Pierre-Clément Timbal *et al.*, *La Guerre de Cent Ans vue à travers les registres du Parlement (1337–1369)*, pp. 503–4.
8. H. J. Hewitt, *The Organisation of War Under Edward III*, pp. 33–4, 36, 52.

Chapter 1

1. Robert of Avesbury, in *English Historical Documents*, vol. 4, 1327–1485, p. 66.
2. *BPR*, vol. 4, p. 253.
3. David Green, *The Battle of Poitiers, 1356*, p. 73.
4. Sumption, *Trial by Fire*, pp. 280–90.
5. Marilyn Livingstone and Morgen Witzel, *The Road to Crécy, The English Invasion of France, 1346*, p. 6.
6. Malcolm Vale, *The Origins of the Hundred Years War, The Angevin Legacy, 1250–1340*, pp. 15, 53–7.
7. See Craig Taylor, 'Edward III and the Plantagenet Claim to the French Throne', in *The Age of Edward III*, ed. J. S. Bothwell, pp. 155–69 for discussion of Edward III's claim and Jonathan Sumption, *Trial by Battle, The Hundred Years War*, vol. 1, pp. 103–11, 116–22 for a description of events surrounding the succession to the French crown on the death of Charles IV.
8. Chandos ll. 3916–20.
9. For events surrounding Robert of Artois, see Sumption, *Trial by Battle*, pp. 170–2 and 184, and Vale, *The Origins of the Hundred Years War*, pp. 259–60.
10. *English Historical Documents*, vol. 4, 1327–1485 – Statutes of the Realm, I, 292, p. 70.
11. For a detailed description of events in the war up until the autumn of 1355, see Sumption, *Trial by Battle*, pp. 152–586, and *Trial by Fire*, pp. 1–102. For a thorough

analysis of the Crécy *chevauchée* and battle see Andrew Ayton and Philip Preston, *The Battle of Crécy 1346*.

12. David Green, *The Black Prince*, p. 53, and *WCS*, p. 293–4.

13. *BPR*, vol. 4, pp. 143–4.

14. For biographical notes on many of the participants in the *chevauchées* and the Battle of Poitiers, see David Green, *The Battle of Poitiers*, Appendix 2, pp. 95–128.

15. *BPE*, pp. 20–1.

16. Craig Lambert, 'Taking the War to Scotland and France: The Supply and Transportation of English Armies by Sea', p. 234.

17. *BPR*, vol. 3, p. 204.

18. *BPR*, vol. 3, p. 493.

19. *BPR*, vol. 3, pp. 145, 153, 156–68.

20. Lambert, 'Taking the War to Scotland and France', p. 235.

21. Pierre-J. Capra, 'Le séjour du Prince Noir, lieutenant du roi, à l'archevêché de Bordeaux', in *Revue Historique de Bordeaux et de la Gironde*, vol. 8, no. 4, pp. 241–52 for residence of the prince in Bordeaux.

22. Robin Neillands, *The Hundred Years War*, p. 120, and Sumption, *Trial by Fire*, pp. 168–9.

23. *WCS*, p. 293, n. 38.

Chapter 2

1. *The Pilgrim's Guide: A 12th Century Guide for the Pilgrim to St James of Compostella*, trans. James Hogarth. The work is commonly attributed to Aimery de Picaud, a cleric from Poitou.

2. A. H. Burne, *The Crécy War*, p. 251.

3. Yves Renouard, *Bordeaux sous les rois d'Angleterre*, vol. 2, p. 369.

4. Henxteworth, pp. 5–7, and 10–12. See David Green, *Edward the Black Prince, Power in Medieval Europe*, p. 131 for the role of Henxteworth.

5. J. M. Tourneur-Aumont, *La Bataille de Poitiers (1356) et la construction de la France*, p. 31.

6. The Musée d'Aquitaine in Bordeaux records a population in the fourteenth century of around 30,000 living in an area of 170 hectares. Malcolm Vale quotes the same figure in *The Origins of the Hundred Years War*, p. 144. For population figures for London in the fourteenth century see George Unwin, ed., *Finance and Trade under Edward III*, p. 43.

7. Baker, p. 129, *WCS*, p. 305, n. 103, and Sumption, *Trial by Fire*, pp. 175–6.

8. Micheline Dupuy, *Le Prince Noir, Edouard, Seigneur d'Aquitaine*, pp. 127–8.

9. *English Historical Documents*, vol. 4, item 294, pp. 483–4.

10. Anne Curry, *Agincourt: A New History*, p. 73, cites the example of the earl of Oxford's retinue: a list for the return shipping indicates that almost all men-at-arms were accompanied by a servant. However, she does point out that possibly this was not the case in the retinues of lesser captains.

11. See Yuval Noah Harari 'Strategy and Supply in Fourteenth-Century Western European Campaigns', *Journal of Military History*, vol. 64, April 2000, pp. 301–2, for an analysis of the size of non-combatant elements for fourteenth-century armies.

12. Andrew Ayton, *Knights and Warhorses: Military Service and the English Aristocracy under Edward III*, p. 58, gives an example from 1340 of transportation allowances of five horses for bannerets, four for knights, three for esquires and one for mounted archers. H. J. Hewitt, *The Horse in Mediaeval England*, pp. 42–3, cites the case of Sir John Chandos' retinue returning from France in 1363 having allowances of four horses for knights, three for esquires and two for men-at-arms.

13. Lambert, 'Taking the War to Scotland and France', p. 236.

14. Timbal *et al.*, *La Guerre de Cent Ans*, p. 73.

15. See Harari, 'Strategy and Supply', pp. 297–334, for an analysis of baggage trains and transport for fourteenth-century armies.

16. Peter Spufford, *Power and Profit: The Merchant in Medieval Europe*, p. 199, describes the load-carrying capacity of pack animals and carts. A pack-horse was expected to carry 400 pounds, a two-wheeled cart drawn by three or four horses between 1,200 and 1,600 pounds, and a four-wheeled cart drawn by six horses up to 3,300 pounds.

17. Burne, *The Crécy War*, p. 252 for the prince taking bridges in 1355. Livingstone and Witzel, *The Road to Crécy*, pp. 132, 143, and 214, and Ayton and Preston, *The Battle of Crécy, 1346*, pp. 38–9, and nn. 12–16 for repair of bridges on the Crécy campaign.

18. Ayton and Preston, *The Battle of Crécy, 1346*, p. 360.

19. Sumption, *Trial by Fire*, p. 185, cites reports of 1,000 carts full of booty.

20. Baker, p. 128.

21. Jean-Marc Soyez, *Quand les anglais vendangeaient l'Aquitaine*, p. 245: 'Si la citée de Bordeaus est une des grosses citiez et bien peuplée de ce royaume elle le doit à l'isle d'Angleterre … les dits anglois apportent de l'or et de l'argent qu'ils convertissent en vins de Gascogne.'

22. *Hugh Johnson's Story of Wine*, pp. 138–49 for an account of viticulture in Gascony in the Middle Ages.

23. Soyez, *Quand les anglais vendangeaient l'Aquitaine*, p. 139.

24. Hewitt, *The Horse in Mediaeval England*, pp. 38 and 59.

25. Léo Drouyn, *La Guyenne militaire*, pp. 270–6.

26. Henxteworth, p. 16.

27. Sumption, *Trial by Fire*, pp. 79 and 550; for events in Bazas in 1345–52, see Kenneth Fowler, *The King's Lieutenant, Henry of Grosmont, First Duke of Lancaster, 1310–1361*, pp. 64–5, and 67.

28. Matthew Strickland and Robert Hardy, *The Great War Bow*, p. 201.

29. Jacques Sargos, *Histoire de la Forêt Landaise, du désert à l'age d'or*, pp. 39 *et seq.* describes the Landes in the period before the reclamation of the nineteenth century.

30. *The Pilgrims' Guide*, p. 18.

31. Denifle, vol. 2–1, p. 87 n. 5.

32. Baker, p. 128; *Life and Campaigns*, p. 61.

33. Drouyn, *La Guyenne militaire*, pp. 285–90; Jacques Gardelles, *Les châteaux du Moyen Age dans la France du sud-ouest – La Gascogne anglaise de 1216 à 1327*, p. 117.

34. Henxteworth, p. 17.

35. Baker, p. 129; *Life and Campaigns*, p. 61.

36. Baker, pp. 128–9; *Life and Campaigns*, pp. 61–2.

Chapter 3

1. Avesbury, p. 437.
2. A. Breuils, 'Jean Ier, Comte d'Armagnac et le mouvement national dans le Midi, au temps du Prince Noir', *Revue des Questions Historiques*, vol. 15, no. 59, p. 55, n. 3, for Vielle-Soubiran.
3. James Bentley, *Fort Towns of France*, pp. 12–14; Vale, *The Origins of the Hundred Years War*, pp. 118 and 152–60; D. Brissaud, *Les anglais en Guyenne*, pp. 264–6; Gardelles, *Les châteaux du Moyen Age*, p. 86.
4. WCS, p. 307.
5. Map 1 in Vale's *The Origins of the Hundred Years War* shows a place with the name of Juliac but does not clarify whether this is a town or a castle.
6. WCS, p. 307, n. 108.
7. *Cassini*, CD-ROM France Sud, sheet 106.
8. Maurice Romieu, *Histoire de la vicomté de Juliac*, pp. 459–71.
9. Baker, p. 129.
10. Breuils, 'Jean Ier, Comte d'Armagnac', p. 55, n. 3, lists a number of places, some of which do not feature in other sources, as receiving the attention of the army, including Gabarret and Roquefort. His complete list of places cited is: Arouille; Graulas or Graulous, the church at Herré, the church of St-Rémy, all near Gabarret; the château of Beroy-de-Juliac in Betbèze, Geu, Ste-Aigne, Mauvezin, Mau, Pouy, Bréchan, all near Labastide-d'Armagnac; Bergonce, and Perquic, near Roquefort; Estang; Panjas; Beyries near Estang; Gontaud near St-Justin-de-Marsan; Saumon, near Mauvezin; Mau near Le Houga.
11. Baker, p. 129.
12. *Oeuvres*, vol. 18, p. 368. 'Et mounseir n'ad en tout ceste viage pardu nul chivaler, ne esquire, sinoun mounseir Johan de Lisle qui fust tués mult merveilousment d'un quarrel le tierce jour que nous entrasmes en les terres de nos enemys, et mourrust le XVe jour octobre.'
13. Green, *The Battle of Poitiers, 1356*, p. 32.
14. Breuils, 'Jean Ier, Comte d'Armagnac', p. 55 n. 3.
15. The details on the village and castle of Panjas are drawn from notes produced locally for tourists. See Green, *The Black Prince*, p. 11 for reference to the apparent portrayal of the Black Prince as one of the Riders of the Apocalypse.
16. Baker, pp. 130, 293–4, states clearly that the army rested for two days and then camped outside the town on 16 October. He makes no mention of any attempt to take the town. Two French secondary sources refer to three days of assaults on the town, J. Moisant, *Le Prince Noir en Aquitaine*, p. 34, and S. Dejean, 'L'incursion du Prince Noir en Agenais et en Toulousain (1355)'.
17. WCS, pp. 307–8.
18. Livingstone and Witzel, *The Road to Crécy*, p. 233.
19. The museum of La Tour de Termes-d'Armagnac publishes a brochure which is contradictory in that it states that the tower was built towards the end of the thirteenth or beginning of the fourteenth century but then attributes its construction to the father of Thibault d'Armagnac Termes who was not born until 1405. Jean Henri Ducos and Jacques Gardelles, *Le guide des châteaux de France, 32, Gers*, p. 150 refer to a first record for the castle in 1317 and judge the architectural style to be contemporary with that date.
20. Baker, p. 130.

21. There are frequent references to Adam de Louches as the Prince's bachelor in *BPR*, vol. 4. See David Green, 'Military Personnel of Edward the Black Prince', *Mediaeval Prosopography*, vol. 21, 2000, p. 152, concerning Adam de Louches; p. 138 on the title bachelor denoting special status within the household.

22. Denifle, vol. 2–1, p. 88.

23. Jean-Justin Monlezun, *Histoire de la Gascogne depuis les temps les plus reculés jusqu'à nos jours*, vol. 3, p. 319.

24. The information relating to Plaisance is drawn from a monograph by the local historian Alain Lagors, *Les étapes de l'evolution de Plaisance au Moyen Age*, and from correspondence with Monsieur Lagors.

25. Monsieur Lagors cites *Glanages ou preuves*, J.-B. Larcher, vol. 6, pp. 235–48, for information concerning the destruction of Plaisance and the Abbey of Case-Dieu.

26. Baker, p. 130.

27. Michael Prestwich, *Armies and Warfare in the Middle Ages: The English Experience*, pp. 13–15, and Maurice Keen, *Chivalry*, p. 168 for an explanation of the rank of banneret and its evolving status during the fourteenth and fifteenth centuries. See Baker, p. 130, and *Life and Campaigns*, p. 62 for Sir Richard Stafford's promotion; Green, 'Military Personnel of Edward the Black Prince', pp. 147 and 152 concerning Sir Richard Stafford.

28. Richard Barber, *Edward, Prince of Wales and Aquitaine: A Biography of the Black Prince*, p. 171.

29. Baker, p. 130.

30. Baker, p. 130. The details on Mirande come from a local publication prepared for the tourist office, *Mirande, Histoire d'une bastide gasconne: Parcours historique*.

Chapter 4

1. B. H. Liddell Hart, *Strategy: The Indirect Approach*, p. 12.

2. Baker, p. 130; *Life and Campaigns*, p. 63.

3. *Life and Campaigns*, p. 63, states that the rearguard lodged at the monastery, the middle guard at Villefranche and the rearguard again at Tournan, and *BPE*, p. 54, has the vanguard at Tournan, the main body at Simorre, and the rearguard at Villefranche. However, Baker, pp. 130–1, records that the rearguard was at Simorre, the middle guard at Villefranche, and the vanguard at Tournan.

4. The information on Simorre is drawn from tourist guides entitled *Si ... Simorre m'était conté – Circuit touristique*, and *L'église abbatiale de Simorre* distributed by the tourist office. There is no obvious reason why Simorre, Villefranche and Tournan should have escaped destruction, other than perhaps the presence of the Dominican abbey at Simorre, but Clifford Rogers, *WCS*, p. 308, makes the only reference that I can find to the destruction of these villages.

5. Baker, p. 131 writes: 'Dominica quarta, die sanctorum Crispini et Crispiniani, transierunt quoddam vadum in terras comitis de Comenge, que extendebantur usque Tolosam; set fuerunt ignibus et gladio depaste.' Richard Barber, *Life and Campaigns*, p. 63, translates this as: 'On the fourth Sunday, St Crispin and Crispinian's day, they crossed a ford in the lands of the count of Comminges, which reached as far as Toulouse; but they had been laid waste by fire and sword.' M. L. de Santi, 'L'expédition du Prince Noir en 1355 d'après le journal d'un de ses Compagnons', *Mémoires de l'Académie des sciences, inscriptions, et belles-lettres de Toulouse*, Series 10, vol. 5, pp. 19–20, interprets this

as the army fording the Save and translates the final clause differently: 'they [the lands of the Count of Comminges] were ravaged by sword and fire' (*Elles furent ravagées par le fer et par la flamme*). This translation, although perhaps less faithful to the Latin is more logical in that it implies that it is the prince's army which was responsible for the ravaging. However, de Santi's supposition that the Save was crossed at this stage does not make sense. *BPE*, p. 55, also considers that they forded the Save en route to Samatan.

6. In his translation of Baker, p. 131, Richard Barber, *Life and Campaigns*, p. 63, states that Pope John XXII was ordained bishop in Lombez. De Santi, 'L'expédition du Prince Noir en 1355', p. 20, in his translation into French, states that Pope John XXII 'avait créé un siège Episcopal' at Lombez. John XXII was first appointed to a bishopric at Fréjus in 1300 and became pope in 1316, creating the diocese of Lombez the following year.

7. Tourneur-Aumont, *La Bataille de Poitiers*, p. 48.

8. Baker, p. 131.

9. Avesbury, pp. 437 and 443.

10. The town website, www.samatan-porte-du-gers.com, states: 'La population épouvantée et dispersée à l'approche du plus terrible des ennemis de la France, qui ne laissait derrière lui que ruines, sang et cendres alla s'établir en grande partie à Lombez.'

11. The destruction of Samatan and the monastery is recorded in Baker, p. 131. See Henxteworth, p. 18, for the payments to the Minorite friars and the groom.

12. See Jean Contrasty, *Histoire de Sainte-Foy-de-Peyrolières, Ancien Prieuré du Moyen-Age et de la Renaissance uni en 1606 au Collège de Toulouse*, p. 131 for Salvetat.

13. See Avesbury, p. 443 for Wingfield's letter and the breaking of the bridges.

14. Jean-Luc Pinol, ed., *Atlas historique des villes de France*, pp. 234–5.

15. See Le Bel, p. 220 for the strength of the French army. Barber, *Edward, Prince of Wales and Aquitaine*, p. 121, describes the army as being only a small royal force under the marshal and the constable together with Armagnac's own mercenaries and untrained local militia.

16. *WCS*, p. 309.

17. Sumption, *Trial by Battle*, p. 1 gives a population for Paris of more than 100,000 in 1328, and Vale, *The Origins of the Hundred Years War*, p. 144 quotes a population of 34,000 for Toulouse in 1335. Even allowing for a major asymmetry in the impact of the Black Death in 1348, Toulouse was not another Paris.

18. Sumption, *Trial by Battle*, pp. 535 and 578.

19. See Sumption, *Trial by Battle*, pp. 58–60 for Lancaster's 1349 *chevauchée*. Baker, p. 132, recounts how the inhabitants east of the rivers felt themselves secure.

20. Quoted in Charles M. Westenhoff, *Military Air Power: The CADRE Digest of Air Power Opinions and Thoughts*, p. 78.

21. Baker, p. 131; Avesbury, p. 437; *Oeuvres*, vol. 5, pp. 339 (first account) and 344–5 (second account).

22. *BPE*, pp. 55–7 and *WCS*, pp. 308–11 with related footnotes for Hewitt's and Rogers' interpretation of events around Toulouse.

23. Breuils, 'Jean Ier, Comte d'Armagnac', p. 57.

24. Avesbury, pp. 437, 443 for Sir John Wingfield and the discovery of the ford. Baker, p. 131. Baker refers to the Geronde, translated by Richard Barber, *Life and Campaigns*, p. 63, as the Gironde. Baker was mistaken. This could only have been the Garonne.

25. Avesbury, pp. 437, 443.

26. Hewitt, *BPE*, p. 56, believes that the crossing was probably made 'between Rogues [*sic*] and Pinsaguel, a little above the confluence', and Rogers, *WCS*, p. 310 and n. 127 takes a similar view.

27. *Oeuvres*, vol. 5, p. 344: 'car elle estoit durement basse, et lisaison belle et sèche'.

28. The *Livret d'accueil de Pinsaguel*, published locally, gives the progressive deformation of the Old French form *Passage à Guet* as one of two possible origins of the name of Pinsaguel.

29. *Cassini*, CD-ROM, France Sud, sheet 38.

30. Baker, p. 131.

31. *BPE*, p. 56; *WCS*, p. 310.

32. See Livingstone and Witzel, *The Road to Crécy*, pp. 90–1, for discussion of the diet of the medieval English soldier. Ayton, *The Battle of Crécy 1346*, p. 101, states the daily need for water for horses. See Harari's 'Strategy and Supply' for a detailed discussion of the nutritional needs of men and horses and the calculation of the means for their provision, and pp. 302–10 for the figures quoted.

33. B. H. Liddell Hart, *Thoughts on War*, p. 218.

34. Baker, p. 131. The modern village of Lacroix-Falgarde, rather than the hamlet of Falgarde, is frequently stated to be the location of the halt on 28 October (Thompson in Baker, p. 294; *BPE*, p. 57; *Life and Campaigns*, p. 63; *WCS*, p. 310) but, according to documentation supplied by the Mairie de Lacroix-Falgarde, habitation adjacent to the river where the modern village is located was first recorded in 1394.

35. P.-E. Ousset and G. Labit, *Clermont sur Ariège: Archéologie et histoire*, p. 25 and n. 2.

36. Dom Claude de Vic and Dom Joseph Vaissete, *Histoire générale de Languedoc*, vol. 7, p. 191.

Chapter 5

1. Carl von Clausewitz, *On War*, p. 621.

2. Barber, *Edward, Prince of Wales and Aquitaine*, p. 122; *BPE*, p. 215; and Yves Dossat, Anne-Marie Lemasson, Philippe Wolff, eds. *Le Languedoc et le Rouergue dans le Trésor des Chartes*, Item 1735.

3. *Oeuvres*, vol. 5, pp. 345–6; and Dossat *et al.*, *Le Languedoc et le Rouergue dans le Trésor des Chartes*, Item 1766. The destruction of the church is according to local tradition recorded in a tourist brochure.

4. Baker, pp. 131–2. Richard Barber, *Edward, Prince of Wales and Aquitaine*, p. 121 and n. 17, refers to part of the Marshal Clermont's forces being deployed at Montauban, citing a reference to de Vic and Vaissete, *L'Histoire générale de Languedoc*.

5. Monsieur Jean Odol, a local historian who has devoted forty years to the study of the period in the region, described the likely construction of the walls and relates the assessment of how many people could be supported by a mill.

6. Nicholas Wright, *Knights and Peasants: The Hundred Years War in the French Countryside*, pp. 101–2, describes the construction and use of underground shelters. Information relating to Montalbiau is contained in a locally produced monograph by Jean Odol, *La Bossa de Montalbiau: Essai de monographie d'une colline d'Ayguesvives*. The information on Corronsac was produced by Monsieur M. Vidal after a survey of the site in 1972 shortly before the refuge was filled in for safety reasons.

7. Léon Galibert, *Histoire de la baronnie et du consulat de Montbrun Lauragais*, p. 18.

8. Baker, p. 132, makes mention of only Bazière, Villefranche and Avignonet as having been destroyed on 30 October. Local historian Jean Odol believes that the other towns and villages listed were also destroyed during the passage of the army through the Lauragais. Antoine-Lucien Cazals, *L'Histoire de la Ville et de la Communauté de Montesquieu-sur-Canal*, p. 32, for the decline in the population of Montesquieu.

9. Baker, pp. 132 and 294; *Life and Campaigns*, p. 64; *Oeuvres*, vol. 5, p. 346 for events from Bazière to Avignonet; Avesbury, p. 438. The information on Avignonet's fortifications and church comes from the town website.

10. *Ordonnances des roys de France de la troisième race*, vol. 3, ed. Mr Secousse, pp. 73–4.

11. Dossat *et al.*, *Languedoc et le Rouergue dans le Trésor des Chartes*, Items 1770 and 1775.

12. Matthew Strickland, writing in *The Great War Bow*, cites a competition at Calais in 1478 over a distance of 260 yards (p. 381), and legislation of 1512 by Henry VIII requiring all men over the age of twenty-four to shoot at a mark not less than 220 yards distant (p. 393). Although both examples are much later than the *chevauchées* of the Black Prince, it is worthy of note that they date from a time when English archery was considered to be in decline.

13. See *Oeuvres*, vol. 5, pp. 346–7; Baker, pp. 132; *Life and Campaigns*, p. 64, for events in Mas-Stes-Puelles and Castelnaudary. Henri Mullot and Joseph Poux, *Nouvelles recherches sur l'itinéraire du Prince Noir à travers les pays de l'Aude*, p. 2 and n. 3 for Castelnaudary.

14. J. F. Jeanjean, *La Guerre de Cent Ans en pays audois: Incursion du Prince Noir en 1355*, pp. 50–1 and nn. 71–4. Dossat *et al.*, *Le Languedoc et le Rouergue dans le Trésor des Chartes*, Item 1764.

15. Roger Maguer, *De la Cocagne au Blé*, pp. 91–2, 99, and 345 concerning the reconstruction of the walls, castle and Carmelite monastery.

16. De Santi, *L'expédition du Prince Noir en 1355*, pp. 20–1, n. 4.

17. Baker, p. 132; *Life and Campaigns*, p. 64. De Santi, *L'expédition du Prince Noir en 1355*, p. 22 adds Lasbordes which is not in Baker.

18. This summary on circulades is drawn from a booklet produced by the Association des Villages Circulaires entitled *Circulades: Sur la route d'un urbanisme de 1000 ans*, which is based on the work of Krzysztof Pawlowski, *Circulades languedociennes de l'an mille: Naissance de l'urbanisme européen*, Montpellier, 1994.

19. Baker, p. 132: 'viculum vocatum Alse'.

20. Baker, p. 294, *Life and Campaigns*, p. 64 and de Santi, *L'expédition du Prince Noir en 1355*, p. 22 all take Alse to be Alzonne. Mullot and Poux, *Nouvelles recherches sur l'itinéraire du Prince Noir*, p. 3, and Jeanjean, *La Guerre de Cent Ans en pays audois*, p. 23, prefer Alzau.

21. See Jeanjean, *La Guerre de Cent Ans en pays audois*, p. 51 for initial exemption of taxes for Alzonne; Dossat, *et al.*, *Languedoc et le Rouergue dans le Trésor des Chartes*, Items 1737 for confirmation in 1359.

22. Local historian Jean-Louis Bonnet explained the changes in the embankments and river management over the centuries.

23. See Thomas Bouges, *Histoire ecclésiastique et civile de la ville et diocèse de Carcassonne*, p. 240, for construction of walls and buildings in the *bourg*.

24. Baker, pp. 132–3; *Life and Campaigns*, pp. 64–5; Avesbury, pp. 438 and 443.

25. *Oeuvres*, vol. 5, pp. 347–9.

26. Jeanjean, *La Guerre de Cent Ans en pays audois*, pp. 26–31, for a discussion of the lack of evidence to support the contention that the *bourg* was defended, and Bouges, *Histoire*

ecclésiastique et civile de la ville et diocèse de Carcassonne, pp. 471 *et seq.* for the record of consuls.

27. See Baker, p. 133, for the sum of 250,000 *écus*; WCS, p. 312 for equivalent value of the ransom. Jeanjean, *La Guerre de Cent Ans en pays audois*, p. 31, quotes a ransom of 25,000 gold *écus*,. He does not give a primary source for the lower sum, but sees it as more credible in the light of the ability of the city to pay such a sum, in particular in view of the ravages of the Black Death only a few years before.

28. Text of the letter of the clergy in Bouges, *Histoire ecclésiastique et civile de la ville et diocèse de Carcassonne*, pp. 241 *et seq.* and Jeanjean, *La Guerre de Cent Ans en pays audois*, pp. 31–2.

29. Jean-Louis Bonnet described the findings of the excavations.

30. Henxteworth, p. 18.

31. James F. Hunnewell, *The Historical Monuments of France*, p. 23.

32. *Archéologie du Midi médiéval*, vol. 22, p. 104.

33. See Barber, *Edward, Prince of Wales and Aquitaine*, p. 123 for Richard Barber's discussion of the *cité* being close to the end of its water supplies, and Bouges, *Histoire ecclesiastique et civile de la ville et diocèse de Carcassonne*, p. 242 for the shortage of water and the defence by Thibaud de Barbasan.

34. Jonathan Sumption, *The Albigensian Crusade*, pp. 94–100.

35. See Livingstone and Witzel, *The Road to Crécy*, p. 204, concerning Vernon, and Mullot and Poux, *Nouvelles recherches sur l'itinéraire du Prince Noir*, p. 5, for tactics at Carcassonne.

36. *BPE*, p. 60; Baker, p. 133.

37. Alphonse Mahul, *Cartulaire et archives des communes de l'ancien diocèse et de l'arrondissement administratif de Carcassonne*, vol. 6, pt 1, p. 21, for reconstruction of Carcassonne *bourg*. See also Bouges, *Histoire ecclésiastique et civile de la ville et diocèse de Carcassonne*, pp. 242–3 also for reconstruction, King Jean's letter in full and the extension of tax exemptions.

38. See *BPE*, p. 60 and Jeanjean, *La Guerre de Cent Ans en pays audois*, p. 34, for the burning of Trèbes; *Oeuvres*, vol. 5, p. 350 for the ransoming of the town and *Récits d'un bourgeois de Valenciennes*, ed. Kervyn de Lettenhove p. 282, for d'Albret acting as godfather. Jeanjean, *La Guerre de Cent Ans en pays audois*, p. 34, mentions the burning of a priory at Milhan, a hamlet which he places close to Trèbes, and Mullot and Poux, *Nouvelles recherches sur l'itinéraire du Prince Noir*, p. 6, n. 3 refer to Millan which is likely to be the same place.

39. See Mullot and Poux, *Nouvelles recherches sur l'itinéraire du Prince Noir*, p. 7, for the case for Syloine being Sérame.

40. Le Bel, p. 221.

41. Mahul, *Cartulaire et archives des communes*, vol. 4, p. 286.

42. Baker, pp. 133 and 295; Le Bel, p. 221; Jeanjean, *La Guerre de Cent Ans en pays audois*, p. 35.

Chapter 6

1. Rogers, 'By Fire and Sword', p. 38.

2. *Cassini*, CD-ROM, France Sud, sheet 58.

3. Jeanjean, *La Guerre de Cent Ans en pays audois*, p. 35, n. 45.

4. Baker, pp. 133–4; *Oeuvres*, vol. 5, p. 351–2; Avesbury, pp. 438 and 444; Paul Carbonel, *Histoire de Narbonne, dès origines à l'époque contemporaine*, p. 193, states that there were 6,000 *feux*, or households, equating to a population of 30,000 for the *bourg* and *cité* combined; see Jacques Michaud and André Cabanis, eds., *Histoire de Narbonne*, pp. 124–5 for a map showing ramparts, gates and bridges in the early fourteenth century.

5. Baker, pp. 133–4, and 295, *Oeuvres*, vol. 5, pp. 351–2. See *BPE*, p. 60, for the report of the wounding of Jean de Pommiers; *Thalamus parvus: Le petit thalamus de Montpellier*, ed. Ferdinand Pegat and Eugène Thomas, p. 351, for the death of Pommiers and up to ten Anglo-Gascons in total; De Vic and Vaissete, *L'histoire générale de Languedoc*, vol. 7, p. 191, for de Tournel.

6. Carbonel, *Histoire de Narbonne*, p. 194; Michaud and Cabanis, *Histoire de Narbonne*, p. 194.

7. *Cassini*, CD-ROM, France Sud, sheet 58.

8. Julien Aussenac provided information relating to Ouveillan, including sketch maps of the defences of the village at different periods, and Fontcalvy. See *Archives communales, Ouveillan, Series GG, parchement no. 3*, for the evidence of Guillaume Bérenger d'Ouveillan.

9. The general accounts of the period after leaving Narbonne give a confusing picture. Baker, p. 134, makes no mention of events at Cuxac d'Aude, Ouveillan or Capestang. *Oeuvres*, vol. 5, pp. 350–2, describes events at Capestang but has them occurring before the army reached Narbonne. Jeanjean, *La Guerre de Cent Ans en pays audois*, pp. 38–41, and Mullot and Poux, *Nouvelles recherches sur l'itinéraire du Prince Noir*, p. 9, give an account of events at Cuxac, Ouveillan and Capestang. De Vic and Vaissete, *L'histoire générale de Languedoc*, vol. 7, p. 191 mention the army reaching Capestang. Le Bel, p. 221, has the army ranging beyond Capestang to Béziers and St-Thibéry.

10. *Oeuvres*, vol. 5, has two versions of the size of the ransom: 20,000 florins (£2,840), p. 341, and 40,000 écus (£5,680), p. 350. Monique Bourin, Michel Adgé, Yves Rouquette and Bernard Nayral, *L'imagier et les poètes au château de Capestang*, for the population of Capestang.

11. Avesbury, p. 438.

12. De Santi, *The Black Prince's Expedition*, p. 61.

13. Le Bel, p. 222. See *Anonimalle*, p. 35 for the numbers quoted.

14. See Avesbury, p. 438, for the pope's embassy, p. 433 for the destruction of walls at Montpellier, and *Oeuvres*, vol. 5, p. 341, for the despatch of moveable wealth from Montpellier.

15. It may seem to be stretching the imagination to go from Baker's 'Ulmes' to the modern Homps, but the town's Latin name was Adulmus, or country of the elms.

16. *Oeuvres*, vol. 5, p. 350.

17. Baker, p. 134.

18. Information on La Redorte is drawn from a locally produced leaflet *Repères Culturels en Minervois: La Redorte*.

19. Mahul, *Cartulaire et archives des communes*, vol. 4, pp. 8 and 257 for the destruction of Azille and Pépieux.

20. Mullot and Poux, *Nouvelles recherches sur l'itinéraire du Prince Noir*, pp. 11 and 14.

21. Avesbury, p. 444.

22. See Baker. p. 134 for a record of the knighting; *BPR*, vol. 4, pp. 207 and 218 for the annuity: on 1 July 1357 an annuity of 200 marks is recorded, but on 2 September 1357 it

is reported that an earlier annuity awarded of £200 had fallen into arrears and payment is ordered to be brought up to date.

23. Mullot and Poux, *Nouvelles recherches sur l'itinéraire du Prince Noir*, pp. 10–15; *WCS*, pp. 317–19; *BPE*, p. 63.

24. *BPE*, p. 63; *WCS*, p. 305. Writing with a regional perspective, Mullot and Poux, *Nouvelles recherches sur l'itinéraire du Prince Noir*, and Jeanjean, *La Guerre de Cent Ans en pays audois*, are strong proponents of the prince seeking to avoid Armagnac. A general perception of battle-avoidance is also found in Tourneur-Aumont, *La Bataille de Poitiers*, pp. 85–7, in particular: 'la chevauchée de pillage, autant que possible, sans bataille vers les villes opulentes, rivales historiques de Bordeaux' (p. 85).

25. There is a wider debate among historians over whether there was a general strategy of battle-avoidance or battle-seeking in the Middle Ages. See, inter alia, Clifford J. Rogers, 'The Vegetian "Science of Warfare" in the Middle Ages', *Journal of Medieval Military History*, vol. 1, pp. 1–19; Stephen Morillo, 'Battle Seeking: The Contexts and Limits of Vegetian Strategy', *Journal of Medieval Military History*, vol. 1, pp. 21–41; and John Gillingham, '"Up with Orthodoxy!" In Defense of Vegetian Warfare', *Journal of Medieval Military History*, vol. 2, pp. 149–58.

26. Mullot and Poux, *Nouvelles recherches sur l'itinéraire du Prince Noir*, p. 14: 'Au départ de Lamyane, au contraire, une marche en colonnes protégées s'impose naturellement à la prudence anglais, par suite du voisinage des troupes françaises solidement établies, comme nous l'avons vu, sur la rive gauche de l'Aude. Ce n'est qu'après avoir été rassuré par l'inaction de l'ennemi, qui reste sur ses postions, dans l'expectative, que le prince de Galles se décide de quitter Lamyane'; and Jeanjean, *La Guerre de Cent Ans en pays audois*, p. 42: 'le Prince ne continua pas sa marche directe vers Carcassonne et l'on comprend pourquoi il tenta de s'éloigner de l'armée du Comte d'Armagnac en remontant vers le Nord.'

27. *WCS*, p. 317.

28. *BPE*, p. 63.

29. Text from *Life and Campaigns*, p. 66 with place-names reinserted within single quotation marks from Baker pp. 134–5.

30. Mullot and Poux, *Nouvelles recherches sur l'itinéraire du Prince Noir*, pp. 10–11.

31. *WCS*, p. 318, n. 165.

32. *WCS*, p. 310.

33. Thompson's conclusion, Baker, p. 295, that 'Esebon' is the now dried-up lake of Marseillette is generally accepted and consistent with other details of the route.

34. Mullot and Poux, *Nouvelles recherches sur l'itinéraire du Prince Noir*, p. 13.

35. Avesbury, p. 438.

36. Avesbury, p. 444.

37. Jeanjean, *La Guerre de Cent Ans en pays audois*, pp. 43–4; Mullot and Poux, *Nouvelles recherches sur l'itinéraire du Prince Noir*, p. 14; *WCS*, p. 318, and nn. 163–6; see *BPE*, p. 63 for discussion of the route between 13 and 15 November.

38. See Jeanjean, *La Guerre de Cent Ans en pays audois*, pp. 50–1, for Alzonne and Castelnaudary; L. H. Fonds-Lamothe, *Notices historiques sur la ville de Limoux*, pp. 14–17 for the destruction and rebuilding of Limoux.

39. Sumption, *Trial by Fire*, pp. 465–88; de Vic and Vaissete, *Histoire générale du Languedoc*, vol. 7, pp. 241–3.

40. Mullot and Poux, *Nouvelles recherches sur l'itinéraire du Prince Noir*, p. 14 n. 2 cite Mahul, *Cartulaire et archives des communes*, vol. 4, p. 51 to support their contention that

Villepeyroux was sacked. The reference refers to the commune of Castans and makes no mention of events in 1355.

41. See Denis Pébernard, *Histoire de Conques-sur-Orvieil et de la Manufacture des Saptes*, p. 250 for destruction of Conques being in local tradition.

42. WCS, p. 318, n. 164.

43. Jean Miquel, *Essai sur l'Arrondissement de Saint-Pons*, p. 135 for Ventajou, and Jeanjean, *La Guerre de Cent Ans en pays audois*, p. 43 for La Lavinière, Siran and Ventajou. See also Archives Municipaux de Cassagnoles (Ref 54 EDT 4), dated 1390, for the instrument by which the *viguier* (magistrat or provost) of Carcassonne, Béziers and Minerve ordered the fortification of Cassagnoles after the devastation of Ventajou, and Joseph Sahuc, *St-Pons-de-Thomières*, pp. 10–11 for reference to fortification after the activities of the Great Company.

44. Preixan has been suggested for Pezence, Baker, p. 295. In view of its spelling Pezens looks much more likely. Pennautier, Pech, and a combination of the two neighbouring hamlets of Pech-Redon and Sauzens have been proposed for Puchsiaucier: Baker, p. 295; WCS, p. 318. *Pech* appears on the large-scale maps in countless place-names, and this does not help in locating Puchsiaucier. Of the proposals only Pennautier is shown as having a bridge on the eighteenth-century Cassini maps, *Cassini*, CD-ROM France Sud, sheet 19. Earlier bridges at the other locations cannot be ruled out, but evidence for them is absent. In addition, in the sixteenth century Pennautier is recorded as having fortifications 'in the style of the Middle Ages'. See Mahul, *Cartulaire et archives des communes*, vol. 6, part 2, p. 419 for the various names for Pennautier and p. 457 for a description of the defences. In sum, Pennautier is the closest fit for a town with a fortified tower and a bridge and the ancient name for Pennautier was Puech Nautier, which could become Puchsiaucier. Pennautier is the most likely location for Puchsiaucier.

45. Mullot and Poux, *Nouvelles recherches sur l'itinéraire du Prince Noir*, p. 14, n. 6.

46. The Occitan name for St-Hilaire is St Ilari, and there is land close to the village named Plan d'Alièro, remarkably close to the spelling of Alieir. It is not difficult to see a corruption of either St-Hilaire or St Ilari to become Alieir, but equally Alieir could be a corruption of Villalier.

47. See Mahul, *Cartulaire et archives des communes*, vol. 5, p. 20 for the route from La Grasse to St-Hilaire.

48. WCS, p. 318, n. 166.

49. Christine de Pizan, *The Book of Deeds of Arms and of Chivalry*, p. 49.

50. See David Buisseret, *The Mapmaker's Quest: Depicting New Worlds in Renaissance Europe*, pp. 1–9 for a summary of medieval mapping; Prestwich, *Armies and Warfare in the Middle Ages*, pp. 189–90 for a discussion of mapping and guides. The payments to the prince's guides are from Henxteworth, pp. 17, 18, 20. See also Spufford, *Power and Profit*, pp. 140 *et seq.* for itineraries.

Chapter 7

1. Prestwich, *Armies and Warfare in the Middle Ages*, p. 229.

2. Richard Barber's translation, *Life and Campaigns*, p. 66, is: 'On Sunday, St Machutus' day, they entered fair open country, and made a long march'. De Santi, 'L'expédition du Prince Noir en 1355', p. 26, translates the same passage as 'Le dimanche, fête de saint Maclou, on déboucha, par un grand chemin, dans un pays riche, largement et longue-

ment ouvert'. The key difference being between Barber's translation of *itinere magno* as a 'long march', and de Santi's version of a 'great road'. If Pennautier were the location for the overnight stop for the prince on 14 November, then the distance travelled of sixteen miles would not seem to merit the description of a long march. The translation by de Santi better fits the route, initially along the Via Aquitania which would certainly be considered a great road, from Pennautier to Prouille.

3.   Mullot and Poux, *Nouvelles recherches sur l'itinéraire du Prince Noir*, p. 15 refer to the destruction of Villasavary but provide no evidence. Baker, p. 135, describes the abbey at Prouille, and states that the army burnt Lemoyns, Falanges, Vularde and Serre. There is evidence for Lemoyns being Limoux in Fonds-Lamothe, *Notices historiques sur la ville de Limoux*, p. 141. n. 1, and *Oeuvres*, vol. 5, p. 352. Falanges seems certain to have been Fanjeaux and there is evidence for the town having been destroyed, with exemption of taxes being confirmed in 1357 to encourage reconstruction (Dossat *et al.*, *Le Languedoc et le Rouergue dans le Trésor des Chartes*, Item 1357). Vularde is proposed by de Santi ('L'expédition du prince Noir en 1355', p. 26) as Villasavary, on the basis that the local name was 'le Villar'. Rogers, *WCS*, p. 318, n. 166, believes Vularde to be Villar-St-Anselme. Serre is generally considered to be Lasserre, or Lasserrre-de-Prouille on modern maps. See *Oeuvres*, vol. 5, p. 353 for Montréal and Routiers.

4.   Denifle, vol. 2-1, p. 91; Fonds-Lamothe, *Notices historiques sur la ville de Limoux*, p. 93.

5.   Denifle, vol. 2-1, p. 92 records a Dominican monastery, by implication inside the walls, and a Franciscan monastery outside the town. Fonds-Lamothe, *Notices historiques sur la ville de Limoux*, p. 146 records Augustinian and Franciscan monasteries outside the town but makes no mention of monasteries inside the walls.

6.   See Fonds-Lamothe, *Notices historiques sur la ville de Limoux*, p. 141 for the letter of Jean d'Armagnac, and A. Sabarthès, *Notes historiques sur la ville de Limoux*, p. 82, for the letter of Philippe VI.

7.   See Fonds-Lamothe, *Notices historiques sur la ville de Limoux*, pp. 141-7 for events in Limoux and the measures for reconstruction, and Denifle, vol. 2-1, p. 92, n. 1, for the letter of Pope Innocent VI.

8.   Dominique Baudreu and Frédéric Loppe, 'Types de forts villageois dans le bassin moyen de l'Aude durant la Guerre de Cent Ans', in *Archéologie du Midi Médiéval*, vol. 22, p. 116.

9.   Mahul, *Cartulaire et archives des communes*, vol. 3, pp. 257, 311 and 340.

10.   See *Circulades, sur la route d'un urbanisme de 1000 Ans*, for Lasserre-de-Prouille.

11.   See Baker, p. 135, for events at Prouille; Henxteworth, p. 19, for payment of alms; *BPR*, vol. 4, p. 255 for the annuity for Richard of Leominster.

12.   See Dossat *et al.*, *Le Languedoc et le Rouergue dans le Trésor des Chartes*, Item 1765, for confirmation of tax exemptions for reconstruction.

13.   *BPE*, p. 72.

14.   Thompson, in Baker, p. 295, suggests Pechluna (*sic*) for Ayollpuhbone.

15.   I am grateful to local historian and Président de la Société d'Histoire de Belpech, Auguste Armengaud, for his description of the village and its bridges, defences and castle.

16.   J. de Lahondès, *Belpech de Garnagois*, pp. 1–7.

17.   The description and location of the ford over the Hers were provided by Auguste Armengaud. The name is thought to come from the Occitan word for monk, *mourge*, since it is believed that there was once a monastery in the vicinity.

18. Pierre Duffaut, *Histoire de Mazères, ville maîtresse et capitale des Comtes de Foix*, p. 120.

19. See Roger Armengaud, *Boulbonne, le Saint Denis des Comtes de Foix*, pp. 165–71 concerning Mazères. The existence of town walls in 1355 is implied by an instruction from the count to the town consuls in 1359 that 'they close existing passages in their buildings neighbouring the fortified curtain wall'.

20. De Santi, 'L'expédition du Prince Noir', p. 27, n. 2, claims that the castle was Roman. A town publication, *Bienvenue à Calmont*, states that the castle dates back to at least the twelfth century.

21. Duffaut, *Histoire de Mazères*, p. 43 concerning fords, p. 76 for bridge, and p. 120 for the passage by way of La Bastide-de-Sérou.

22. Roger Ycart, *Cintegabelle, Un village dans l'histoire*, pp. 19–20, for the ownership of the village, and p. 69 for the assault by Phoebus in 1359.

23. The information on the ford at La Muraillette was provided by local historian Roger Ycart. For the use of the ford by Simon de Montfort see Roger Armengaud and Roger Ycart, *Cintegabelle: Châtellenie royale en pays toulousain*, pp. 154–80.

24. C. Barrière-Flavy, *Cintegabelle au XV siècle*, pp. 4–5, 7–9. Roger Armengaud, 'Le Passage du Prince Noir', *La Croix du Midi*, 9 February 1967.

25. The information on Cintegabelle was given orally by local historian Roger Ycart.

26. The information on Auterive is based on discussion with Louis Latour, a member of the Société Archéologique du Midi de la France, and two of his articles for the society's journal, *Mémoires*, including 'Le grand pont romain d'Auterive', vol. 51, 1991, and 'Le castrum d'Auterive: Ses origines, son histoire, ses fortifications', vol. 54, 1994.

27. Baker, p. 136: 'et media custodia fuit ospitata in magna villa Miremont, que cum castro fuerat combusta.'

28. Information on the village, its fortifications and castle was provided orally by two local historians, Jean-Yves Canal and Francis Bop, both of whom are closely involved with the archaeological research in the village.

29. Much of the information on the silos was given orally, but there is a report, Catherine Poulain-Martel and Jean-Yves Canal, 'Des silos médiévaux à Miremont', *Gardarem Miremont*, Bulletin No. 4, 2002.

30. See Ycart, *Cintegabelle*, pp. 17, 18, 46 and 50 for a description of diet, farming and feudal obligations in Cintegabelle.

31. Baker, p. 136. It is probable that, since Baker's account relates to the middle guard, the mounted elements of the prince's division passed by Montaut, but, as discussed below, the prince himself was on this occasion with the vanguard passing by way of Rieux.

32. Baker, p. 136, states: 'Aquam de Geronde cum gracia Dei petransitam relacione castellanorum nullus potuisset petransivisse post inundacionem pluvie diurne, unde eius transitus Dei virtuti iuste fuerat ascriptus.' Due to the ambiguity of the subjunctive and of *diurne* (which can mean either 'daily' or 'of the day'), it is impossible to be certain whether Baker means here to indicate that they crossed just before the day's rain *would have* made the ford impassable, or that they crossed after the flooding caused by daily rain *should have* (already) made the crossing impossible. De Santi, 'L'expédition du Prince Noir en 1355', inclines to the former interpretation, but the context (Baker's emphasis on divine aid) tends to support the latter (cf. *Life and Campaigns*, p. 67). De Santi's reading implies that there was a degree of urgency to get mounted troops across the river to provide protection for the crossing over the bridge at Carbonne before conditions

deteriorated to the extent that the river became impassable. The other interpretation makes the matter perhaps less urgent, but no less important, since without such cover the entire army would risk being faced with forcing a crossing on a narrow bridge with the French arrayed on the other bank. My thanks to Clifford J. Rogers and John France for their advice on translation of the Latin in preparation of my 'The Itineraries of the Black Prince's *Chevauchées* of 1355 and 1356: Observations and Interpretations', *Journal of Medieval Military History*, vol. 7, 2009, pp. 12–37.

33. Blaise Binet, quoted in Henri Ménard, *Carbonne: Huit siècles d'histoire*, p. 36, from *Mémoire de Blaise Binet*, probably published around 1768. Binet, a member of the Société Royale des Sciences de Montpellier and of l'Académie Royale des Sciences de Toulouse, and a member of the local administration, contributed to the work of a Benedictine monk, Dom Bourotte: 'chargé par les Etats de Languedoc de la description historique de cette province commencée par dom Vaissete.'

34. Information concerning the wooden bridge provided by the society Histoire et Traditions Carbonnaises. A map showing the location of town in the thirteenth century is in Ménard, *Carbonne: Huit siècles d'histoire*, p. 142. There is also provision for the rebuilding of the bridge in orders signed by Jean II in August 1356 (*Ordonnances des Roys de France de la Troisième Race*, vol. 3, ed. Secousse, p. 82).

35. Jean Contrasty, *Histoire de la cité de Rieux-Volvestre et de ses évêques*, p. 98, does not produce evidence for his claim. However, it should not be dismissed out of hand in view of the strong oral tradition in the Languedoc relating to the *chevauchée* of 1355.

Chapter 8

1. Avesbury, p. 439.
2. Avesbury, p. 438.
3. The term lance was occasionally used to describe a tactical unit in the medieval period. However, in the English armies of the fourteenth century it was used more as an administrative term for pay and recruiting purposes. There is an example of a lance in 1379 consisting of two men-at-arms, an archer and a page. See Prestwich, *Armies and Warfare in the Middle Ages*, p. 49, and Ayton and Preston, *The Battle of Crécy, 1346*, p. 354, n. 10. I am grateful to both Professor Clifford Rogers and Dr Andrew Ayton for their advice on the status of the 'lance'. The prince probably used the term here as synonymous with man-at-arms.
4. See *WCS*, p. 320, n. 174, concerning the size of French army; Le Bel, vol. 2, p. 222 describes the French army as three times the size of that of the prince. Delachenal, vol. I, p. 130, n. 1, for King Jean's letter: 'quod numerus gencium nostrarum in armis numerum hostium nostrorum ibidem multiper excedbat, nec poterant evadere sine bello.'
5. Jean-Pierre Dehoey, 'Carbonne sous l'Ancien Régime', in *Histoire et traditions carbonnaises*, vol. 4, pp, 59–61, and Ménard, *Carbonne: Huit siècles d'histoire*, pp. 37–9 and 142. See Joseph Dedieu, *Histoire de Carbonne: Les institutions communales d'une bastide sous l'Ancien Régime*, p. 33 for destruction of the charter and p. 53 for King Jean's letter; *Ordonnances des Roys de France de la Troisième Race*, vol. 3, p. 82, for the provisions for the rebuilding of the bridge.
6. See Ménard, *Carbonne: Huit siècles d'histoire*, p. 39, for the reconstruction of the town.
7. Baker, p. 137.

8. Avesbury, p. 439.

9. See Jean Castan, *Marestaing: Ancienne commanderie des Templiers*, pp. 17–19 for the location of the ford and the construction of the first bridge in 1846.

10. Baker, p. 137; see *Life and Campaigns*, p. 68, for the passage in translation.

11. *BPE*, p. 67.

12. *WCS*, p. 321, n. 179.

13. Baker, p. 137: 'parvam villam ab hostibus uno miliari distantem.'

14. *Cassini*, CD-ROM, France Sud, sheet 38.

15. Baker, p. 137.

16. Breuils, 'Jean 1er, Comte d'Armagnac', p. 58.

17. See Baker, pp. 136–7, and Avesbury, p. 439, for events from Mauvezin to Gimont.

18. Avesbury, p. 439.

19. Baker, p. 137, refers to 'Realmont'. Réjaumont derives its modern name from the origins of the town as 'Mont Royal', and it is clear that this was Baker's Realmont.

20. Rogers, *WCS*, p. 322, n. 184 opts for St-Lary while Barber, *Life and Campaigns*, p. 69, prefers Ste-Radegonde.

21. The *bastides* website, http://bastides.free.fr, attributes the foundation to Beaumarchais in 1285, while the town website www.rejaumont.net attributes the foundation, or at least the confirmation of privileges, to John of Havering in 1292. Bentley, *Fort Towns of France*, p. 196, concurs with 1285 as the year of foundation but attributes the origins to the Cistercian order. The town website is the source for information on the castle and defences, and the story of the siege.

22. Baker, p. 138: 'Die veneris transierunt, et districte, magnam aquam, et residuo diei inter villas muratas et castra forcia.' *Life and Campaigns*, p. 69.

23. See the town brochure, *Valence/Baise: Bastide du XIII siècle*.

24. Rogers, *WCS*, p. 322, n. 184, opts for Lasserre. Barber is undecided between Lasserre (*Life and Campaigns*, p. 69), and Lagardère (*Edward, Prince of Wales and Aquitaine*, map 3, p. 118). Hewitt, *BPE*, map p. 51 prefers Lagardère, as does Thompson in Baker, p. 296. De Santi, 'L'expédition du Prince Noir', p. 31, prefers La Ressingle (Larressingle). According to a tourist guide, *Larressingle en Condomois*, the village of Larressingle, whose perimeter dates from the thirteenth century, was not attacked during the Hundred Years War.

25. Henxteworth, pp. 18–20.

26. J. Queyrou, *Casteljaloux et sa région* (preliminary page – not numbered), records that in the sixteenth century Casteljaloux was still known as Castrum Gelosium which is close enough to Baker's text of Castro Gelous to remove any doubt over the lodgings for 30 November.

27. See Bentley, *Fort Towns of France*, p. 204, for Durance; Baker, p. 138, for the itinerary from 27 November to 2 December.

28. Queyrou, *Casteljaloux et sa région*, pp. 4 and 8, and the town guide, *Connaître et aimer Casteljaloux*, concerning Casteljaloux's history and monuments.

29. *Life and Campaigns*, p. 69, takes Baker's 'Melan' as Meulan without attempting to identify it, although in *Edward, Prince of Wales and Aquitaine*, map p. 118, Barber does show the town as Meilhan. Thompson in Baker, p. 296 opts for Meilhan-sur-Garonne. Both Barber, *Life and Campaigns*, p. 69, and Thompson in Baker, p. 296, interpret 'Montguilliam' as Montpouillon (*sic*). Denifle, vol. 2-1, p. 93, n. 3, argues for Fontguilhem.

30. *WCS*, p. 326 and map p. 327.

31. *Oeuvres*, vol. 4, pp. 278–9 for the assault on Meilhan, variously called Rocemillon by Froissart and Roche-Millon, or Rulle-Millant, in Henri Ribadieu, *Les campagnes du Comte Derby en Guyenne*, p. 41.
32. See Sumption, *Trial by Battle*, pp. 474–5 for an account of the taking of La Réole. The town's tourist brochures, *Visiter la Réole* and *Circuit urbain médiéval Leo Drouyn à la Réole* give information on the historic monuments. See Fowler, *The King's Lieutenant*, p. 62 for the settlement made by Lancaster for the people of the town.
33. Moisant, *Le Prince Noir en Aquitaine*, p. 43.

Chapter 9

1. Avesbury, p. 445.
2. Sumption, *Trial by Fire*, p. 185.
3. Avesbury, p. 445.
4. Sumption, *Trial by Fire*, p. 186.
5. Sumption, *Trial by Fire*, pp. 204 and 212–13.
6. Timbal *et al.*, *La Guerre de Cent Ans*, pp. 108–9.
7. Timbal *et al.*, *La Guerre de Cent Ans*, p. 127.
8. Timbal *et al.*, *La Guerre de Cent Ans*, p. 240.
9. Barber, *Edward, Prince of Wales and Aquitaine*, pp. 129–30.
10. Sumption, *Trial by Fire*, p. 185.
11. See BPE, pp. 68–73, for a summary of the arguments surrounding the concept of the *chevauchée*. Rogers sets out the underlying arguments for strategic objectives in *WCS*, pp. 5–8, 'By Fire and Sword', pp. 56–7, and 'Edward III, the Dialectics of Strategy', in *The Wars of Edward III, Sources and Interpretations*, pp. 265–83.
12. See Sumption, *Trial by Battle*, pp. 1–68 for the state of France and England at the start of the reign of Edward III, p. 24 for relative incomes and pp. 10 and 35 for the populations of France and England.
13. Pizan, *The Book of Deeds of Arms and of Chivalry*, p. 53.
14. For the division of spoils see Ayton, *The Battle of Crécy 1346*, p. 193 and Prestwich, *Armies and Warfare in the Middle Ages*, p. 103.
15. Denifle, vol. 2–1, p. 93.
16. BPE, p. 75.
17. Timbal *et al.*, *La Guerre de Cent Ans*, p. 260.
18. Pizan, *The Book of Deeds of Arms and of Chivalry*, pp. 171–2.
19. Dupuy, *Le Prince Noir*, p. 136.
20. *WCS*, pp. 260 and 324.
21. Avesbury, p. 448.
22. Sumption, *Trial by Fire*, p. 192.
23. Avesbury, p. 457.
24. Sumption, *Trial by Fire*, p. 193.
25. BPR, vol. 3, pp. 223–4, for reinforcements and the order for bows, arrows and bowstrings. Barber, *Edward Prince of Wales and Aquitaine*, p. 130.
26. BPE, pp. 92 and 94.
27. Sumption, *Trial by Fire*, pp. 102–42 and 198–207 for a detailed account of the confrontation between Charles and Jean.
28. BPE, pp. 92–4.

Chapter 10

1. H. T. Riley, *Memorials of London and London Life, in the XIIIth, XIVth, and XVth Centuries*, p. 285.
2. Black Prince's letter to the bishop of Worcester, 20 October 1356, *Oeuvres*, vol. 18, pp. 389–91.
3. *Anonimalle*, p. 35.
4. Fowler, *The King's Lieutenant*, p. 58, and Joseph du Lac, *Bergerac et son arrondissement*, p. 32.
5. See Bentley, *Fort Towns of France*, p. 104, and Brissaud, *Les anglais en Guyenne*, pp. 266–8, for details of the governance of Monségur.
6. M. H. Guyot and M. Cheyron, *Château des ducs de Duras et la ville*, pp. 12–13.
7. See Vale, *The Origins of the Hundred Years War*, p. 101, for a summary of Gaillard de Durfort's career; Fowler, *The King's Lieutenant*, p. 63 for Gaillard's cross-over to the English in 1345; Avesbury, p. 449, for Gaillard's return to the English cause in April 1356; Moisant, *Le Prince Noir en Aquitaine*, pp. 47–8 for the forfeiture of his lands in 1354 and their return in 1356; and René Blanc, *La douloureuse histoire de la ville de Duras*, p. 15 for his death at Poitiers.
8. Sumption, *Trial by Battle*, pp. 463–5.
9. Fowler, *The King's Lieutenant*, p. 71.
10. *BPE*, p. 90.
11. See Sumption, *Trial by Fire*, pp. 195–226 for a summary of events in 1356 leading up to the prince's departure from Bergerac on 4 August.
12. *BPE*, p. 71.
13. Tourneur-Aumont, *La Bataille de Poitiers*, p. 97–8: 'Devant les Anglo-Gascons de 1356, ne parlons donc pas de "forces servant la couronne d'Angleterre", il ne s'agit que de brigandage.'
14. *WCS*, pp. 348–50.
15. Ayton and Preston, *The Battle of Crécy 1346*, pp. 38–108.
16. Riley, *Memorials of London and London Life*, p. 285.
17. See Baker, p. 140 and *BPE*, p. 102 for the measures taken for the defence of Gascony; Sumption, *Trial by Fire*, p. 225 for the estimate of the strength of the force left to defend Gascony.
18. See Chapter 13 for discussion on the size of the prince's army at Poitiers.
19. *WCS*, pp. 353–4 summarises the various accounts of the routes taken. See *Oeuvres*, vol. 18, pp. 385–6 for Burghersh's letter for the route through the Agenais, Limousin, Auvergne and Berry; *Oeuvres*, vol. 5 pp. 377–80 for his general account of the route; Matteo Villani, 'Cronica', in *Cronisti del Trecento*, ed. Roberto Palmarocchi, p. 526, for his version including an approach to Orléans, and Riley, *Memorials of London and London Life*, p. 285 for the prince's description.
20. Arlette Higounet-Nadal, *Périgueux aux XIV et XV siècles: Etude de démographie historique*, pp. 25–6, 29, 31, 51 n. 236, 106 n. 135, and accompanying maps and charts for details of Périgueux, its population, defences, suburbs, roads from Bergerac and bridges.
21. Guy Penaud, *Histoire de Périgueux dès origines à nos jours*, pp. 131–2.
22. Delachenal, vol. 1, p. 197 and Tourneur-Aumont, *La Bataille de Poitiers*, p. 90 both refer to the prince having stayed at Château-l'Evêque but no evidence is cited.
23. Gérard Durand de Ramefort, *Le Château de Ramefort*, pp. 8–12, 16–17, 19–20 and 41–2.

24. Information on Quinsac from L. Grillon, *Un peu d'histoire de Quinsac, dès celtes à la Révolution*, and local historian Francis Reix.

25. Le Comte de Bruc-Chabans, *Le Château de la Chapelle-Faucher*, p. 8.

26. Hervé Gaillard, *Carte archéologique de la Gaule: La Dordogne*, Fig. 5, p. 47.

27. *WCS*, p. 353, n. 24 summarises the various views on the location of *Merdan* and *Quisser*.

28. Abbé Adolphe Mondon, 'Notes historiques sur la baronnie de Marthon en Angoumois', *Bulletin de la Société Archéologique et Historique de la Charente*, 1895, 1896, and 1897, for a compilation of the archival records for Marthon.

29. *Eulogium*, p. 216.

30. The ruins of the twelfth-century abbey at St-Estephe are listed as an historic monument. Details of the origins and purpose of the lakes are given in *Visite commentée de la communauté de communes du Périgord vert granitique*, published by the Office de Tourisme Intercommunal du Périgord Vert Granitique, Piégut-Pluviers. See also Dominique Audrerie and Yannick Couland, *Sites naturels en Périgord*, Section 13, for the construction and purpose of the lakes. Information on the Grandmontain order from the Groupe d'Etudes et de Recherches sur les Grandmontains. R. Laugardière, 'Essais topographiques, historiques et bibliographiques sur l'arrondisement de Nontron', *Bulletin de la Société Historique et Archéologique du Périgord*, vol. 14, p. 325, surmises that the lakes were much older than the monasteries.

31. Laugardière, 'Essais topographiques, historiques et bibliographiques sur l'arrondisement de Nontron', *Bulletin de la Société Historique et Archéologique du Périgord*, vol. 16, p. 65.

32. Sumption, *Trial by Fire*, pp. 48 and 120.

33. Laugardière, 'Essais topographiques, historiques et bibliographiques sur l'arrondisement de Nontron', *Bulletin de la Société Historique et Archéologique du Périgord*, vol. 12, p. 431.

34. *Eulogium*, p. 216.

35. Pierre Boulanger, *Manot: Quelques pages de notre histoire*, p. 5, and Nicole Raynaud, 'La chevauchée du Prince Noir en 1356: Recherche de son itinéraire entre La Péruse et Le Dorat', *Travaux d'Archéologie Limousine*, vol. 18, pp. 86, 88.

36. Baker, p. 142, relates how heavy rains had made the Loire impassable.

37. The Pont Notre Dame over the River Vienne at St-Junien, recorded as an historic monument, dates from the thirteenth century. For the castle and bridge at Chabanais see José Délias, *Chabanais*, pp. 69, 70 and 85.

38. Villani, 'Cronica', p. 526 quoted in *WCS*, p. 355, n. 26 makes general comments on widespread destruction; although as an Italian family seemingly remote from the events of the Hundred Years War, the Villani were widely involved in banking and commerce and the *Cronica* of Giovanni and subsequently Matteo Villani is well respected as a source for events during the war. *Anonimalle Chronicle*, cited in Rogers, *The Wars of Edward III, Sources and Interpretations*, p. 164 refers to the devastation of Périgord. See *Eulogium*, p. 215 for Burghersh taking unnamed towns. None of these sources, however, gives names for towns taken or destroyed, in contrast to the detailed account in the *Eulogium* after the crossing of the Vienne.

39. Denifle, vol. 2-1, p. 117.

40. *Eulogium*, p. 216: 'Die Dominica, hoc est XIIII die Augusti, princeps transivit prae-

dictam aquam et continuo displicavit vexilla sua et venit ad quamdam villam Litherp vocatam.'

41. *WCS*, p. 353.

42. *WCS*, p. 353, n. 23.

Chapter 11

1. Chandos, ll. 704–15.

2. Raynaud, 'La chevauchée du Prince Noir', p. 89 for the existence of the road through St-Maurice-de-Lyons between Manot and Le Dorat.

3. See S. Verpaalen-Bessaguet, *Lesterps, chef-d'oeuvre de l'art roman*, for a history of the abbey and a description of the fortifications of the town.

4. *Eulogium*, pp. 216–17.

5. Moisant, *Le Prince Noir en Aquitaine*, app. 16, pp. 192–4.

6. Raynaud, 'La chevauchée du Prince Noir', pp. 77–90.

7. The Marquis du Fraisse asserts that the destruction of the castle by the Black Prince's troops is recorded in the family archives. Nicole Raynaud (see nn. 2 and 6) has had extensive access to the archives and has not found supporting evidence. However, the construction of a new castle in the fifteenth century to replace a thirteenth-century building provides some circumstantial evidence in support of the claim.

8. Raynaud, 'La chevauchée du Prince Noir', p. 83 and n. 19.

9. Raynaud, 'La Chevauchée du Prince Noir', p. 77.

10. The Augustinian and Carmelite convents and the castle are all listed historic monuments. René Rougerie, *Histoires de Mortemart, suivie de légendes racontées par Paul Lauvergne*, pp. 12–13, and 19, and Lorgue, *Histoire de Mortemart (Haute-Vienne)*, p. 87.

11. *Eulogium*, p. 217.

12. Delachenal, vol. 2, p. 198, n. 1.

13. Listed historic monument dating from the thirteenth century.

14. Denifle, vol. 2-1, p. 118.

15. Chris Given-Wilson and Françoise Briac, 'Edward III's Prisoners of War: The Battle of Poitiers and Its Context', *English Historical Review*, September 2001, pp. 815 and 831.

16. See J. Font-Réaulx, *Le Dorat, ancienne capitale de la Basse Marche*, vol. 1, p. 52, entries 69 and 70; Michel Courivaud, *Le Dorat en Basse Marche*, pp. 58 and 276–9; and J. Nouaillac, *Le Dorat à travers son passé*, pp. 19–21 for the defences of Le Dorat, its castle and the Bourbon ownership.

17. Denifle, vol. 2-1, p. 118 and n. 2.

18. *Eulogium*, p. 217.

19. *Eulogium*, p. 217.

20. Laurence Lechaux, *Argenton-sur-Creuse en Berry: Au fil des rues*, pp. 12, 35–7 and 39.

21. Sumption, *Trial by Fire*, pp. 219 and 222.

22. Delachenal, vol. 1, p. 199 and n. 4.

23. Sumption, *Trial by Fire*, pp. 222 and 226–7.

24. M. Grillon des Chapelles, *Esquisses biographiques du Département de l'Indre*, containing 'Historique des Princes de Déols', pp. 394–7, written by Frère Jean de la Gogue, a Benedictine monk at the Priory of St Gildas in Châteauroux in the fifteenth century, and 'Histoire du chronique des Princes de Déols et Barons de Châteauroux', pp. 450–1, believed to have been written by Père Péan, Superior of the Convent of Cord-

eliers in Châteauroux in the seventeenth century, for accounts of events in Châteauroux. See p. 396 for assessment of the risks: 'que si ledict prince faisoit faire l'assault, qu'il perdroit moult de ses gens, et toutefois n'estoit-il pas seur de gaigner la place. Ceux qui avoient parlé à monseigneur André confirmèrent le dict d'icelluy chevalier, et pour ce fust visé que veu que les Anglois devoient avoir la bataille contre le roy de France, qu'ills n'avoient encore nul mestier de faire l'assault.'

25. Guy Gross, *Le Prince Noir en Berry*, pp. 45–6 for lodgings and the death of Chauvigny. See Baker, pp. 313–14 for a list of those captured and killed at the Battle of Poitiers.

26. *Eulogium*, p. 218.

27. Hilaire de Vesvre, *Le Bas Berry: Déols et Châteauroux dès origines à nos jours*, pp. 20 and 30. Denifle, vol. 2–1, p. 118.

28. WCS, pp. 354–5, and BPE, p. 104, prefer Villedieu for Burgo Dei. Denifle, vol. 2-1, p. 118, and Delachenal, vol. 1, p. 198, opt for Déols. Barber, *Edward, Prince of Wales and Aquitaine*, p. 134, also prefers Déols but considers that Seynt Yman was St-Maur.

29. Gross, *Le Prince Noir en Berry*, p. 50 and Louis Raynal, *Histoire du Berry, depuis les temps les plus anciens jusqu'en 1789*, vol. 2, pp. 294–5.

30. *Oeuvres*, vol. 5, pp. 384–6 for the Berry and Bourges.

31. Gross, *Le Prince Noir en Berry*, p. 46 for Blet and p. 49 for Dun-sur-Auron.

32. John Gillingham, *Richard I*, pp. 123–4.

33. Gillingham, *Richard I*, pp. 83–4, 104, 142, 294 and 296–7.

34. See Claudine Risselin-Nin and Olivier Ruffier, 'Le rempart médiéval d'Issoudun: Etude topographique', *Cahiers d'Archéologie et d'Histoire du Berry*, no. 101, pp. 13–14 for a description of the fortifications of Issoudun.

35. *Oeuvres*, vol. 5, pp. 384–6; Armand Pérémé, *Recherches historiques et archéologiques sur la ville d'Issoudun*, pp. 130–2, and Romain Guignard, *Issoudun dès origines à 1850: Aperçu des chroniques locales*, pp. 44–5 for the defence of Issoudun and the impact of the destruction. *Eulogium*, p. 218.

36. *Eulogium*, p. 218, records the owner of the castle at La Ferté as the Viscount de Todard. However, this seems to have a been a corruption of Thouars (in the modern *département* of Deux-Sèvres) – see Louis Gueneau, 'Aubigny-sur-Nère (Cher) pendant la Guerre de Cent Ans: Les incursions anglaises', *Cahiers d'Archéologie et d'Histoire du Berry*, no. 6, p. 18.

37. Gross, *Le Prince Noir en Berry*, p. 48.

38. J.-B. E. Tausserat, *Chroniques de la châtellenie de Lury*, pp. 43 and 89.

39. Gross, *Le Prince Noir en Berry*, p. 48.

40. *Eulogium*, p. 218.

41. See Alain Rives, *A la recherche des remparts du vieux Vierzon*, pp. 13 and 21, for the events of 1197 and subsequent reconstruction, the attack from Puits Berteau, and the reconstruction between 1358 and 1460; M. Lemaitre, *Mémoires sur Vierzon*, p. 82, for the possible constructions made during the attack; Jean Chaumeau, *Histoire de Berry*, p. 113, for the suggestion that the town was lightly defended. Gross, *Le Prince Noir en Berry*, p. 54, is dismissive of the idea of the prince's army having built any redoubts, pointing out that there are references going back to the tenth century for these constructions.

42. Denifle, vol. 2–1, p. 119 states that the abbey in question was that of St Pierre, but alludes to the possibility that the Benedictine abbey at Massay, about eight miles southwest of Vierzon, may also have been destroyed. However, Joseph Lacueille, *Histoire de*

Massay, p. 21, attributes the destruction of the abbey in Massay to English troops in 1360, possibly at this stage members of one of the companies of routiers.

43. *Eulogium*, p. 218.

44. Le Bel, vol. 2, p. 230, n. 2, for King Jean at Chartres on 28 August. *Eulogium*, p. 219, gives the strength of the French as eighty lances and that of the Anglo-Gascons as ten lances. Baker, p. 141, gives the French strength as 200 men.

45. See Marcel Aubert, *Mennetou-sur-Cher*, pp. 6–7, for fortifications, J. Branger and R. Tripeau, *Mennetou-sur-Cher: Histoire du canton*, p. 17 for the requirement to mount guard and p. 23 for the prince raising his banner, and J. Branger and R. Tripeau, *Châtres-sur-Cher: Notre village*, pp. 44 and 47–8, for the route of the Chemin de la Fringale.

46. See *Eulogium*, pp. 219–20, Le Bel, vol. 2, pp. 230–1, *Oeuvres*, vol. 5, pp. 387–91 and Riley, *Memorials of London and London Life*, p. 286, for accounts of events on 29 August.

47. R. Crozet, 'Siège de Romorantin par le Prince de Galles (1356)', *Revue Historique*, vol. 153, p. 190.

48. For accounts of the assault on Romorantin see *Eulogium*, pp. 219–20, Baker, p. 141, and *Oeuvres*, vol. 5, pp. 387–95.

49. E. Montrot, *Sainte-Maure-de-Touraine*, pp. 67–8.

50. Denifle, vol. 2-1, p. 120, n. 2; *BPE*, p. 158.

51. Alexandre Dupré, *Recherches historiques sur Romorantin et la Sologne*, p. 27.

52. Baker, p. 141, *Eulogium*, p. 220.

Chapter 12

1. Chandos, ll. 236–9.

2. Clifford Rogers has been the leading exponent of the argument that the prince sought battle during this phase while at the same time avoiding being trapped. In *WCS*, pp. 361–6, he sets out the arguments for his view and summarises the position of the other school of thought.

3. For debate over battle avoidance versus battle seeking strategies see, *inter alia*, Rogers, 'The Vegetian "Science of Warfare in the Middle Ages"', Morillo, 'Battle Seeking', and Gillingham, '"Up with Orthodoxy!"'.

4. Riley, *Memorials of London and London Life*, p. 286, letter of Black of the Black Prince to the Mayor, Aldermen, and Commonalty of the City of London.

5. Le Bel, p. 231.

6. M. le colonel Babinet, 'Etude de la Bataille de Poitiers-Maupertuis', Part 1, *Bulletin de la Société des Antiquaires de l'Ouest*, Series 2, vol. 3, p. 107.

7. Delachenal, vol. 1, p. 202, n. 2.

8. René Guyonnet, *Saint-Aignan: Mille ans d'histoire*, vol. 3, p. 105.

9. *Montrichard*, a guide published by Office Municipal de Tourisme de Montrichard, pp. 5–6, and C. Labreuille, *Etude historique sur Montrichard et Nanteuil*, pp. 65–7, 99.

10. Raymond Chevallier, *Les voies romaines*, p. 215.

11. The debate took place through the *Bulletin de la Société des Antiquaires de l'Ouest* between M. le colonel Babinet, a prominent local historian of the Battle of Poitiers, and M. Charles de Grandmaison, a local archivist. M. Grandmaison had the last word when he produced a fifteenth-century account of the passage of the prince with specific reference to Montlouis: Grandmaison, 'Note sur un point de l'itinéraire du Prince de Galles avant la Bataille de Poitiers', *Bulletin de la Société des Antiquaires de l'Ouest*, series

2, vol. 3, 1883, pp. 360–3; Babinet, 'Note en réponse à M. de Grandmaison', *Bulletin de la Société des Antiquaires de l'Ouest*, series 2, vol. 3, 1883, pp. 364–6; Grandmaison, 'Seconde note sur un point de l'itinéraire du Prince de Galles avant la Bataille de Poitiers', with Babinet's 'Réponse à la seconde note de M. Ch. de Grandmaison', *Extrait du Bulletin de la Société des Antiquaires de l'Ouest*, 1er Trimestre, 1896, pp. 1–8; and Grandmaison, 'Séjour du Prince Noir à Montlouis, près Tours', *Bulletin de la Société des Antiquaires de l'Ouest*, series 2, vol. 8, 1898, pp. 150–5.

12. See *Eulogium*, pp. 220–1, for the itinerary from Romorantin to Montlouis.

13. E. Giraudet, *Histoire de la ville de Tours*, vol. 1, pp. 142–6, and 145, n. 1.

14. The prince in his letter to the City of London, *Memorials of London and London Life*, pp. 285–8, states that the count of Angers was at Tours, while Bartholomew de Burghersh in his letter to the bishop of Worcester, *Oeuvres*, vol. 18, pp. 389–92 reports that it was the count of Poitiers.

15. Grandmaison, citing a manuscript in vol. 156 of the catalogue of archives in Tours library written in the fifteenth century and reproduced in the *Bulletin de la Société des Antiquaires de l'Ouest*, series 2, vol. 8, 1898, pp. 150–5.

16. Denifle, vol. 2–1, p. 121, n. 2, and Giraudet, *Histoire de la ville de Tours*, vol. 1, p. 146.

17. Denifle, vol. 2–1, p. 121; Delachenal, vol. 1, pp. 202–3; *Oeuvres*, vol. 5, pp. 383–4 and 395–7 for the gathering of the Fench army and its movement across the Loire.

18. Riley, *Memorials of London and London Life*, p. 286.

19. J. Maurice, *Montbazon et Veigné aux temps jadis: Synthèse historique*, p. 42. Sources are not cited for this routing.

20. Maurice, *Montbazon et Veigné aux temps jadis*, pp. 31 and *Montbazon et Veigné aux temps jadis: Synthèse historique*, p. 36.

21. Maurice, *Montbazon et Veigné aux temps jadis: Synthèse historique*, p. 142.

22. See *Oeuvres*, vol. 5, p. 397, *Eulogium*, p. 221 and Riley, *Memorials of London and London Life*, pp. 287–8 for the prince's letter to the City of London for the negotiations with the cardinal.

23. *BPR*, vol. 4, p. 145.

24. Gillingham, *Richard I*, p. 69. M. L. Rédet, ed., *Dictionnaire topographique du département de la Vienne*, p. 514, for confirmation that St-Rémi-sur-la-Haie is the same village as St-Rémy-sur-Creuse.

25. Tourneur-Aumont, *La Bataille de Poitiers*, p. 182, A. Bretaudeau, *Histoire des Ponts-de-Cé*, p. 47, and 'Chronicon Briocense 377–1415', 'Chronicon Britannicum, 211–1356' and 'Chronicon Britannicum Alterum, 593–1463' in *Memoires pour servir de preuves à l'histoire ecclesiastique et civile de Bretagne*, ed. P. H. Morice, vol. 1, pp. 7, 43 and 113.

26. *Anonimalle*, p. 37.

27. Letter of Bartholomew de Burgersh in *Oeuvres*, vol. 18, p. 386.

28. Given-Wilson and Briac, 'Edward III's Prisoners of War', p. 831.

29. *Eulogium*, p. 222, and the prince in his letter to the City of London (Riley, *Memorials of London and London Life*, p. 287); *Oeuvres*, vol. 5, pp. 399–401. The *Anonimalle*, p. 37, asserts that the army camped in a wood by a small river near the site of the engagement. There are no watercourses marked on modern large-scale maps in the vicinity, and on balance the prince's statement can be taken at face value.

30. See *Oeuvres*, vol. 18, pp. 385–7 for Burghersh's letter; *Chartulary of Winchester Cathedral*, Item 370, ed. A. W. Goodman, pp. 159–61 for Peverel. Examples of general locations are: *Chronica Johannis de Reading et anonymi Cantuariensis, 1346–67*, ed. James Tait, p.

124 which records the place as 'prope La Chaveney [near Chauvigny]', and Avesbury, p. 471 which says 'in via ducente de Chaveny versus Peyters [on the road which led from Chauvigny to Poitiers]'.

31. Detailed arguments for Savigny-Lévescault as the location of this engagement can be found in WCS, pp. 364–5, n. 91.

32. Anonimalle, pp. 36–7: 'et puis mounterent lour chyvalles et passerent le pount du dit chastelle Heraude et lesserent lour haut chemyn dvers Poyters et tournerent lour chemyn devers Chavene'; Sir Thomas Gray, Scalacronica, ed. and trans. Andy King, p. 29: 'he went through the country in great haste with his three divisions in battle order, to get there before the King of France crossed the river at Chauvigny'; and the prince in his letter (Riley, Memorials of London and London Life, p. 287): 'And the King came with his force to Chaveny, five leagues from us, to pass the same river [Vienne] in the direction of Peytiers. And thereupon we determined to hasten towards him.'

33. WCS, p. 365 and n. 95.

34. Petite chronique françoise, de l'an 1270 à l'an 1356, ed. M. Douet d'Arcq, pp. 27–8: 'Dont il advent que le XXe [sic] jour de septembre ensuivant, les deux os prisrent terre assez près de Poitiers aussi que à que lieue, c'est à savoir que entre ung manoir de l'éveque de Poitiers qui a nom Savigny le Vestal, et un bois hault qui est de l'Abbay de Noally et est appellé Borneau, auquel bois s'éstoient embuchez la plus grant partie des ennemis.'

35. Rédet, Dictionnaire topographique du département de la Vienne, p. 81, records La Chaboissière as La Chabucère in the Cartulaire de l'Abbaye de la Trinité in 1334.

36. The evidence is thin. In his account of his travels in France in the mid-nineteenth century, Lord William Pitt Lennox, Recreations of a Sportsman, vol. 2, p. 255, relates that he was accommodated at the Château de la Chaboissière, close to the battlefield at Maupertuis. The current occupant recounts that there was a château which was burnt down sometime before her family acquired the property in 1925. There are also reported to be photographs of the castle before the fire which I have not been able to trace.

37. Examples of the general statements taken to show the prince's intention to avoid combat are: Chronique de Jean II et de Charles V, p. 70: 'Et quant le dit prince scot que le Roy li aloit en l'encontre, il s'en retourna en alant droit vers Poitiers', and Chronique Normande, p. 112: 'Le prince de Galles se print à retraire quant il seut la venue du roy Jehan.'

38. Oeuvres, vol. 5, p. 396.

39. Baker, p. 141; Life and Campaigns, p. 71.

40. Chandos, ll. 738–44.

41. Le Bel, p. 232.

42. Oeuvres, vol. 18, p. 390: 'et avions nouvelles que le roy de France ove grant povear bien près de celles marches venoit pour combattre ove nous, et approchasmes tant que la bataille se prist entre nous.'

43. Riley, Memorials of London and London Life, pp. 285–7; Oeuvres, vol. 18, pp. 386–9; Chartulary of Winchester Cathedral, Items 370 and 371, pp. 159–64, and p. 162 n. 1.

44. Riley, Memorials of London and London Life, p. 286.

45. BPE, p. 106.

46. WCS, p. 363.

Chapter 13

1. Chandos, ll. 1338–40.
2. Riley, *Memorials of London and London Life*, p. 287.
3. I cite sources for information given, and in some cases, where I can do so briefly, explain the conclusions which I have reached. However, there is not the space here, and indeed it is not the purpose of this book, to set out an exhaustive analysis of either the primary sources or the varying interpretations given in secondary works. The most detailed analyses of the battle and the battlefield are those by Tourneur-Aumont, *La Bataille de Poitiers*, pp. 239–53, Babinet, 'Etude de la Bataille de Poitiers-Maupertuis', Parts 1 and 2, A. H. Burne, 'The Battle of Poitiers', *English Historical Review*, vol. 53, no. 209, 1938, pp. 21–52, and *WCS*, pp. 366–84.
4. The detail can be found on the Institut Géographique National 1:25,000 scale Carte de Randonnée, Sheet 1727E, Poitiers.
5. *Oeuvres*, vol. 5, p. 458, and *Chroniques*, p. 52.
6. *Chroniques*, p. vi, n. 1.
7. Tourneur-Aumont, *La Bataille de Poitiers*, pp. 239–40.
8. Larousse, *Dictionnaire de l'Ancien Français*, p. 454, and Larousse, *Dictionnaire du Moyen Français*, p. 471.
9. *Oeuvres*, vol. 5, p. 526, n. 'Le roi Jean fait reconnoitre la position des Anglais.'
10. *Eulogium*, p. 224.
11. *Oeuvres*, vol. 5, p. 411.
12. Baker, pp. 146–7, trans. Burne, 'The Battle of Poitiers', pp. 27– 8.
13. Burne, 'The Battle of Poitiers', p. 42, has an alternative view of the location of the marsh and suggests that there was a minor watercourse and marshy area in the re-entrant near the settlements of La Cadrousse and Bernon. There is now no trace of a watercourse here, but the nature of the vegetation certainly indicates that it could be marshy in wet periods. He concludes that the army was deployed behind a hedge, orientated along a track running across the north-west edge of the area called Tourageau, with its left flank anchored on the marsh and the right flank protected by trenches and wagons. It is difficult to see how this squares with other elements of Baker's description, including the 'broad deep valley' and the hill occupied by the prince's column which 'lay higher than the enemy', or indeed a ford in the vicinity unless the now absent watercourse was once much more significant. Also, Burne's location of the prince's army places the gap in the hedge described by Baker on the axis of current D12 road to Nouaillé. This does not fit with the statement that the gap was opened by carters in the autumn, which implies that the gap was opened in a hedge alongside a road to allow access either into the forest for wood gathering or into cultivated land at harvest time. The case for the marsh and the deployment of the armies being where Burne suggested is not convincing.
14. Clifford J. Rogers, 'The Battle of Agincourt', in *The Hundred Years War (Part II)*, p. 51 and n. 41.
15. *WCS*, p. 266–7.
16. *Oeuvres*, vol. 5, p. 421.
17. *Chronique normande du XIVième siècle*, ed. A. and E. Molinier, p. 114.
18. Rogers, 'The Battle of Agincourt', p. 52. I am grateful for Clifford Rogers' views on the possible depth of archers which he believes would, for practical purposes, range from between four and seven ranks depending to a degree on the terrain.
19. Babinet, 'Etude de la Bataille de Poitiers-Maupertuis', Part 1, p. 112, n. 1.

20. See note 13 above.

21. Babinet, 'Etude de la Bataille de Poitiers-Maupertuis', p. 112, suggests that the French army was positioned with its right flank in the vicinity of the farms of La Bertandinière, Asnières and La Minière, and its left towards La Cardinerie and Beauvoir.

22. *Anonimalle*, p. 37.

23. Chandos, ll. 761–5.

24. Estimates for the Anglo-Gascon army range from 6,000 to 8,000. Sir Henry Peverel writing to the prior of Winchester Cathedral (*Chartulary of Winchester Cathedral*, pp. 159–61), and Bartholomew de Burghersh in his letter to Jean de Beauchamp (*Oeuvres*, vol. 18, pp. 385–7), both state that the prince had 3,000 men-at-arms, 2,000 archers and 1,000 sergeants. Baker, p. 143, states that the army was 7,000 strong. The upper limit of estimates of the strength of the Anglo-Gascon army is given by Froissart who gives a figure of no more than 8,000 (*Oeuvres*, vol. 5, p. 424). For estimates of the French army see *Oeuvres*, vol. 5, p. 424, and Chandos, ll. 949–52, 993, 1002, and 1037–8. There are other figures for the French army quoted in numerous sources, notably 12,000 men-at-arms in the *Chronique normande*, p. 114, 14,000 men-at-arms plus unquantified infantry in Matteo Villani's 'Cronica', p. 529. Rogers, *WCS*, p. 377 and n. 150, concludes that the overall strength was probably between 14,000 and 16,000; Hewitt, *BPE*, p. 114 comes to a figure of 15–16,000. Delachenal, vol. 1, pp. 215–18, concludes that if we assume that the French army was twice the size of the prince's 'we shall not perhaps be very far from the truth'.

25. Baker, p. 144.

26. Chandos, ll. 906–17.

27. *Chronique des Quatre Premiers Valois (1327–1393)*, ed. Siméon Luce, p. 51.

28. Baker, pp. 144 and 301.

29. Chandos, ll. 920–1.

30. *Oeuvres*, vol. 5, p. 406.

31. *Oeuvres*, vol. 5, pp. 418–19.

32. The main accounts of events on 18 September are: Baker, pp. 142–; *Oeuvres*, vol. 5, pp. 404–20; Le Bel, pp. 232–4; *Chronique normande*, pp. 112–14; Riley, *Memorials of London and London Life*, p. 287; *Anonimalle*, pp. 36–7; *Eulogium*, pp. 222–3; Gray, *Scalacronica 1272–1363*, p. 145; Chandos, ll. 766–1119; Matteo Villani, 'Cronica', pp. 531–3; and *Chronique des quatre premiers Valois*, pp. 49–52.

33. Riley, *Memorials of London and London Life*, pp. 287–8.

34. Chandos, ll. 1082–94.

35. See Rogers, 'The Battle of Agincourt', pp. 74–5, and 127–9 for analysis and calculations on the speed of a cavalry charge of the period.

36. Chandos, ll. 1174–8.

37. *Chronique de Richard Lescot*, ed. Jean Lemoine, Appendix 14.

38. *BPE*, p. 134 nn. 55 and 56; *Oeuvres*, vol. 5, pp. 428, 436, 439, 447 and 454.

39. *BPR*, vol. 3, p. 237, vol. 4, pp. 203, 206, 209, 215, and 261–2. There is a range of spellings of names used in the *BPR*. The names above are conventional spellings used in *BPE*. Examples of original spellings are: Sir Neel Loheryn (Nigel Loring), John del Hay (de la Haye), Sir William Trussell, Sir Alan Cheynee (Cheyne), and Sir Baldwin Botetourt (Buttecourt).

40. Baker, p. 150; *Life and Campaigns*, p. 78.

41. Baker, p. 151; *Life and Campaigns*, p. 79.

42. See Delachenal, vol. 1, p. 238, n. 5 for origins of the name Champ d'Alexandre.

43. *BPE*, pp. 133 n. 52 and 150.

44. For accounts of the battle and events on the 19 September: Baker, pp. 146–55, 300–6; *Oeuvres*, vol. 5, pp. 424–63; Le Bel, pp. 234–5; *Knighton's Chronicle 1337–96*, ed. and trans. G. H. Martin, pp. 144–9; *Anonimalle*, pp. 38–9, and nn., pp. 165–6; *Eulogium*, pp. 224–5; *Chronique normande*, pp. 114–16; Chandos, ll. 1060–1467; Matteo Villani, 'Cronica', pp. 537–8; *Chronique des quatre premiers Valois*, pp. 52–7; Gray, *Scalacronica*, pp. 144–8.

45. *Oeuvres*, vol. 5, pp. 448–51.

46. *BPR*, vol. 4, pp. 338–41 and 379.

47. For details of casualties see *Chartulary of Winchester Cathedral*, pp. 159–64; *Oeuvres*, vol. 18, pp. 385–92. For French reports see *Chronique des Règnes de Jean II et de Charles V*, ed. R. Delachenal, pp. 73–4.

48. Babinet, 'Etude de la Bataille de Poitiers-Maupertuis', Part 1, p. 129, n. 1.

49. *Chronique des quatre premiers Valois*, p. 58.

50. *BPE*, p. 136, nn. 67 and 69 referring to the Issue Rolls and Close Rolls of Edward III. The letters that survive are in Riley, *Memorials of London and London Life*, pp. 285–8, *Oeuvres*, vol. 18, pp. 385–92 and *Chartulary of Winchester Cathedral*, pp. 159–64.

51. Andrew Ayton, 'Armies and Military Communities in Fourteenth Century England', in *Soldiers, Nobles and Gentlemen, Essays in Honour of Morris Keen*, ed. Peter Cross and Christopher Tyerman, pp. 238–9.

52. *Eulogium*, p. 225.

Chapter 14

1. Sumption, *Trial by Fire*, p. 249.

2. *Oeuvres*, vol. 5, p. 465. Le Bel, p. 238, also reports that they returned to Bordeaux without burning or pillaging. This should not come as a surprise, however, since Froissart made much use of Jean Le Bel's work.

3. Philippe Durand and Jean-Pierre Andrault, eds, *Châteaux, manoirs, et logis – La Vienne*, p. 264: the first recorded authorisation to fortify at Prémaire was in 1453.

4. Froissart, *Oeuvres*, vol. 5, pp. 465–6.

5. Christophe Evrard, *Le château médiéval de Gençay, Vienne*, p. 21 claims, without citing sources, that King Jean was held in the castle before moving on to Couhé. See Durand and Andrault, *Châteaux, manoirs, et logis – La Vienne*, p. 301 for the capture of the seigneur. Somewhat oddly they cite two names: Bouchard VIII, and Barthélémy de l'Ile.

6. Durand and Andrault, *Châteaux, manoirs, et logis – La Vienne*, p. 316.

7. F. Picat, *Ruffec: Son histoire d'après les documents recueillis par un vieux ruffecois*, pp. 37 and 54.

8. *Château de Verteuil – Notice* (author not indentified), pp. 1 and 6; Robert Ducluzeau, *Le Connétable du Prince Noir, Jean Chandos*, p. 111.

9. Haydon, *Eulogium*, p. 226 prefers Mouton while Hewitt, *BPE*, map, p. 103 prefers Moutonneau. Barber, *Edward Prince of Wales and Aquitaine*, shows Moutonneau on his Map 4, p. 133, but opts for Mouton in the text, p. 147.

10. Jean-Paul Gaillard, *Châteaux, logis, et demeures anciennes de la Charente*, p. 510.

11. Gaillard, *Châteaux, logis, et demeures anciennes de la Charente*, pp. 578–81, and 586–7.

12. Gaillard, *Châteaux, logis, et demeures anciennes de la Charente*, pp. 819–22.

13. *Eulogium*, p. 226.

14. *Cassini*, CD-ROM, France Sud, sheet 71.

15. Brissaud, *Les anglais en Guyenne*, p. 247.

16. *Cassini*, CD-ROM, France Sud, sheet 104.

17. Brissaud, *Les anglais en Guyenne*, p. 248.

18. Raymond Guinodie, *Histoire de Libourne et des autres villes et bourgs de son arrondissement*, vol. 1, pp. 57 and 424–5.

19. *Oeuvres*, vol. 5, p. 468; Barber, *Edward, Prince of Wales and Aquitaine*, p. 148.

Chapter 15

1. *English Historical Documents*, vol. 4, 1327–1485, p. 209.

2. *Oeuvres*, vol. 6, pp. 15–16; Le Bel, pp. 238–9.

3. See Clifford J. Rogers, 'The Anglo-French Peace Negotiations of 1354–60 Reconsidered', in *The Age of Edward III*, ed. J. S. Bothwell, pp. 199–208, for analysis of the terms of the First and Second Treaty of London.

4. For accounts of events from the Battle of Poitiers until the renewal of war in 1359, see Sumption, *Trial by Fire*, pp. 250–404; Delachenal, vol. 1, pp. 245–470, and vol. 2, pp. 47–88; Ian Mortimer, *The Perfect King: The Life of Edward III, Father of the English Nation*, pp. 330–6; and Barber, *Edward, Prince of Wales and Aquitaine*, pp. 149–58.

5. Rogers, 'The Anglo-French Peace Negotiations', pp. 210–13.

6. Rogers, 'The Anglo-French Peace Negotiations', pp. 210–13; *Oeuvres*, vol. 6, p. 280.

7. For accounts of events from the return to war in 1359 through to the signing of the treaty at Calais, see Barber, *Edward, Prince of Wales and Aquitaine*, pp. 158–69; Delachenal, vol. 2, pp. 141–266; Sumption, *Trial by Fire*, pp. 424–54.

8. For events from the signing of the Treaty Brétigny until the renewal of war in 1369, see Barber, *Edward, Prince of Wales and Aquitaine*, pp. 170–221; Sumption, *Trial by Fire*, pp. 455–585.

9. Barber, *Edward, Prince of Wales and Aquitaine*, pp. 192–237; Jonathan Sumption, *Divided Houses*, pp. 3, 20, 50–1, 95–6 and 156. See *Oeuvres*, vol. 8, p. 382 for the French service in commemoration of the death of the Black Prince.

Appendix 1

1. This assumes a march initially towards Lombez and then turning back to Aurimont.

2. The resting place on this night is unnamed, but it is likely to have been close to Montaut.

Appendix 2

1. See Chapter 12; the *Eulogium* does not name St-Aignan, but this is the likely location.

2. See Chapter 12; the *Eulogium* does not name Montrichard, but from the description given this is the likely location.

Bibliography

Unpublished Primary Sources

Archives Communales, Ouveillan, Series GG.

Journal of John Henxteworth, trans. Edmund Rollo Laird Clowes, Duchy of Cornwall Archives.

Municipal archives for Cassagnoles, 45 EDT4, Archives Départementales de l'Hérault.

Printed Primary Records and Narrative Sources

Anonimalle Chronicle 1333–1381, ed. V. H. Galbraith, Manchester, 1927.

Avesbury, Robertus de, *De gestis mirabilibus Regis Edwardi Tertii*, ed. E. M. Thompson, London, 1889.

Carte de Cassini, La France du XVIIIe siècle, d'après les originaux d'IGN, CD-ROM, 2 vols, France Sud and France Nord.

Chartulary of Winchester Cathedral, ed. A. W. Goodman, Winchester, 1927.

'Chronicon Briocense 377–1415', *Memoires pour servir de preuves à l'histoire ecclésiastique et civile de Bretagne*, ed. P. H. Morice, vol. 1, pp. 1–7, Paris, 1742.

'Chronicon Britannicum, 211–1356', *Memoires pour servir de preuves à l'histoire ecclésiastique et civile de Bretagne*, ed. P. H. Morice, vol. 1, pp. 7–101, Paris, 1742.

'Chronicon Britannicum Alterum, 593–1463', *Memoires pour servir de preuves à l'histoire ecclésiastique et civile de Bretagne*, ed. P. H. Morice, vol. 1, pp. 101–18, Paris, 1742.

Chronique des quatre premiers Valois (1327–1393), ed. Siméon Luce, Paris, 1861.

Chronique de Richard Lescot, ed. Jean Lemoine, Paris, 1896.

Chronique normande du XIVième siècle, ed. A. and E. Molinier, Paris, 1882.

Chronique des règnes de Jean II et Charles V, ed. R. Delachenal, Paris, 1910.

Dossat, Yves, Lemasson, Anne-Marie, and Wolff, Philippe, eds, *Le Languedoc et le Rouergue dans le Trésor des Chartes*, Paris, 1983.

English Historical Documents, vol. 4: 1327–1485, ed. David C. Douglas, London and New York, 1969.

Eulogium Historiarum, vols 1 and 3, ed. F. S. Haydon, London, 1863.

Froissart, Jean, *Chroniques*, vol. 5, ed. Siméon Luce, Paris, 1874.

Froissart, Jean, *Oeuvres de Froissart, Chroniques*, vols 4, 5, 17, and 18, ed. Kervyn de Lettenhove, Brussels, 1867–77.

Galfridi Le Baker de Swynebroke, Chronicon, ed. E. M. Thompson, Oxford, 1889.

Gray, Sir Thomas, *Scalacronica, 1272–1363*, ed. and trans. Andy King, Woodbridge, 2005.

Knighton's Chronicle 1337–1396, ed. and trans. G. H. Martin, Oxford, 1995.

Larcher, J.-B. *Glanages ou preuves*, vol. 6, Tarbes, 1747.

Le Bel, Jean, *Chronique*, ed. J. Viard and E. Déprez, Paris, 1904–5.

Mahul, Alphonse, *Cartulaire et archives des communes de l'ancien diocese et de l'arrondissement administratif de Carcassonne*, Paris, 1857–1882.

Murimuth, Adam, *Adae Murimuth. Continuato Chronicarum*, ed. E. M. Thompson, London, 1889.

Ordonnances des roys de France de la troisième race, vol. 3, ed. Mr Secousse, Paris, 1732.

Petit chronique françoise, de l'an 1270 à l'an 1356, ed. M. Douet d'Arcq, Paris, 1866.

Récits d'un bourgeois de Valenciennes, ed. Kervyn de Lettenhove, Louvain, 1877.

Riley, H. T., ed., *Memorials of London and London Life, in the XIIIth, XIVth, and XVth Centuries*, London, 1868.

Thalamus Parvus: Le Petit Thalamus de Montpellier, ed. Ferdinand Pegat and Eugène Thomas, Montpellier, 1840.

The Black Prince's Register, vols 2, 3, and 4, London, 1933.

The Life and Feats of Arms of Edward the Black Prince by Chandos Herald, trans. Francisque-Michel, London and Paris, 1883.

The Pilgrim's Guide: A 12th Century Guide for the Pilgrim to St James of Compostella, trans. James Hogarth, London, 1992.

Timbal, P.-C., in collaboration with Monique Gilles, Henri Martin, Josette Metman, Jacques Payen and Brigitte Poussin, *La Guerre de Cent Ans vue à travers les registres du Parlement (1337–1369)*, Paris, 1961.

Villani, Matteo, 'Cronica', in *Cronisti del Trecento*, ed. Roberto Palmarocchi, Milan, 1935.

Walsingham, *Chronicon Angliae*, ed. E. M. Thompson, London, 1874.

Secondary Sources

Les Amis du Vieux Montrichard, *Montrichard*, Montrichard, 1986.

Archéologie du Midi medieval, vol. 22, Carcassonne, 2004.

Armengaud, Roger, 'Le passage du Prince Noir', *La Croix du Midi*, Toulouse, 9 February 1967 (rebranded as *La Voix du Midi* in 2009).

Armengaud, Roger, *Boulbonne, le Saint-Denis des Comtes de Foix*, Mazères, 1993.

Armengaud, Roger, and Ycart, Roger, *Cintegabelle: Châtellenie royale en pays toulousain*, Aucamville, 1981.

Association des Villages Circulaires, *Circulades: Sur la route d'un urbanisme de 1000 ans*, Paulhan, undated.

Aubert, Marcel, *Mennetou-sur-Cher*, Blois, 1921.

Audrerie, Dominique, and Couland, Yannick, *Sites naturels en Périgord*, Périgueux, 1993.

Ayton, Andrew, *Knights and Warhorses: Military Service and the English Aristocracy under Edward III*, Woodbridge, 1994.

Ayton, Andrew, 'Armies and Military Communities in Fourteenth Century England', in *Soldiers, Nobles and Gentlemen: Essays in Honour of Morris Keen*, ed. Peter Cross and Christopher Tyerman, Woodbridge, 2009, pp. 215–39.

Ayton, Andrew, and Preston, Philip, *The Battle of Crécy 1346*, Woodbridge, 2005.

Babinet, M. le colonel, 'Etude de la Bataille de Poitiers-Maupertuis', *Bulletin de la Société des Antiquaires de l'Ouest*, series 2, vol. 3, 1883; Part 1, pp. 95–147 and Part 2, pp. 167–213.

Babinet, M. le colonel, 'Note en réponse à M. de Grandmaison', *Bulletin de la Société des Antiquaires de l'Ouest*, series 2, vol. 3, 1883, pp. 364–6.

Babinet, M. le Colonel, 'Réponse à la seconde note de M. Ch. de Grandmaison sur un point de l'itinéraire du Prince de Galles avant la Bataille de Poitiers', *Extrait du Bulletin de la Société des Antiquaires de l'Ouest*, 1er trimestre, 1896, pp. 5–8.

Barber, Richard, *Edward, Prince of Wales and Aquitaine: A Biography of the Black Prince*, Woodbridge, 1978.

Barber, Richard, *Life and Campaigns of the Black Prince*, Woodbridge, 1979.

Barrière-Flavy, C., *Cintegabelle au XV siècle*, Toulouse, 1888.

Baudreu, Dominique, and Loppe, Frédéric, 'Types de forts villageois dans le bassin moyen de l'Aude durant la Guerre de Cent Ans', *Archéologie du Midi Médiéval*, vol. 22, 2004, pp. 103–40.

Bentley, James, *Fort Towns of France*, London, 1993

Blanc, René, *La douloureuse histoire de la ville de Duras*, Mazères, 2003

Bouges, Thomas, *Histoire ecclesiastique et civile de la ville et diocèse de Carcassonne*, Paris, 1741, reprinted Marseille, 1978.

Boulanger, Pierre, *Manot: Quelques pages de notre histoire*, Manot, 1992.

Bourin, Monique, Adgé; Michel, Rouquette, Yves; and Nayral, Bernard, *L'imagier et les poètes au Château de Capestang*, Portet-sur-Garonne, 1991.

Branger, Jean, and Tripeau, Robert, *Châtres-sur-Cher: Notre village*, St-Armand-Montrond, 1992.

Branger, Jean, and Tripeau, Robert, *Mennetou-sur-Cher: Histoire du canton*, St-Armand-Montrond, 1992.

Bretaudeau, A., *Histoire des Ponts-de-Cé*, Angers, 1904.

Breuils, A., 'Jean 1er, Comte d'Armagnac et le mouvement national dans le Midi, au temps du Prince Noir', *Revue des Questions Historiques*, new series, vol. 15, no. 59, 1896, pp. 44–102.

Brissaud, D., *Les anglais en Guyenne*, Paris, 1875.

Bruc-Chabans, Comte de, *Le Château de la Chapelle-Faucher*, Le Bugue, 1992.

Buisseret, David, *The Mapmakers' Quest: Depicting New Worlds in Renaissance Europe*, Oxford, 2003.

Burne, A. H., 'The Battle of Poitiers', *English Historical Review*, vol. 53, no. 209, 1938, pp. 21–52.

Burne, A. H., *The Crécy War*, London, 1955, reprinted Ware, 1999.

Capra, Pierre-J., 'Le séjour du Prince Noir, lieutenant du roi, a l'archevêché de Bordeaux', *Revue Historique de Bordeaux et de la Gironde*, vol. 8, no. 4, 1958, pp. 241–52.

Carbonel, Paul, *Histoire de Narbonne, dès origines à l'époque contemporaine*, Narbonne, 1956.

Castan, Jean, *Marestaing: Ancienne commanderie des Templiers*, Toulouse, 2005.

Cazals, Antoine-Lucien, *Histoire de la ville et de la communauté de Montesquieu-sur-Canal*, Toulouse, 1883.

Château de Verteuil – Notice, Ruffec, 1950.

Chaumeau, Jean, Seigneur de Lassay, *Histoire de Berry*, Lyon, 1566, reproduced Argenton, 1985.

Chevallier, Raymond, *Les voies romaines*, Paris, 1997.

Clausewitz, Carl von, *On War*, ed. and trans. Michael Howard and Peter Paret, Princeton, NJ, 1976.

Connaître et Aimer Casteljaloux, tourist guide, unattributed and undated, Casteljaloux.

Contrasty, Jean, *Histoire de Sainte-Foy-de-Peyrolières, ancien prieuré du Moyen-Âge et de la Renaissance uni en 1606, au ollège de Toulouse*, Toulouse, 1917.

Contrasty, Jean, *Histoire de la cité de Rieux-Volvestre et de ses évêques*, Toulouse, 1936.

Courivaud, Michel, *Le Dorat en Basse Marche*, Autremencourt, 2004.

Crozet, R., 'Siège de Romorantin par le Prince de Galles (1356)', *Revue Historique*, vol. 153, 1926, pp. 187–92.

Curry, Anne, *Agincourt: A New History*, Stroud, 2006.

Dedieu, Joseph, *Histoire de Carbonne: Les institutions communales d'une bastide sous l'Ancien Régime*, Carbonne, 1953.

Dehoey, Jean-Pierre, 'Carbonne sous l'Ancien Régime', *Histoire et traditions carbonnaises*, vol. 4, 1998, pp. 59–61.

Dejean, S., 'L'incursion du Prince Noir en Agenais et en Toulousain (1355)', in *La guerre au Moyen-Age*, fiftieth anniversary compilation by the Académie Toulousaine d'Histoire et d'Arts Militaires, Toulouse, 1994, pp. 36–53.

Delachenal, R., *Histoire de Charles V*, vols 1 and 2, Paris, 1909.

Délias, José, *Chabanais*, Paris, 1997.

Denifle, Henri, *La désolation des monastères, eglises, et hôpitaux en France pendant la Guerre de Cent Ans*, Paris, 1899.

Drouyn, Léo, *La Guyenne militaire*, Marseille, 1977.

Ducluzeau, Robert, *Le Connétable du Prince Noir, Jean Chandos*, Saint-Cyr-sur-Loire, 2004.

Ducos, Jean Henri, and Gardelles, Jacques, *Le guide des châteaux de France*, 32, Gers, Paris, 1985.

Duffaut, Pierre, *Histoire de Mazères, ville maîtresse et capitale des Comtes de Foix*, Mazères, 1988.

Dupré, Alexandre, *Recherches historiques sur Romorantin et la Sologne*, Paris, 1994.

Dupuy, Micheline, *Le Prince Noir, Edouard, Seigneur d'Aquitaine*, Paris, 1970.

Durand, Philippe, and Andrault, Jean-Pierre, eds, *Châteaux, manoirs, et logis – La Vienne*, Chauray, 1995.

Durand de Ramefort, Gérard, *Le Château de Ramefort*, Périgueux, 2001.

L'église abbatiale de Simorre, distributed by the tourist office of Simorre, undated.

Evrard, Christophe, *Le château médiéval de Gençay, Vienne*, Gençay, 1992.

Fonds-Lamothe, L.-H., *Notices historiques sur la ville de Limoux*, Limoux, 1838.

Font-Réaulx, J. de, *Le Dorat, ancienne capitale de la Basse Marche*, Limoges, 1940.

Fowler, Kenneth, *The King's Lieutenant: Henry of Grosmont, First Duke of Lancaster 1310–1361*, London, 1969.

Gaillard, Hervé, *Carte archéologique de la Gaule: La Dordogne*, Paris, 1997.

Gaillard, Jean-Paul, ed., *Châteaux, logis, et demeures anciennes de la Charente*, Paris, 2005.

Galibert, Léon, *Histoire de la baronnie et du consulat de Montbrun-Lauragais*, 1863, reprinted Toulouse, 1986.

Gardelles, Jacques, *Les châteaux du Moyen Age dans la France du sud-ouest – La Gascogne anglaise de 1216 à 1327*, Paris, 1972.

Gillingham, John, *Richard I*, New Haven, CT, and London, 1999.

Gillingham, John, "'Up with Orthodoxy!" In Defense of Vegetian Warfare', *Journal of Medieval Military History*, vol. 2, 2004, pp. 149–58.

Giraudet, E., *Histoire de la ville de Tours*, vol. 1, Tours, 1873.

Given-Wilson, Chris, and Briac, Françoise, 'Edward III's Prisoners of War: The Battle of Poitiers and Its Context', *English Historical Review*, September 2001, pp. 802–33.

Grandmaison, Charles de, 'Note sur un point de l'itinéraire du Prince de Galles avant la Bataille de Poitiers', *Bulletin de la Société des Antiquaires de l'Ouest*, series 2, vol. 3, 1883, pp. 360–3

Grandmaison, Charles de, 'Seconde note sur un point de l'itinéraire du Prince de Galles avant la Bataille de Poitiers', *Extrait du Bulletin de la Société des Antiquaires de l'Ouest*, 1er trimestre, 1896, pp. 1–4.

Grandmaison, Charles de, 'Séjour du Prince Noir à Montlouis, près Tours', *Bulletin de la Société des Antiquaires de l'Ouest*, series 2, vol. 8, 1898, pp. 150–5.

Green, David, 'The Military Personnel of Edward the Black Prince', *Mediaeval Prosopography*, vol. 21, 2000, pp. 133–52.

Green, David, *The Black Prince*, Stroud, 2001.

Green, David, *The Battle of Poitiers, 1356*, Botley, 2004.

Green, David, *Edward the Black Prince, Power in Medieval Europe*, Harlow, 2007.

Grillon, L., *Un peu d'histoire de Quinsac, dès celtes à la Révolution*, published privately, undated.

Grillon des Chapelles, M., *Esquisses biographiques du Département de l'Indre*, Paris, 1864.

Gross, Guy, *Le Prince Noir en Berry*, Bourges, 2004.

Gueneau, Louis, 'Aubigny-sur-Nère (Cher) pendant la Guerre de Cent Ans: Les incursions anglaises', *Cahiers d'Archéologie et d'Histoire du Berry*, no. 6, 1966, pp. 13–26.

Guignard, Romain, *Issoudun dès origines à 1850: Aperçu des chroniques locales*, Issoudun, 1943.

Guinodie, Raymond, *Histoire de Libourne et des autres villes et bourgs de son arrondissement*, vol. 1, Paris, 2004.

Guyonnet, René, *Saint-Aignan: Mille ans d'histoire*, vol. 3, *De Guy du Chatillon à Marie de Parthenay. Les Comtes d'Auxerre et de Tonnerre, Seigneurs de Saint-Aignan (1222 à 1432)*, Saint-Aignan, 1979

Guyot, M. H., and Cheyron, M., *Château des ducs de Duras et la ville*, Bayac, 1989.

Harari, Yuval Noah, 'Strategy and Supply in Fourteenth-Century Western European Invasion Campaigns', *Journal of Military History*, vol. 64, April 2000, pp. 297–333.

Hewitt, H. J., *The Black Prince's Expedition of 1355–1357*, Manchester, 1958, reprinted Barnsley, 2004.

Hewitt, H. J., *The Organisation of War under Edward III*, Manchester and New York, 1966.

Hewitt, H. J., *The Horse in Medieval England*, London, 1983.

Higounet-Nadal, Arlette, *Périgueux aux XIV et XV siècles: Etude de démographie historique*, Bordeaux, 1978.

Hoskins, Peter, 'The Itineraries of the Black Prince's Chevauchées of 1355 and 1356: Observations and Interpretations', *Journal of Medieval Military History*, vol. 7, 2009, pp. 12–37.

Hunnewell, James F., *The Historical Monuments of France*, Boston and New York, 1898.

Jeanjean, J. F., *La Guerre de Cent Ans en pays audois: Incursion du Prince Noir en 1355*, Carcassonne, 1946.

Johnson, Hugh, *Hugh Johnson's Story of Wine*, London, 1989.

Keen, Maurice, *Chivalry*, New Haven, CT, and London, 1984.

Labreuille, C., *Etude historique sur Montrichard et Nanteuil*, vol. 1, Tours, 1896.

Lac, Joseph du, *Bergerac et son arrondissement*, Paris, 1872, reprinted 1992.

Lacueille, Joseph, *Histoire de Massay*, Saint Armand, 1931.

Lagors, Alain, *Les étapes de l'evolution de Plaisance au Moyen Age*, Auch, undated.

Lahondès, J. de, *Belpech de Garnagois*, Toulouse, 1886.

Lambert, Craig, 'Taking the War to Scotland and France: The Supply and Transportation of English Armies by Sea', PhD Thesis, University of Hull, March 2009.

Latour, Louis, 'Le grand pont romain d'Auterive', *Mémoires de la Société Archéologique du Midi de la France*, vol. 51, 1991, pp. 143–75.

Latour, Louis, 'Le castrum d'Auterive: Ses origines, son histoire, ses fortifications', *Mémoires de la Société Archéologique du Midi de la France*, vol. 54, 1994, pp. 85–111.

Laugardière, R. de, 'Essais topographiques, historiques et biographiques sur l'arrondissement de Nontron', *Bulletin de la Société Historique et Archéologique du Périgord*, vols 12, 14, and 16, 1885, pp. 242–93, 412–47, 1887, pp. 110–55, 231–52, 321–35, 390–400, and 1888, pp. 65–74, 115–32, 194–211.

Lechaux, Laurence, ed, *Argenton-sur-Creuse en Berry: Au fil des rues*, Argenton-sur-Creuse, 2002.

Lemaitre, M., *Memoires sur Vierzon*, Bourges, 1836.

Lennox, Lord William Pitt, *Recreations of a Sportsman*, vol. 2, London, 1862.

Liddell Hart, B. H., *Thoughts on War*, London, 1944.

Liddell Hart, B. H., *Strategy: The Indirect Approach*, revised edn, London, 1967.

Livingstone, Marilyn, and Witzel, Morgen, *The Road to Crécy: The English Invasion of France 1346*, Harlow, 2005.

Lorgue, *Histoire de Mortemart (Haute-Vienne)*, Limoges, 1893.

Maguer, Roger, *De la Cocagne au Blé*, Estadens, 2003.

Maurice, Jacques, *Montbazon et Veigné aux temps jadis*, Paris, 1970.

Maurice, J., *Montbazon et Veigné aux temps jadis: Synthèse historique*, new edition, Tours, 1976.

Ménard, Henri, *Carbonne: Huit siècles d'histoire*, Saint-Girons, 1985.

Michaud, Jacques, and Cabanis, André, eds, *Histoire de Narbonne*, Toulouse, 1981.

Miquel, Jean, *Essai sur l'arrondissement de Saint-Pons*, Montpellier, 1895.

Mirande, histoire d'une bastide gasconne: Parcours historique, prepared by l'Office de Tourisme de Mirande, undated.

Moisant, J., *Le Prince Noir en Aquitaine*, Paris, 1894.

Mondon, Adolphe, 'Notes historiques sur la baronnie de Marthon en Angoumois', *Bulletin de la Société Archéologique et Historique de la Charente*, 1895, pp. 233–504, 1896, pp. 1–220, and 1897, pp. 1–80.

Monlezun, Jean-Justin, *Histoire de la Gascogne depuis le temps les plus reculés jusqu'à nos jours*, vol. 3, Auch, 1847.

Montrot, E., *Sainte-Maure-de-Touraine*, Chambray-les-Tours, 1978.

Morillo, Stephen, 'Battle Seeking: The Contexts and Limits of Vegetian Strategy', *Journal of Medieval Military History*, vol. 1, 2003, pp. 21–41.

Mortimer, Ian, *The Perfect King: The Life of Edward III, Father of the English Nation*, London, 2006.

Mullot, Henry, and Poux, Joseph, *Nouvelles recherches sur l'itinéraire du Prince Noir à travers les pays de l'Aude*, Toulouse, 1909.

Neillands, Robin, *The Hundred Years War*, London and New York, 1990.

Nouaillac, J., *Le Dorat à travers son passé*, Le Dorat, 1932.

Odol, Jean, *La Bossa de Montalbiau: Essai de monographie d'une colline d'Ayguesvives*, Nailloux, undated.

Ousset, P.-E., and Labit, G., *Clermont sur Ariège: Archéologie et histoire*, Toulouse, 1934.

Pébernard, Denis, *Histoire de Conques-sur-Orvieil et de la manufacture des saptes*, Carcassonne, 1899.

Penaud, Guy, *Histoire de Périgueux dès origines à nos jours*, Périgueux, 1983.

Pérémé, Armand, *Recherches historiques et archéologiques sur la ville d'Issoudun*, Paris, 1847.

Picat, L., *Ruffec: Son histoire d'après les documents recueillis par un vieux ruffecois*, Ruffec, 1925.

Pinol, Jean-Luc, ed., *Atlas historique des villes de France*, Paris, 1996.

Pizan, Christine de, *The Book of Deeds of Arms and of Chivalry*, trans. Sumner Willard, ed. Charity Cannon Willard, Philadelphia, 1999.

Poulain-Martel, Catherine, and Canal, Jean-Yves, 'Des silos médiévaux à Miremont', *Gardarem Miremont*, Bulletin no. 4, 2002.

Prestwich, Michael, *Armies and Warfare in the Middle Ages: The English Experience*, New Haven, CT, and London, 1996.

Queyrou, J., *Casteljaloux et sa région*, Casteljaloux, 1982.

Raynal, Louis, *Histoire du Berry depuis les temps les plus anciens jusqu'en 1789*, vol. 2, Paris, 1884.

Raynaud, Nicole, 'La chevauchée du Prince Noir en 1356: Recherche de son itinéraire entre La Péruse et Le Dorat', *Travaux d'Archéologie Limousine*, vol. 18, 1998, pp. 77–90.

Rédet, M. L., ed., *Dictionnaire topographique du département de la Vienne*, Paris, 1881.

Renouard, Yves, *Bordeaux sous les rois d'Angleterre*, Bordeaux, 1965.

Repères culturels en Minervois: La Redorte, La Redorte tourist information leaflet, undated.

Ribadieu, Henry, *Les campagnes du Comte Derby en Guyenne*, Paris, 1865.

Risselin-Nin, Claudine, and Ruffier, Olivier, 'Le rempart médiéval d'Issoudun: Etude topographique', *Cahiers d'Archéologie et d'Histoire du Berry*, no. 101, March 1990, pp. 13–24.

Rives, Alain, *A la recherche des remparts du vieux Vierzon*, 3rd edition, Bourges, 1997.

Rogers, Clifford J., 'Edward III and the Dialectics of Strategy', in *The Wars of Edward III: Sources and Interpretations*, Woodbridge, 2000, pp. 265–84.

Rogers, Clifford J., *War Cruel and Sharp: English Strategy Under Edward III, 1327–1360*, Woodbridge, 2000.

Rogers, Clifford J., 'The Anglo-French Peace Negotiations of 1354–60 Reconsidered', in *The Age of Edward III*, ed. J. S. Bothwell, York, 2001, pp. 193–213.

Rogers, Clifford J., 'By Fire and Sword: *Bellum Hostile* and "Civilians" in the Hundred Years War', in *Civilians in the Path of War*, ed. Mark Grimsley and Clifford J. Rogers, Lincoln, NE, 2002, pp. 33–78.

Rogers, Clifford J., 'The Vegetian "Science of Warfare" in the Middle Ages', *Journal of Medieval Military History*, vol. 1, 2003, pp. 1–19

Rogers, Clifford J., 'The Battle of Agincourt', *The Hundred Years War (Part II)*, Villalon, L. J. Andrew and Kagay, Donald J., ed., Leiden, 2008, pp. 37–132.

Romieu, Maurice, *Histoire de la vicomté de Juliac*, Romorantin, 1894.

Rougerie, René, *Histoires de Mortemart, suivie de légendes racontées par Paule Lauvergne*, Limoges, undated.

Sabarthès, A., *Notes historiques sur la ville de Limoux*, Limoux, 1933.

Sahuc, Joseph, *St-Pons-de-Thomières*, Nimes, 1994, facsimile of 1895–1902 edition.

Santi, M. L. de, 'L'expédition du Prince Noir en 1355, d'après le journal d'un de ses compagnons', *Mémoires de l'Academie des Sciences, Inscriptions, et Belles-Lettres de Toulouse*, series 10, vol. 4, 1904, pp. 181–223.

Sargos, Jacques, *Histoire de la Fôret Landaise, du désert à l'age d'or*, Bordeaux, 1997.

Si....Simorre m'était conté – circuit touristique, published by the Mairie of Simorre, undated.

Soyez, Jean-Marc, *Quand les anglais vendangeaient l'Aquitaine*, Paris, 1979.

Spufford, Peter, *Power and Profit: The Merchant in Medieval Europe*, London, 2002.

Strickland, Matthew, and Hardy, Robert, *The Great War Bow*, Stroud, 2005.

Sumption, Jonathan, *The Albigensian Crusade*, London, 1978.

Sumption, Jonathan, *Trial by Battle: The Hundred Years War*, vol. 1, London, 1990.

Sumption, Jonathan, *Trial by Fire: The Hundred Years War*, vol. 2, London, 1999.

Sumption, Jonathan, *Divided Houses: The Hundred Years War*, vol. 3, London, 2009.

Tausserat, J.-B. E., *Chroniques de la chatellenie de Lury*, Bourges and Vierzon, 1878.

Taylor, Craig, 'Edward III and the Plantagenet Claim to the French Throne', in *The Age of Edward III*, ed. J. S. Bothwell, York, 2001, pp. 155–69.

Tourneur-Aumont, J. M., *La Bataille de Poitiers (1356) et la construction de la France*, Paris, Tours and Poitiers, 1943.

Unwin, George, ed., *Finance and Trade under Edward III*, Manchester, 1918.

Vale, Malcolm, *The Origins of the Hundred Years War: The Angevin Legacy 1250–1340*, Oxford, 1996.

Verpaalen-Bessaguet, S., *Lesterps, chef-d'oeuvre de l'art roman*, Saint-Maurice-des-Lyons, 2002.

Vesvre, Hilaire de, ed., *Le Bas-Berry: Déols et Châteauroux, dès origines à nos jours*, Verneuil-sur-Igneraie, 1950.

Vic, Dom Claude de and Vaissete, Dom Joseph, *Histoire générale du Languedoc*, vol. 7, Toulouse, 1844, reprinted Nimes, 1994.

Weir, Alison, *Eleanor of Aquitaine, By the Wrath of God Queen of England*, London, 1999.

Westenhoff, Lt-Col. Charles M., *Military Air Power: The CADRE Digest of Air Power Opinions and Thoughts*, Washington, DC, 1990.

Wright, Nicholas, *Knights and Peasants: The Hundred Years War in the French Countryside*, Woodbridge, 1998

Ycart, Roger, *Cintegabelle: Un village dans l'histoire*, Auterive, 1998.

Index

Warfare in History